cheery

DR
CO

PLUTO CRACY
Chronicles of a Global Monopoly

My thanks to Eloisa and my parents for their support.
To Fabio for his encouragement and contribution.
To Alex for his technical aide.
To Laura, Omar and Eloy for their points of view.
And to Stef for the opportunity.
Without them, this book would have been different
or wouldn't have been.

ISBN 9781681122687
Originally published as PLUTOCRACIA
© Text & Illustrations: Abraham Martínez, 2017
© Bang. ediciones, 2017
English translation rights arranged through S.B.Rights Agency – Stephanie Barrouillet.
Library of Congress Control Number 2020943135
© 2020 NBM for the English translation
Translation by Montana Kane
Lettering by Ortho

Printed in Malaysia
First printing October 20

This book is also available digitally wherever e-books are sold
(ISBN 9781681122694)

PLUTO CRACY
Chronicles of a Global Monopoly

A GRAPHIC NOVEL BY
ABRAHAM MARTÍNEZ

nbm GRAPHIC NOVELS

Nantier • Beall • Minoustchine
NEW YORK

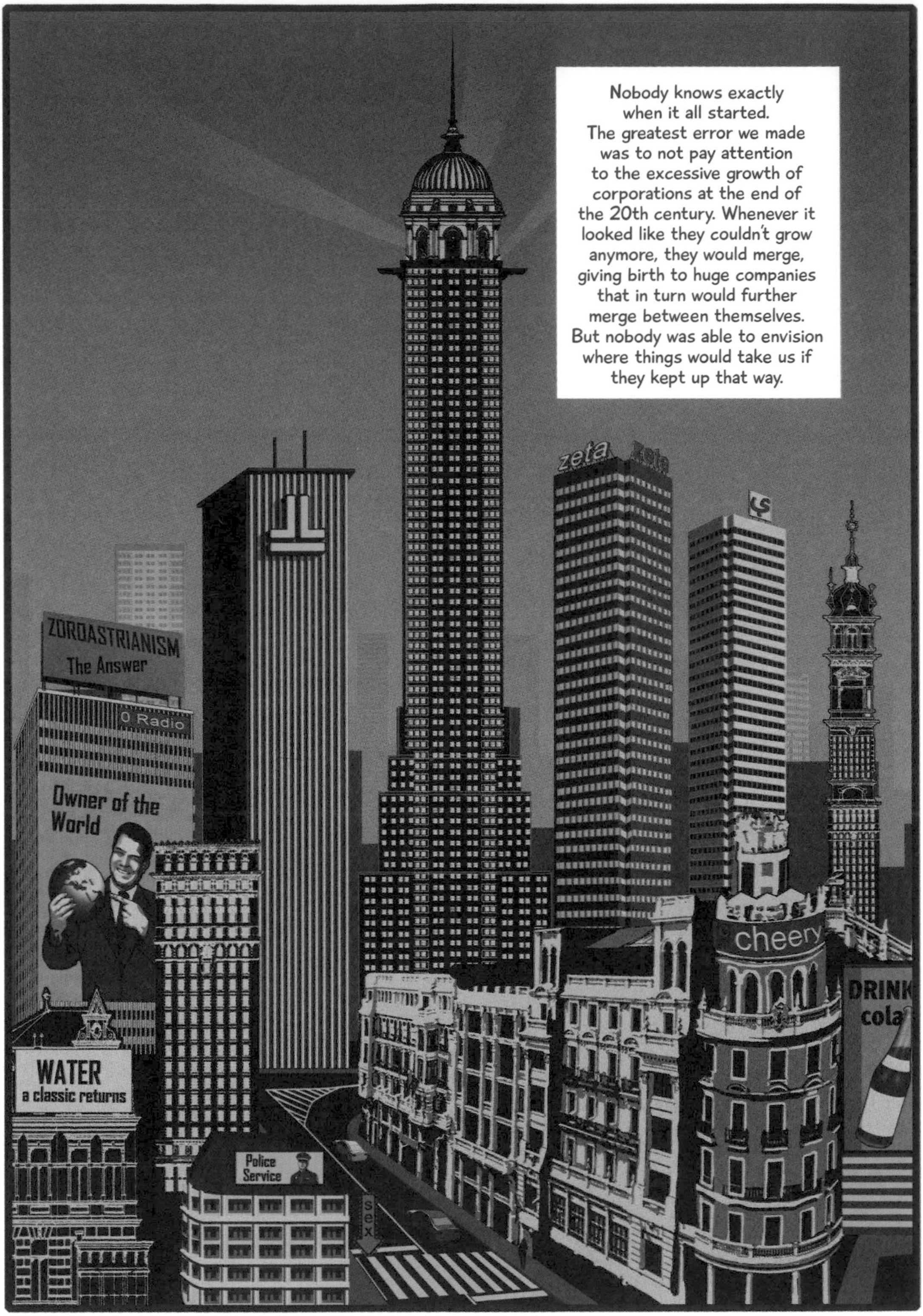
Nobody knows exactly when it all started. The greatest error we made was to not pay attention to the excessive growth of corporations at the end of the 20th century. Whenever it looked like they couldn't grow anymore, they would merge, giving birth to huge companies that in turn would further merge between themselves. But nobody was able to envision where things would take us if they kept up that way.
zeta
zeta
ZOROASTRIANISM
The Answer
0 Radio
Owner of the World
cheery
DRINK
cola
WATER
a classic returns
Police
Service
sex

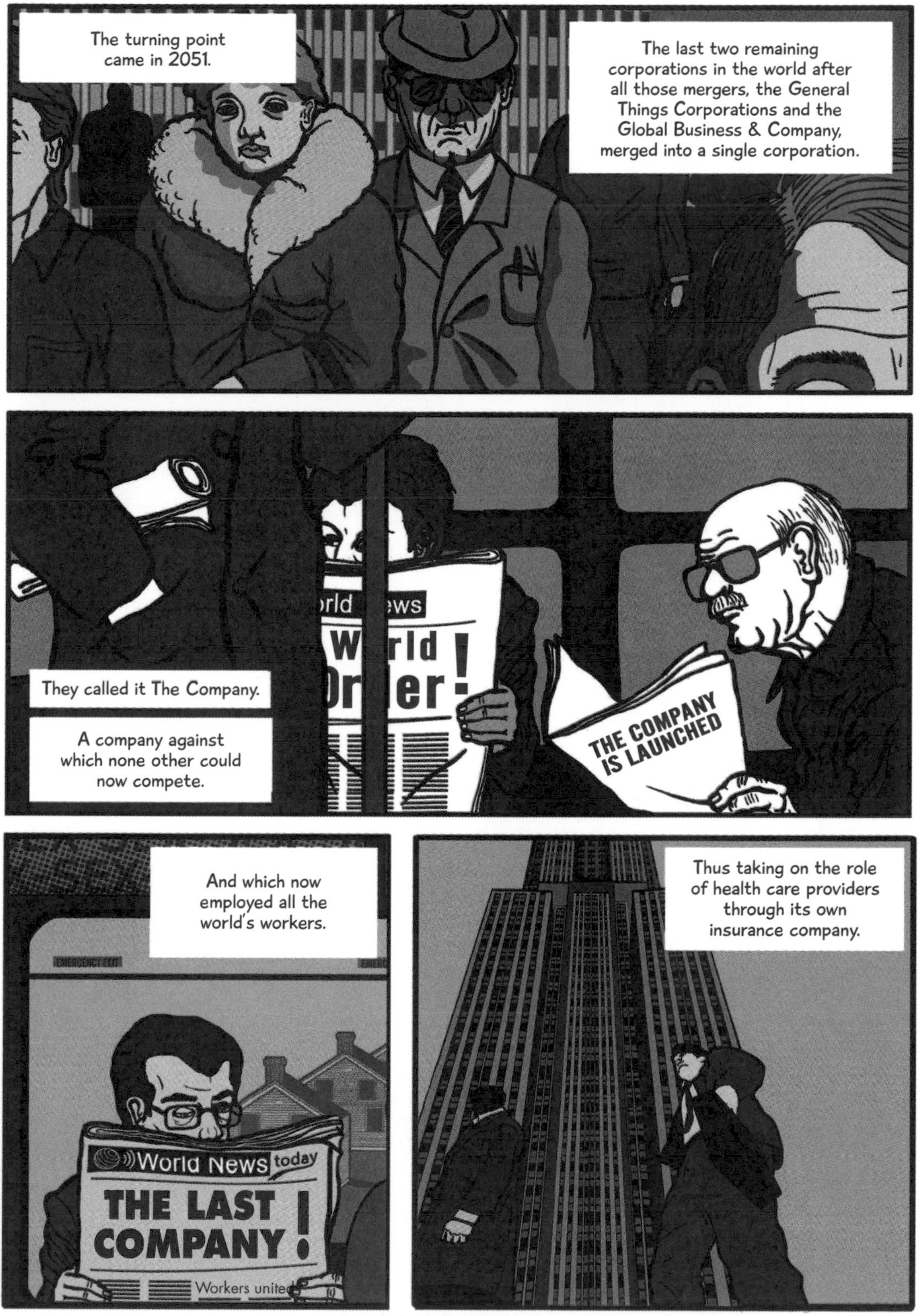

The turning point came in 2051.
The last two remaining corporations in the world after all those mergers, the General Things Corporations and the Global Business & Company, merged into a single corporation.
They called it The Company.
A company against which none other could now compete.
THE COMPANY IS LAUNCHED
And which now employed all the world's workers.
World News today
THE LAST COMPANY!
Thus taking on the role of health care providers through its own insurance company.

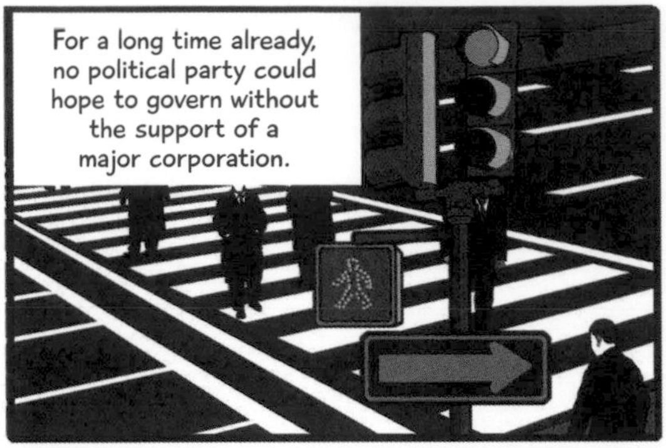
For a long time already, no political party could hope to govern without the support of a major corporation.

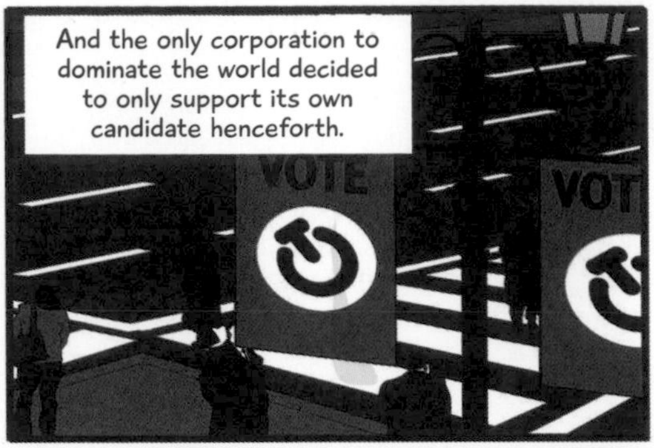
And the only corporation to dominate the world decided to only support its own candidate henceforth.
VOTE
VOT

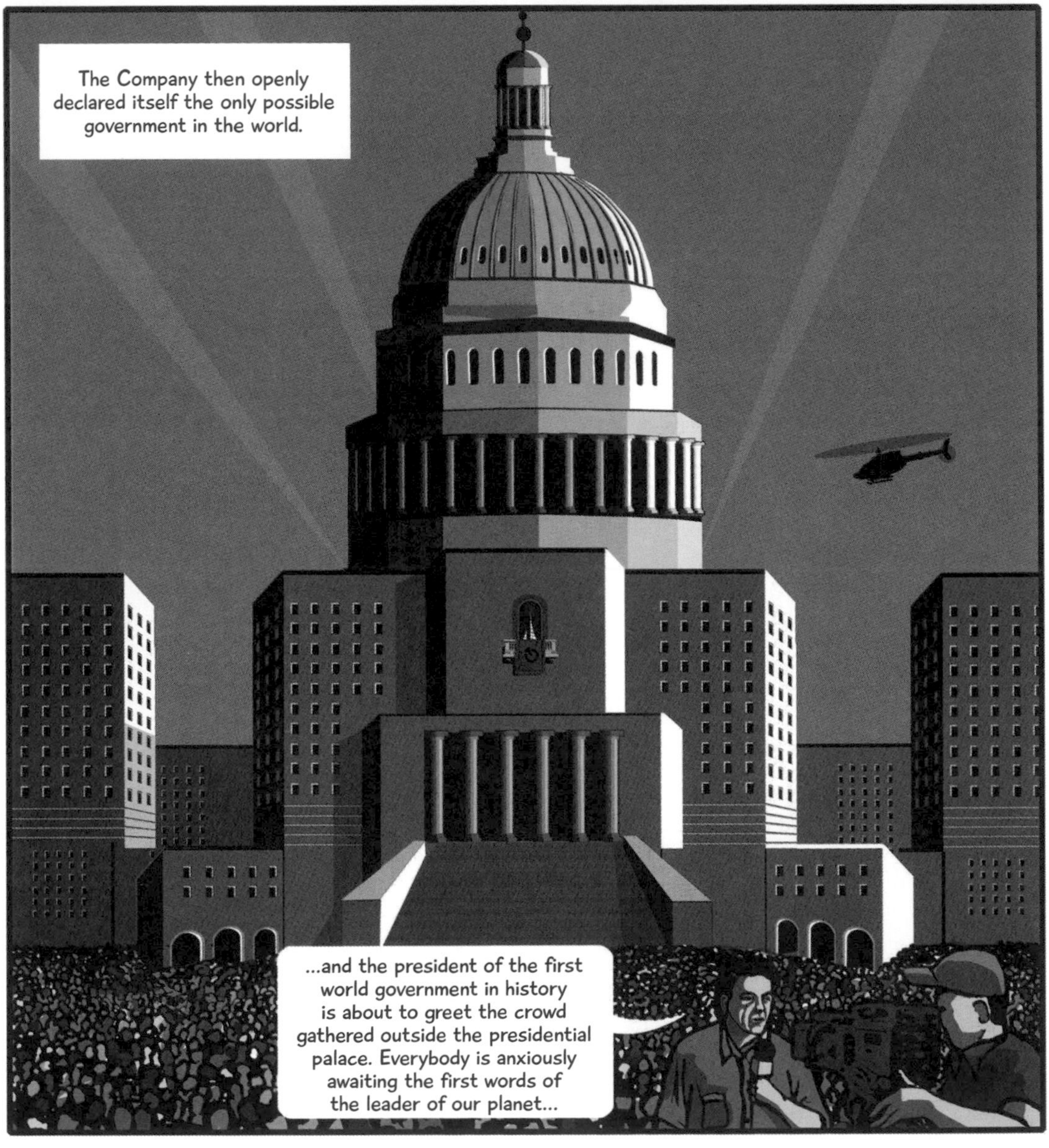
The Company then openly declared itself the only possible government in the world.
...and the president of the first world government in history is about to greet the crowd gathered outside the presidential palace. Everybody is anxiously awaiting the first words of the leader of our planet...

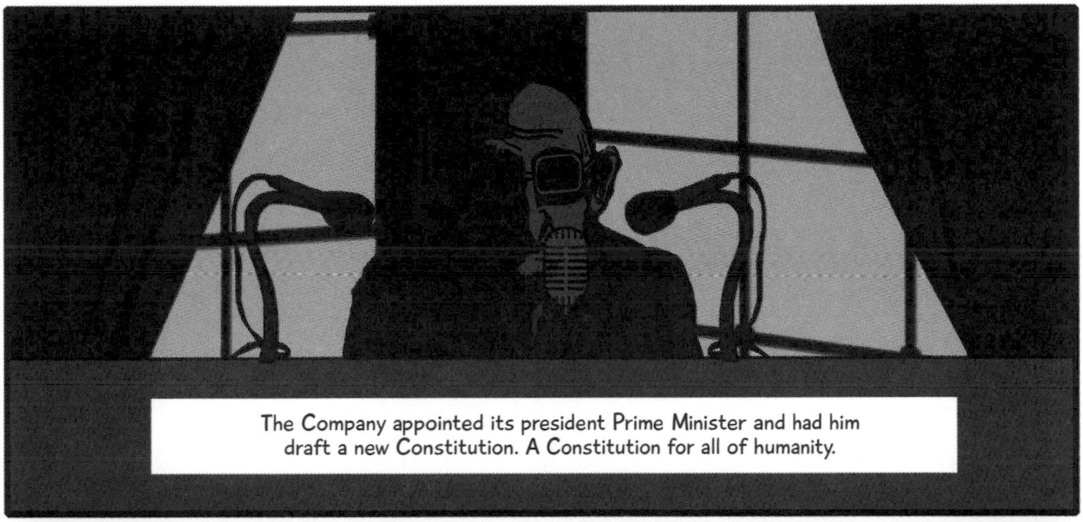
The Company appointed its president Prime Minister and had him draft a new Constitution. A Constitution for all of humanity.

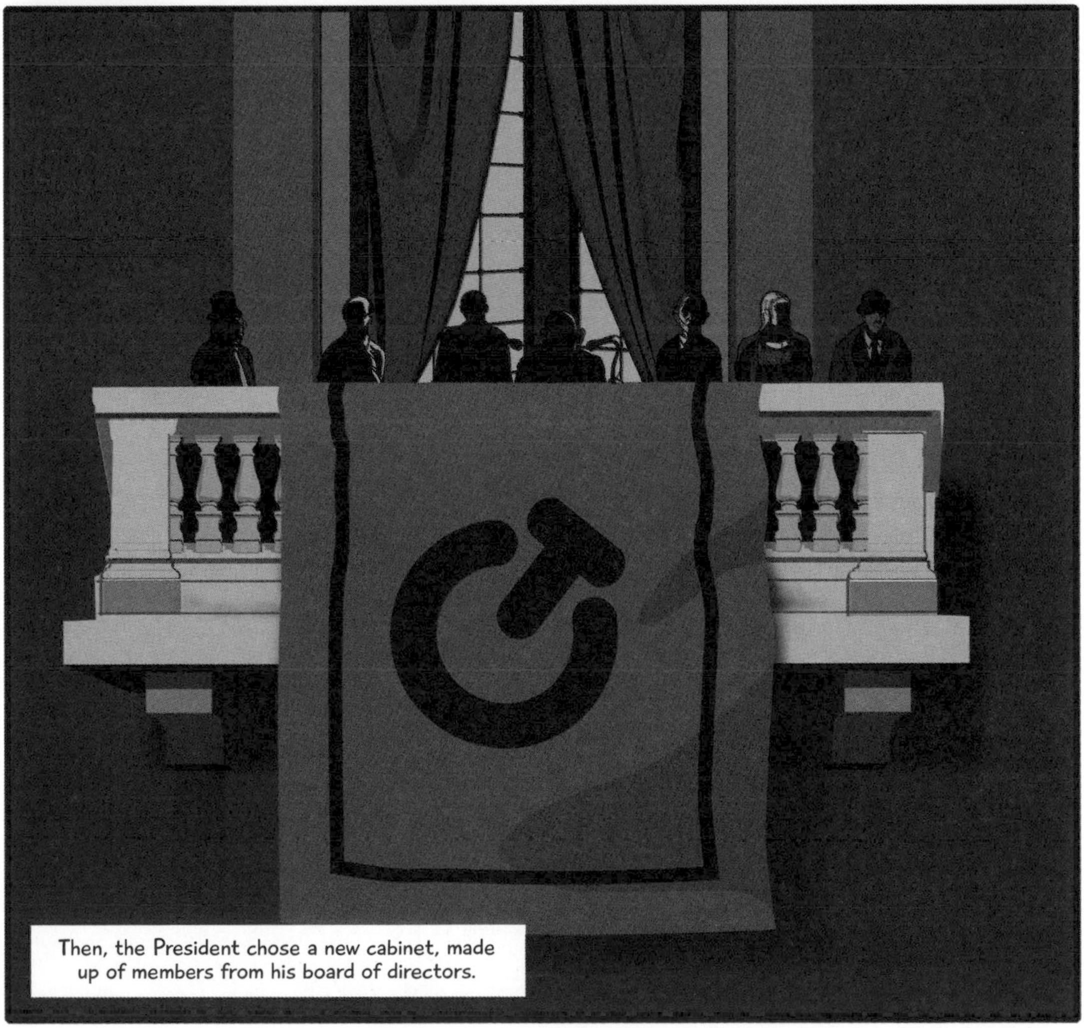
Then, the President chose a new cabinet, made up of members from his board of directors.

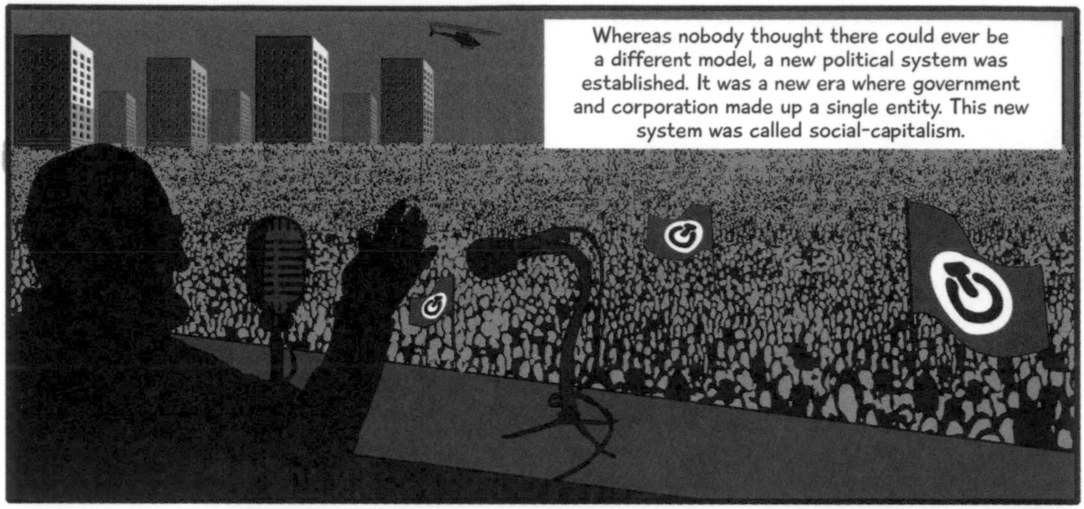
Whereas nobody thought there could ever be a different model, a new political system was established. It was a new era where government and corporation made up a single entity. This new system was called social-capitalism.

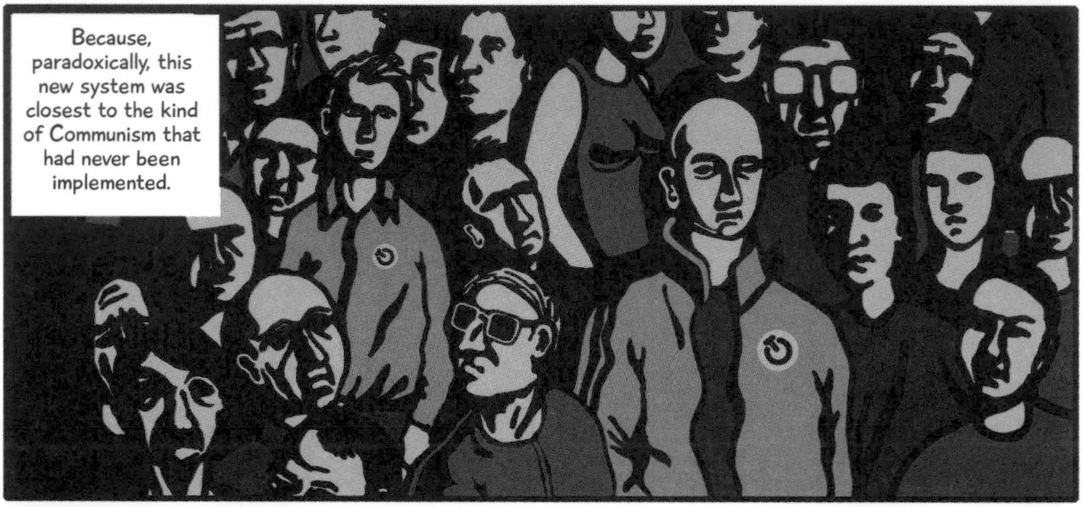
Because, paradoxically, this new system was closest to the kind of Communism that had never been implemented.

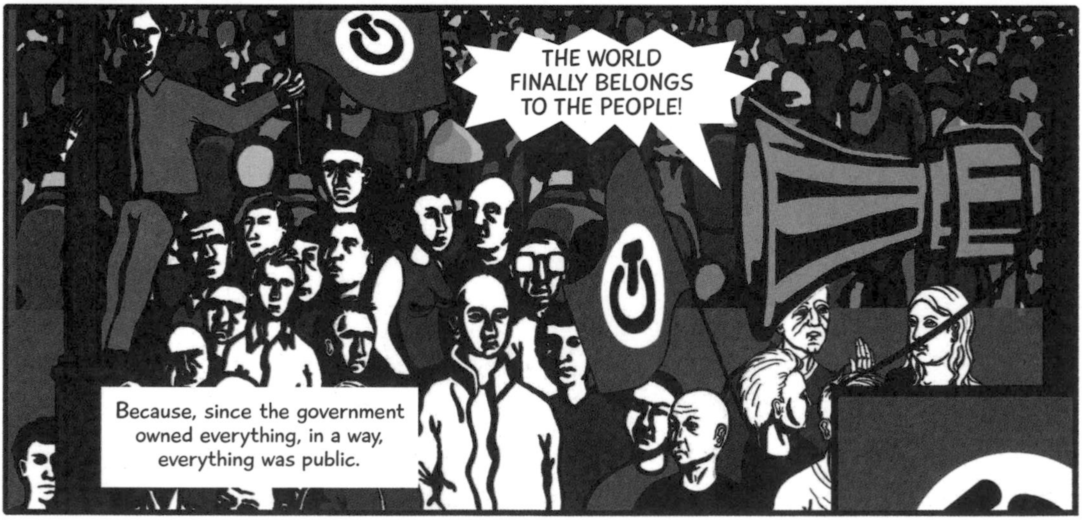
THE WORLD FINALLY BELONGS TO THE PEOPLE!
Because, since the government owned everything, in a way, everything was public.

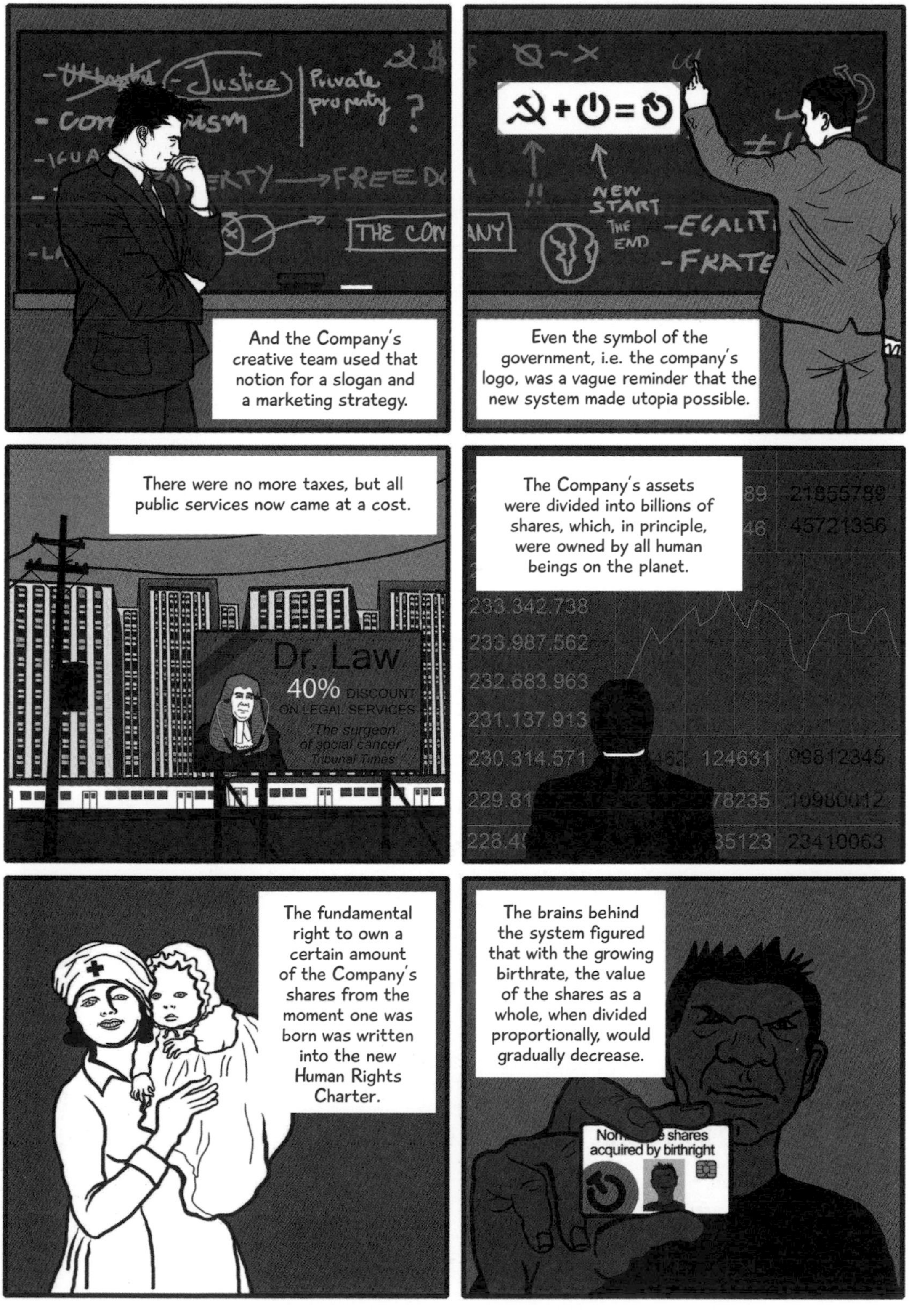
Justice
Private property ?
And the Company's creative team used that notion for a slogan and a marketing strategy.
NEW START
THE END
Even the symbol of the government, i.e. the company's logo, was a vague reminder that the new system made utopia possible.
There were no more taxes, but all public services now came at a cost.
Dr. Law
40% DISCOUNT
ON LEGAL SERVICES
"The surgeon of social cancer"
Tribunal Times
The Company's assets were divided into billions of shares, which, in principle, were owned by all human beings on the planet.
233.342.738
233.987.562
232.683.963
231.137.913
230.314.571
124631
The fundamental right to own a certain amount of the Company's shares from the moment one was born was written into the new Human Rights Charter.
The brains behind the system figured that with the growing birthrate, the value of the shares as a whole, when divided proportionally, would gradually decrease.
acquired by birthright

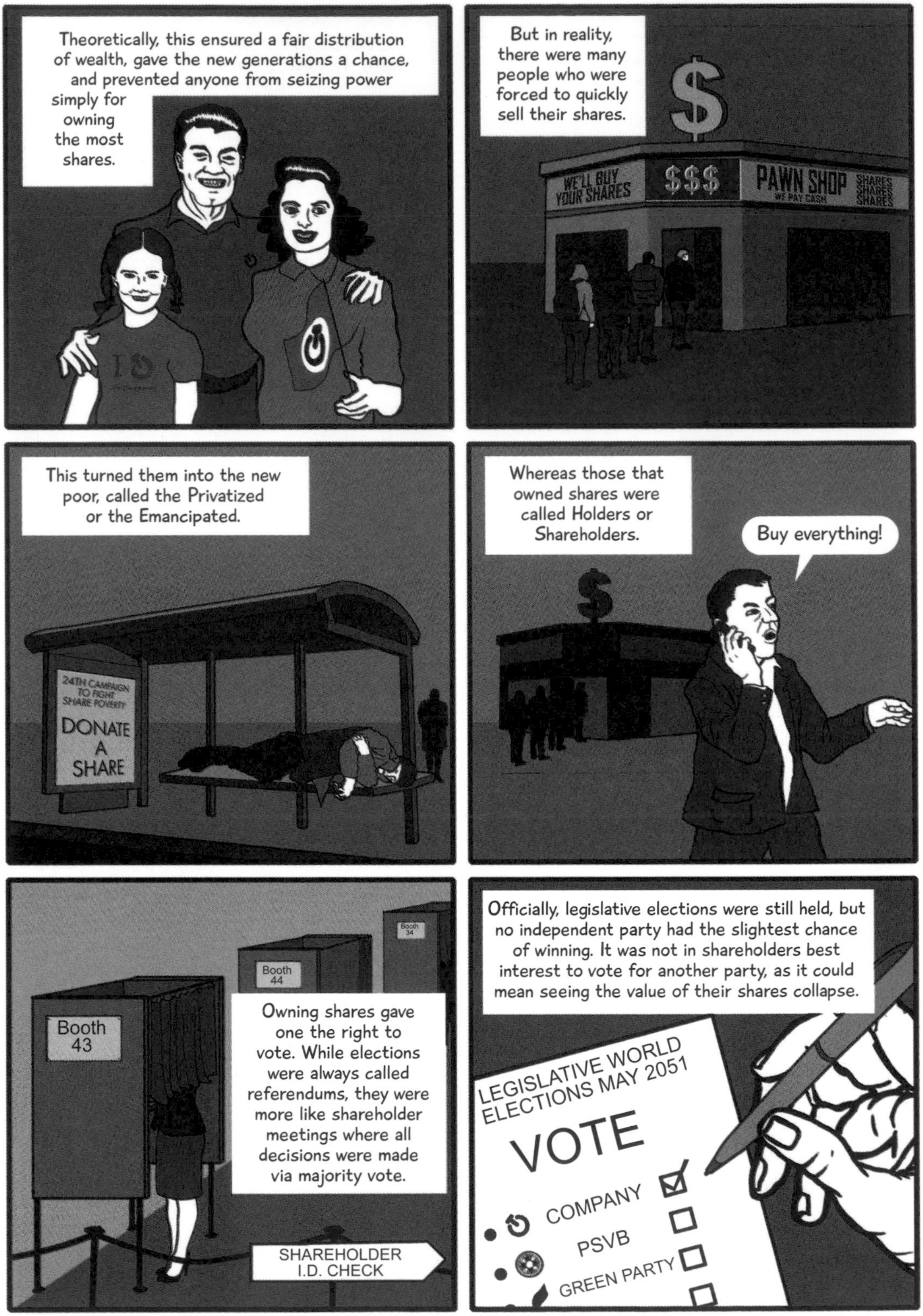
Theoretically, this ensured a fair distribution of wealth, gave the new generations a chance, and prevented anyone from seizing power simply for owning the most shares.
But in reality, there were many people who were forced to quickly sell their shares.
$
WE'LL BUY YOUR SHARES
$$$
PAWN SHOP
WE PAY CASH
SHARES SHARES SHARES
This turned them into the new poor, called the Privatized or the Emancipated.
24TH CAMPAIGN TO FIGHT SHARE POVERTY
DONATE A SHARE
Whereas those that owned shares were called Holders or Shareholders.
Buy everything!
Booth 34
Booth 44
Booth 43
Owning shares gave one the right to vote. While elections were always called referendums, they were more like shareholder meetings where all decisions were made via majority vote.
SHAREHOLDER I.D. CHECK
Officially, legislative elections were still held, but no independent party had the slightest chance of winning. It was not in shareholders best interest to vote for another party, as it could mean seeing the value of their shares collapse.
LEGISLATIVE WORLD ELECTIONS MAY 2051
VOTE
COMPANY
PSVB
GREEN PARTY

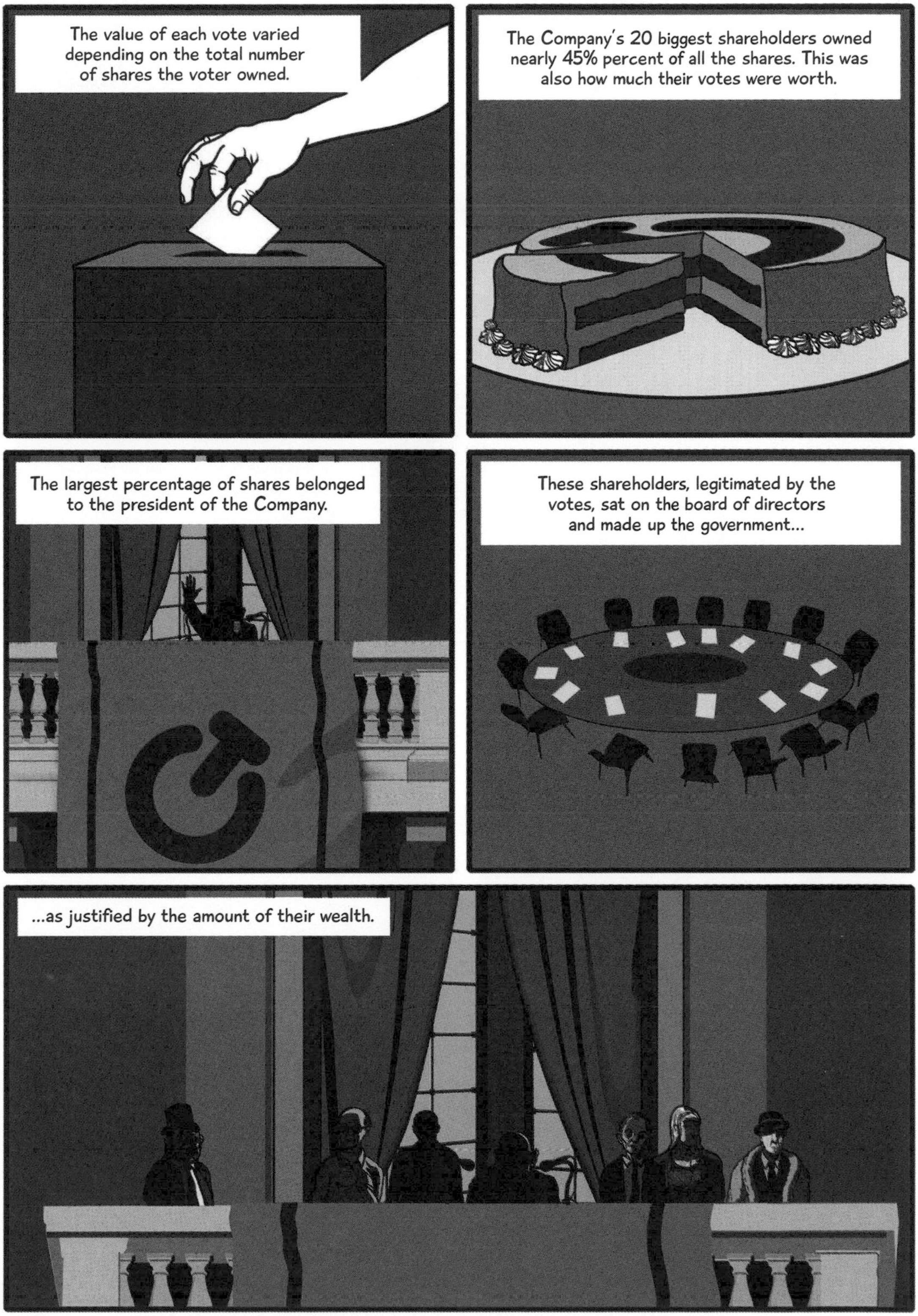
The value of each vote varied depending on the total number of shares the voter owned.
The Company's 20 biggest shareholders owned nearly 45% percent of all the shares. This was also how much their votes were worth.
The largest percentage of shares belonged to the president of the Company.
These shareholders, legitimated by the votes, sat on the board of directors and made up the government...
...as justified by the amount of their wealth.

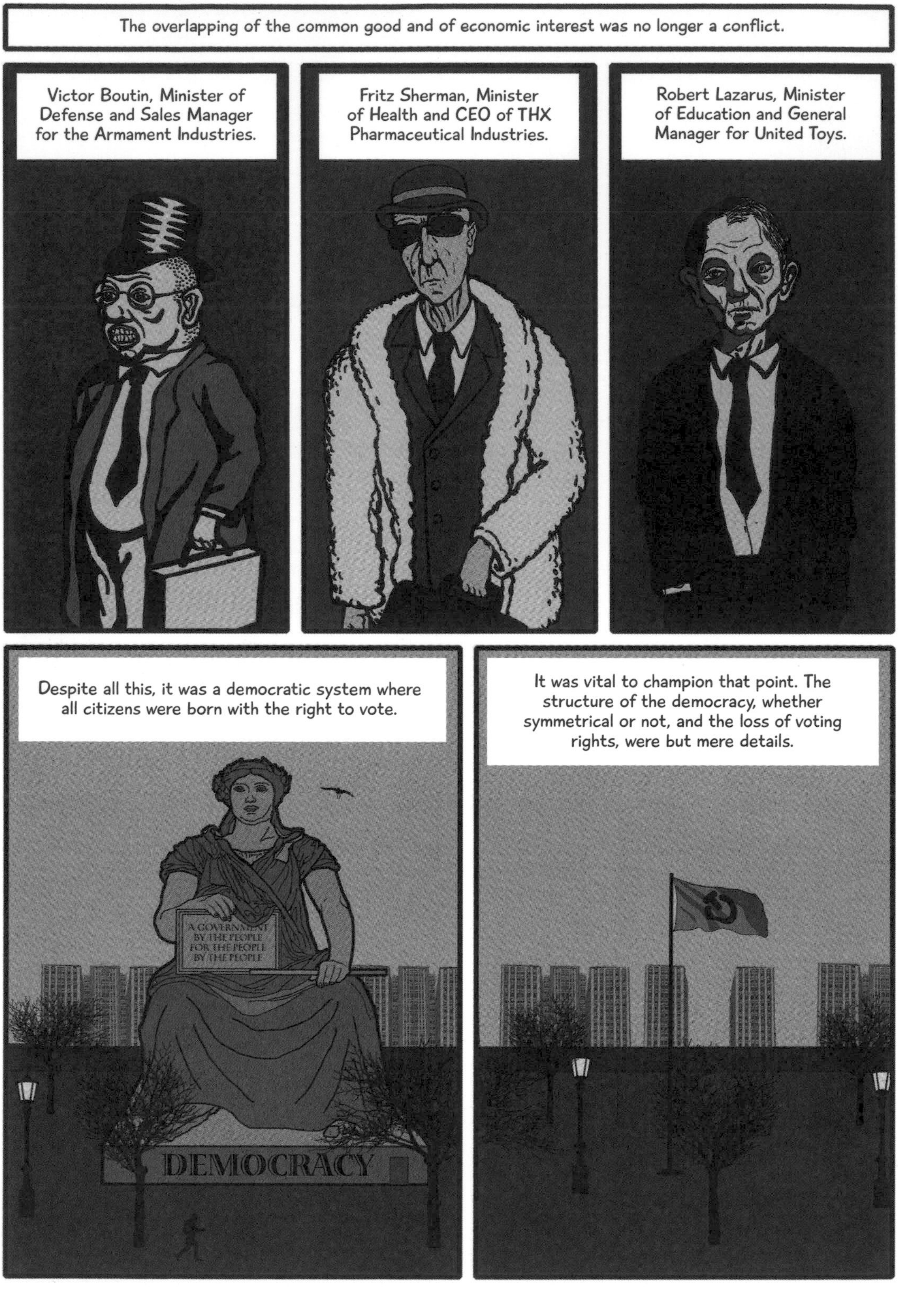
The overlapping of the common good and of economic interest was no longer a conflict.
Victor Boutin, Minister of Defense and Sales Manager for the Armament Industries.
Fritz Sherman, Minister of Health and CEO of THX Pharmaceutical Industries.
Robert Lazarus, Minister of Education and General Manager for United Toys.
Despite all this, it was a democratic system where all citizens were born with the right to vote.
BY THE PEOPLE
FOR THE PEOPLE
BY THE PEOPLE
DEMOCRACY
It was vital to champion that point. The structure of the democracy, whether symmetrical or not, and the loss of voting rights, were but mere details.

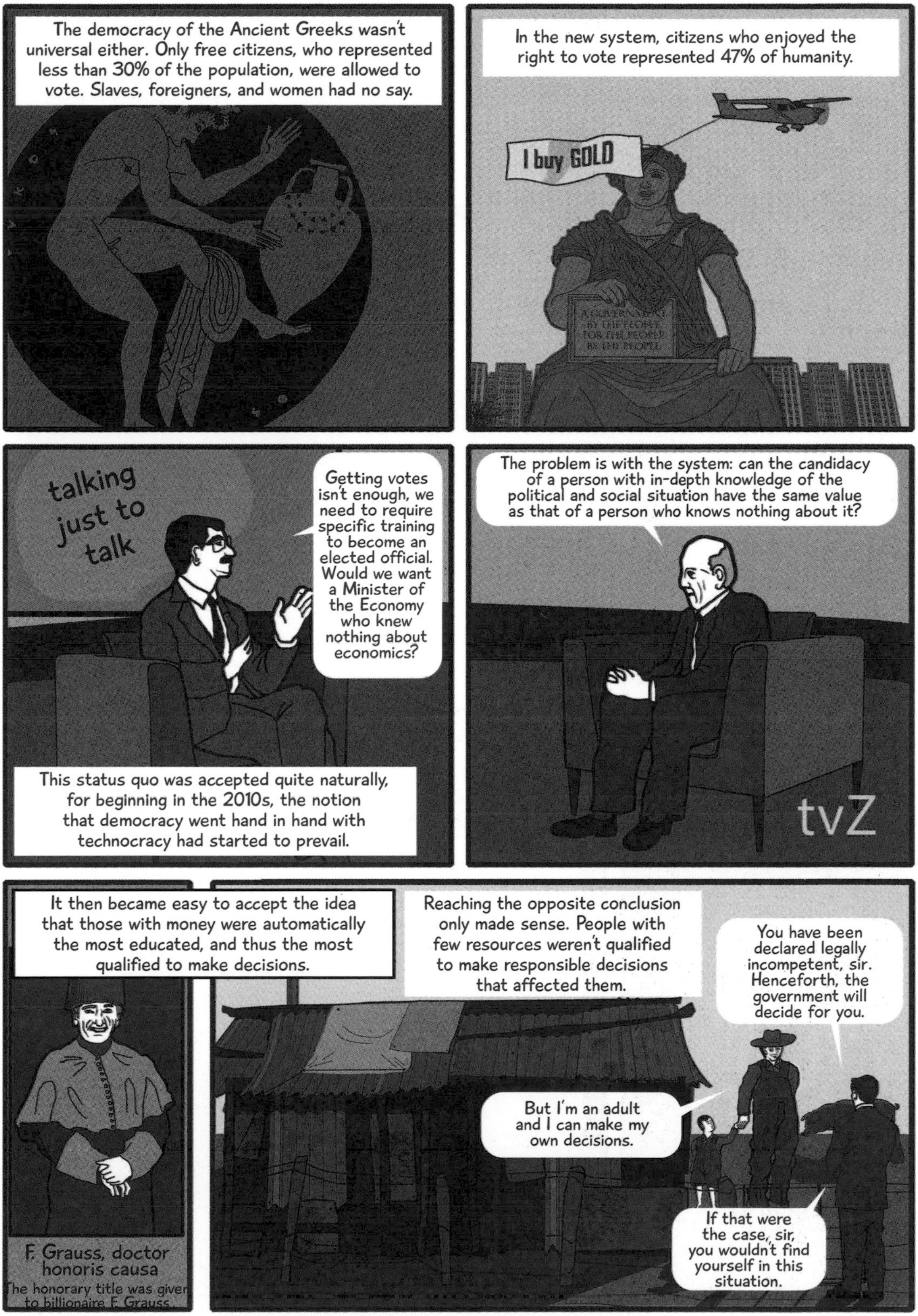
The democracy of the Ancient Greeks wasn't universal either. Only free citizens, who represented less than 30% of the population, were allowed to vote. Slaves, foreigners, and women had no say.
In the new system, citizens who enjoyed the right to vote represented 47% of humanity.
I buy GOLD
talking just to talk
Getting votes isn't enough, we need to require specific training to become an elected official. Would we want a Minister of the Economy who knew nothing about economics?
This status quo was accepted quite naturally, for beginning in the 2010s, the notion that democracy went hand in hand with technocracy had started to prevail.
The problem is with the system: can the candidacy of a person with in-depth knowledge of the political and social situation have the same value as that of a person who knows nothing about it?
tvZ
It then became easy to accept the idea that those with money were automatically the most educated, and thus the most qualified to make decisions.
F. Grauss, doctor honoris causa
The honorary title was given to billionaire F. Grauss.
Reaching the opposite conclusion only made sense. People with few resources weren't qualified to make responsible decisions that affected them.
You have been declared legally incompetent, sir. Henceforth, the government will decide for you.
But I'm an adult and I can make my own decisions.
If that were the case, sir, you wouldn't find yourself in this situation.

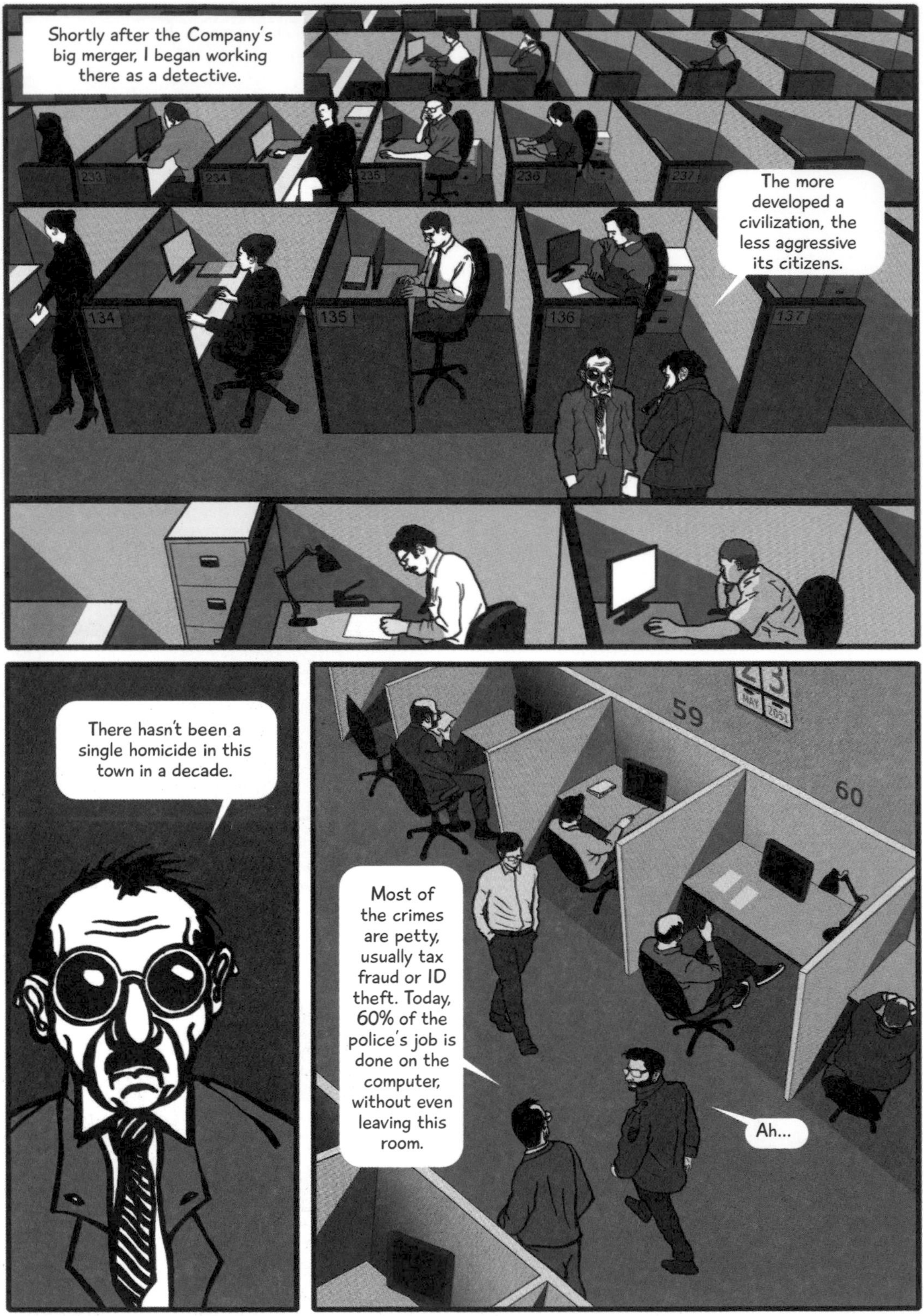
Shortly after the Company's big merger, I began working there as a detective.
The more developed a civilization, the less aggressive its citizens.
There hasn't been a single homicide in this town in a decade.
Most of the crimes are petty, usually tax fraud or ID theft. Today, 60% of the police's job is done on the computer, without even leaving this room.
Ah...

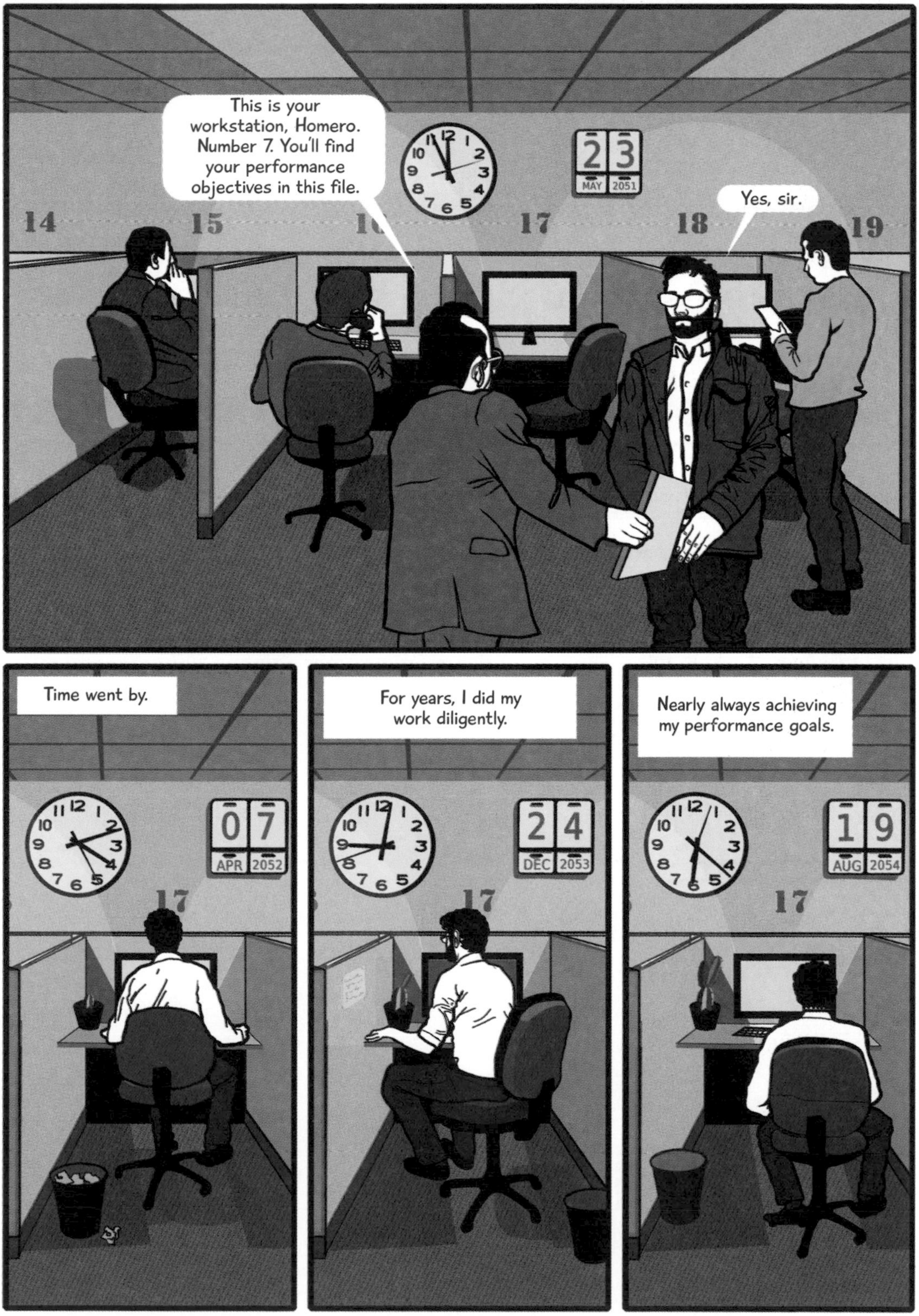
This is your workstation, Homero. Number 7. You'll find your performance objectives in this file.
Yes, sir.
Time went by.
For years, I did my work diligently.
Nearly always achieving my performance goals.

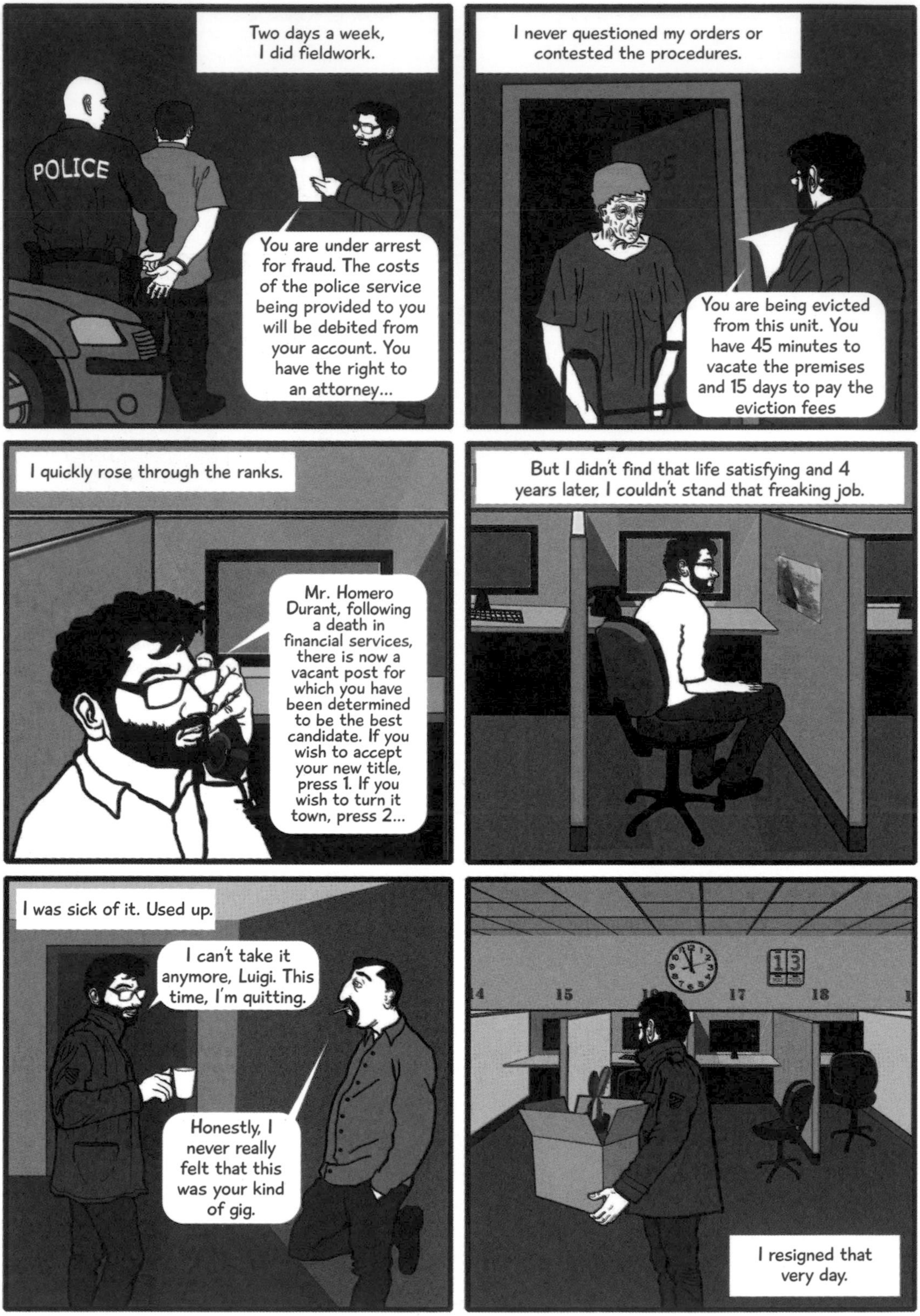
Two days a week, I did fieldwork.
POLICE
You are under arrest for fraud. The costs of the police service being provided to you will be debited from your account. You have the right to an attorney...
I never questioned my orders or contested the procedures.
35
You are being evicted from this unit. You have 45 minutes to vacate the premises and 15 days to pay the eviction fees
I quickly rose through the ranks.
Mr. Homero Durant, following a death in financial services, there is now a vacant post for which you have been determined to be the best candidate. If you wish to accept your new title, press 1. If you wish to turn it town, press 2...
But I didn't find that life satisfying and 4 years later, I couldn't stand that freaking job.
I was sick of it. Used up.
I can't take it anymore, Luigi. This time, I'm quitting.
Honestly, I never really felt that this was your kind of gig.
13
15
17
18
I resigned that very day.

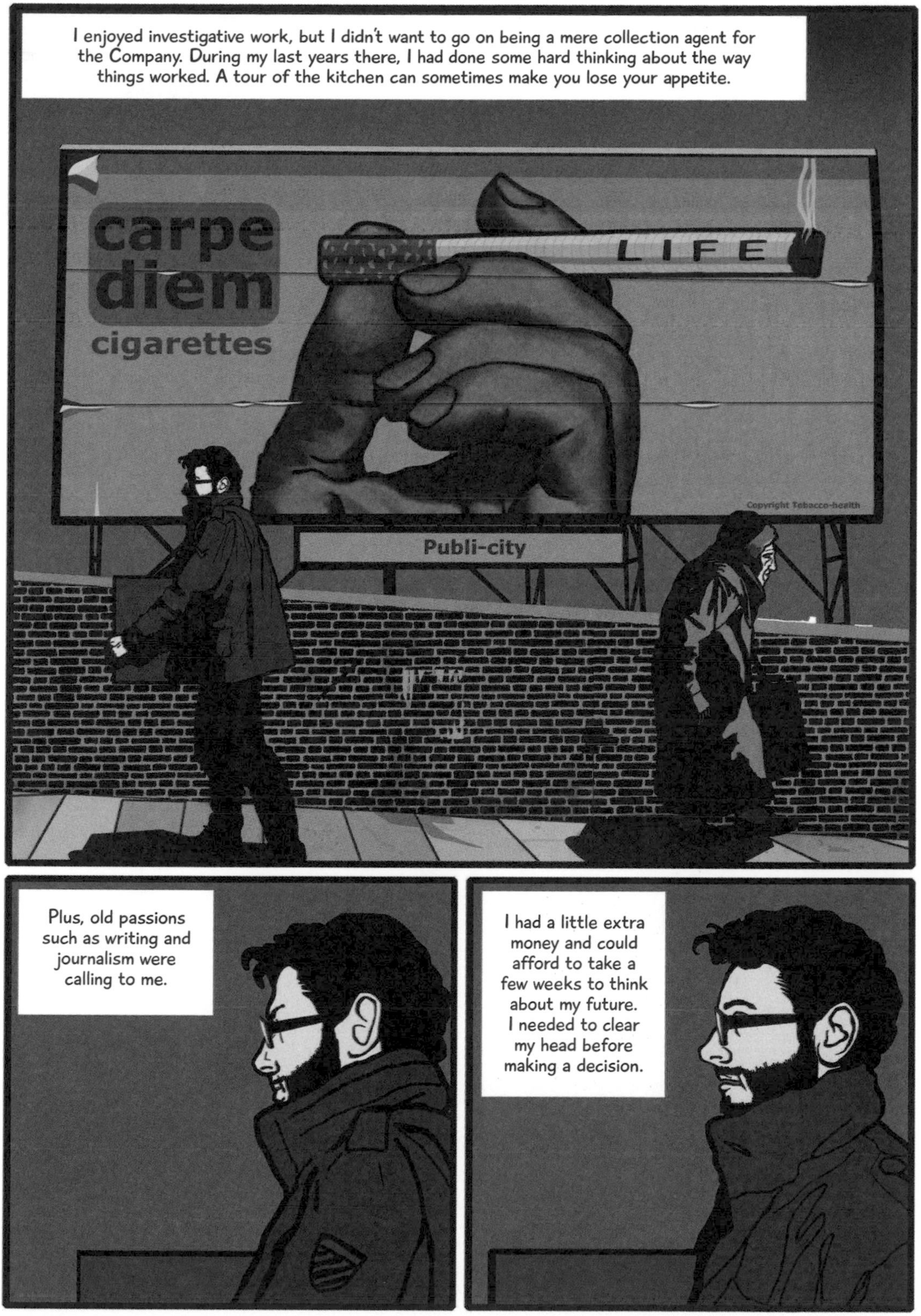
I enjoyed investigative work, but I didn't want to go on being a mere collection agent for the Company. During my last years there, I had done some hard thinking about the way things worked. A tour of the kitchen can sometimes make you lose your appetite.
carpe diem
cigarettes
LIFE
Copyright Tobacco-health
Publi-city
Plus, old passions such as writing and journalism were calling to me.
I had a little extra money and could afford to take a few weeks to think about my future. I needed to clear my head before making a decision.

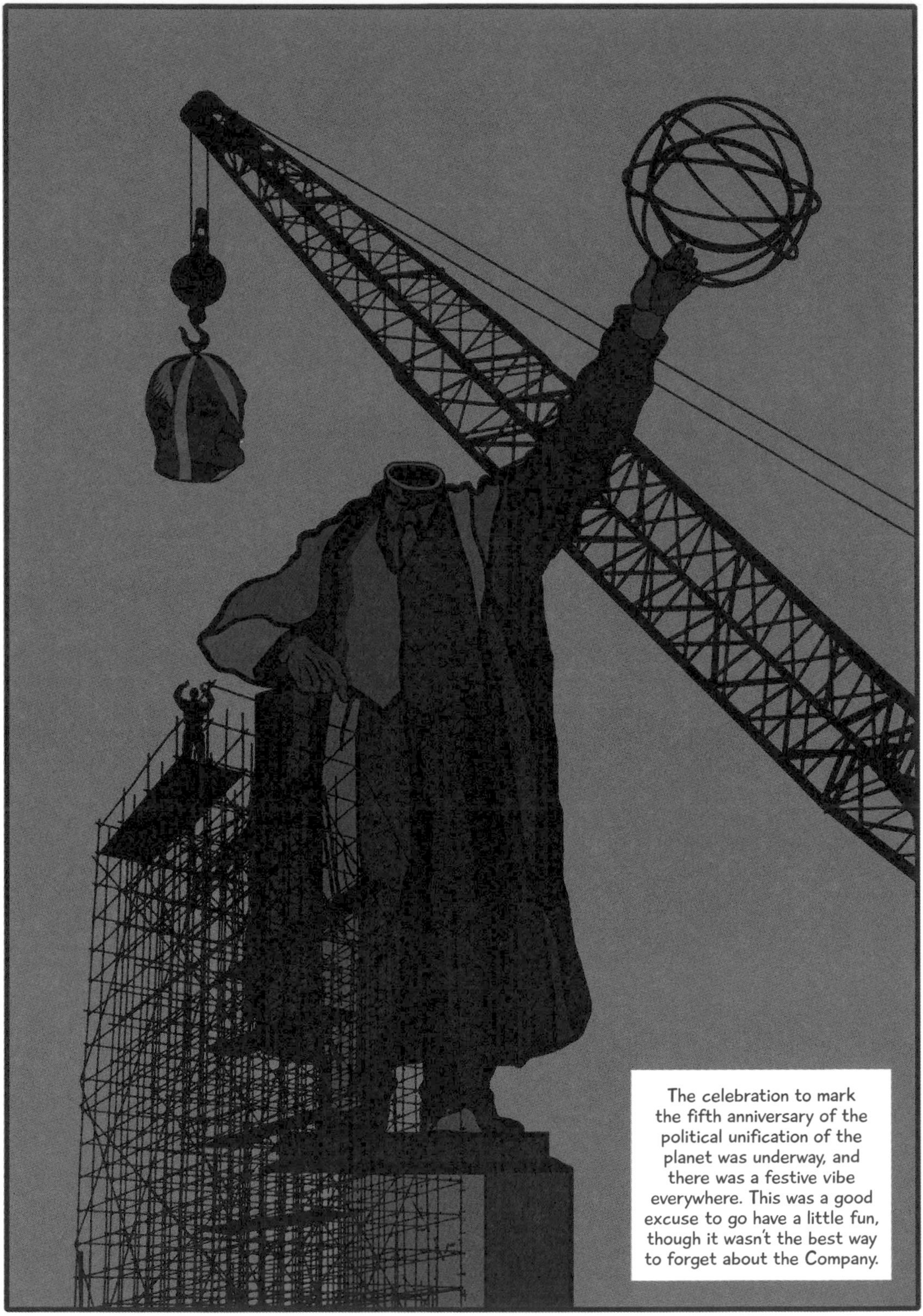
The celebration to mark the fifth anniversary of the political unification of the planet was underway, and there was a festive vibe everywhere. This was a good excuse to go have a little fun, though it wasn't the best way to forget about the Company.

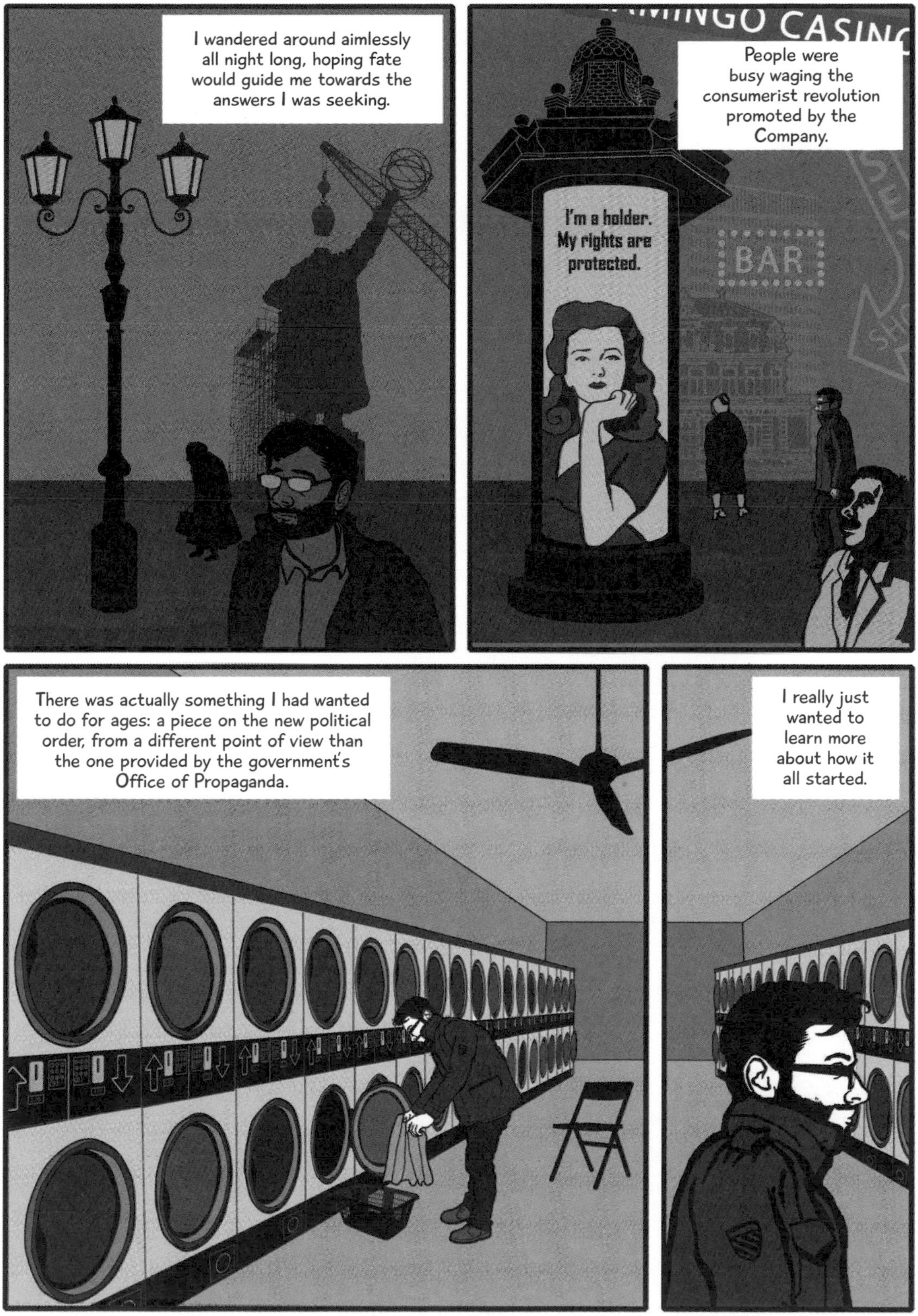
I wandered around aimlessly all night long, hoping fate would guide me towards the answers I was seeking.
MINGO CASIN
People were busy waging the consumerist revolution promoted by the Company.
I'm a holder. My rights are protected.
BAR
There was actually something I had wanted to do for ages: a piece on the new political order, from a different point of view than the one provided by the government's Office of Propaganda.
I really just wanted to learn more about how it all started.

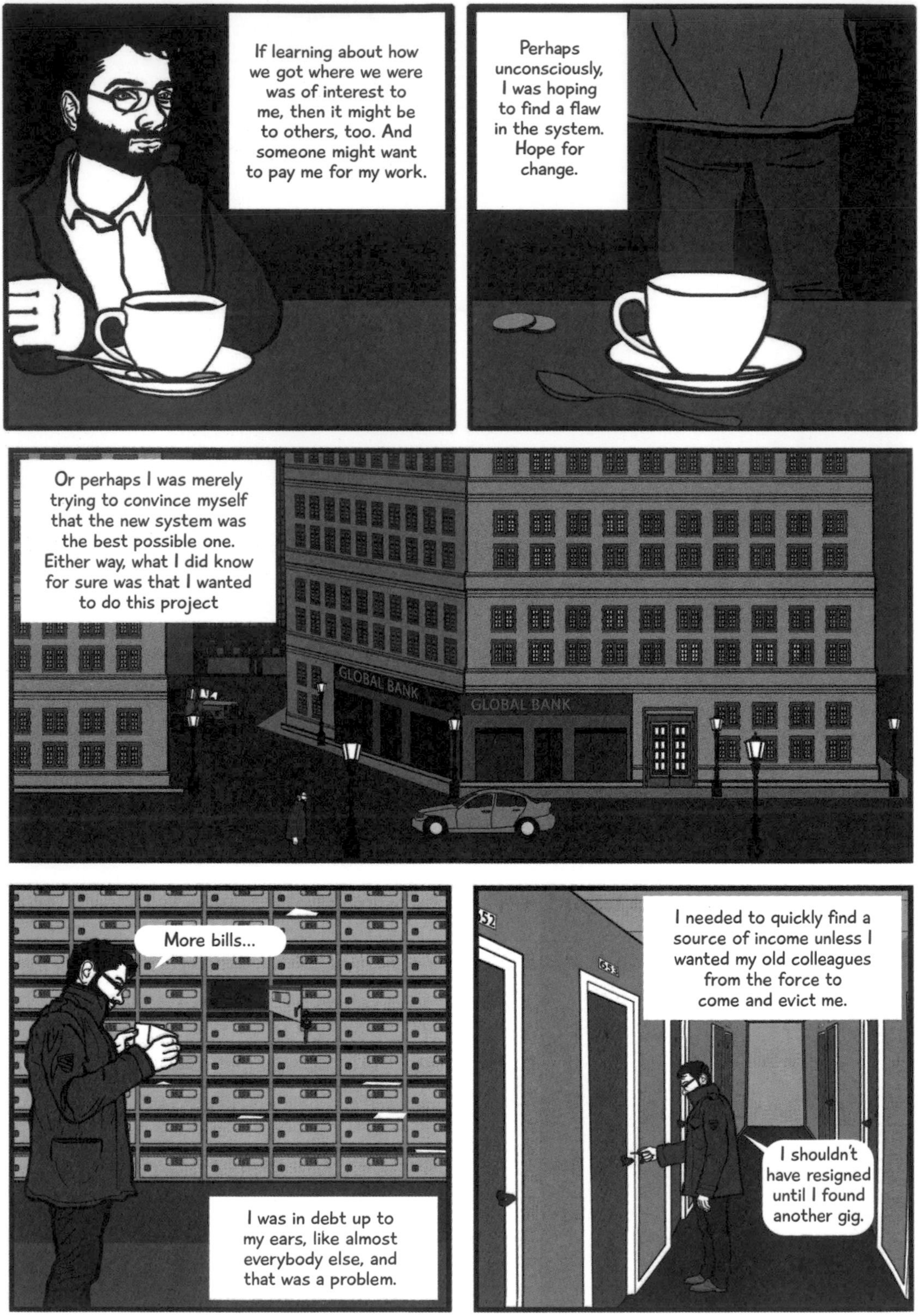
If learning about how we got where we were was of interest to me, then it might be to others, too. And someone might want to pay me for my work.
Perhaps unconsciously, I was hoping to find a flaw in the system. Hope for change.
Or perhaps I was merely trying to convince myself that the new system was the best possible one. Either way, what I did know for sure was that I wanted to do this project
GLOBAL BANK
GLOBAL BANK
More bills...
I was in debt up to my ears, like almost everybody else, and that was a problem.
I needed to quickly find a source of income unless I wanted my old colleagues from the force to come and evict me.
I shouldn't have resigned until I found another gig.

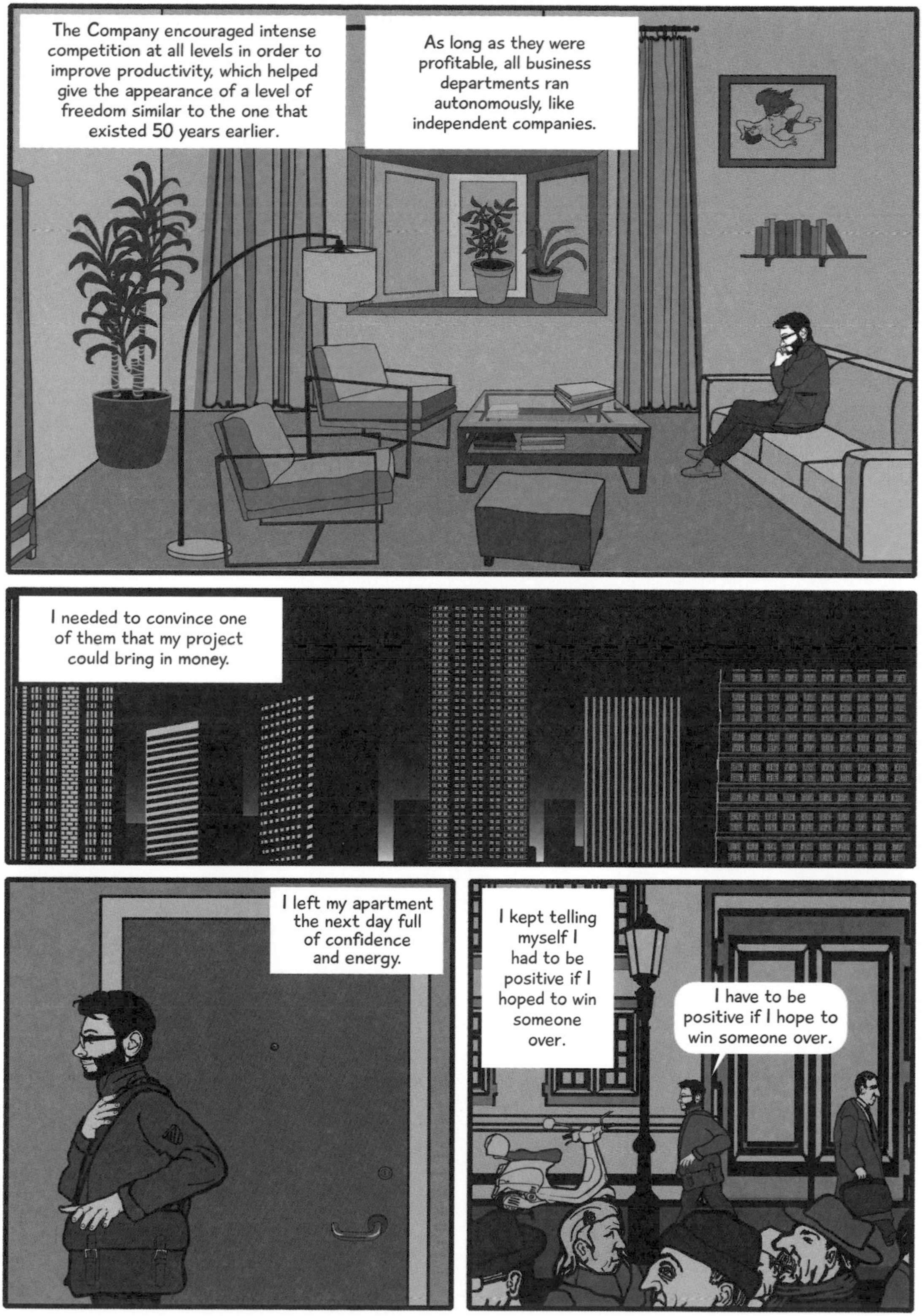
The Company encouraged intense competition at all levels in order to improve productivity, which helped give the appearance of a level of freedom similar to the one that existed 50 years earlier.
As long as they were profitable, all business departments ran autonomously, like independent companies.
I needed to convince one of them that my project could bring in money.
I left my apartment the next day full of confidence and energy.
I kept telling myself I had to be positive if I hoped to win someone over.
I have to be positive if I hope to win someone over.

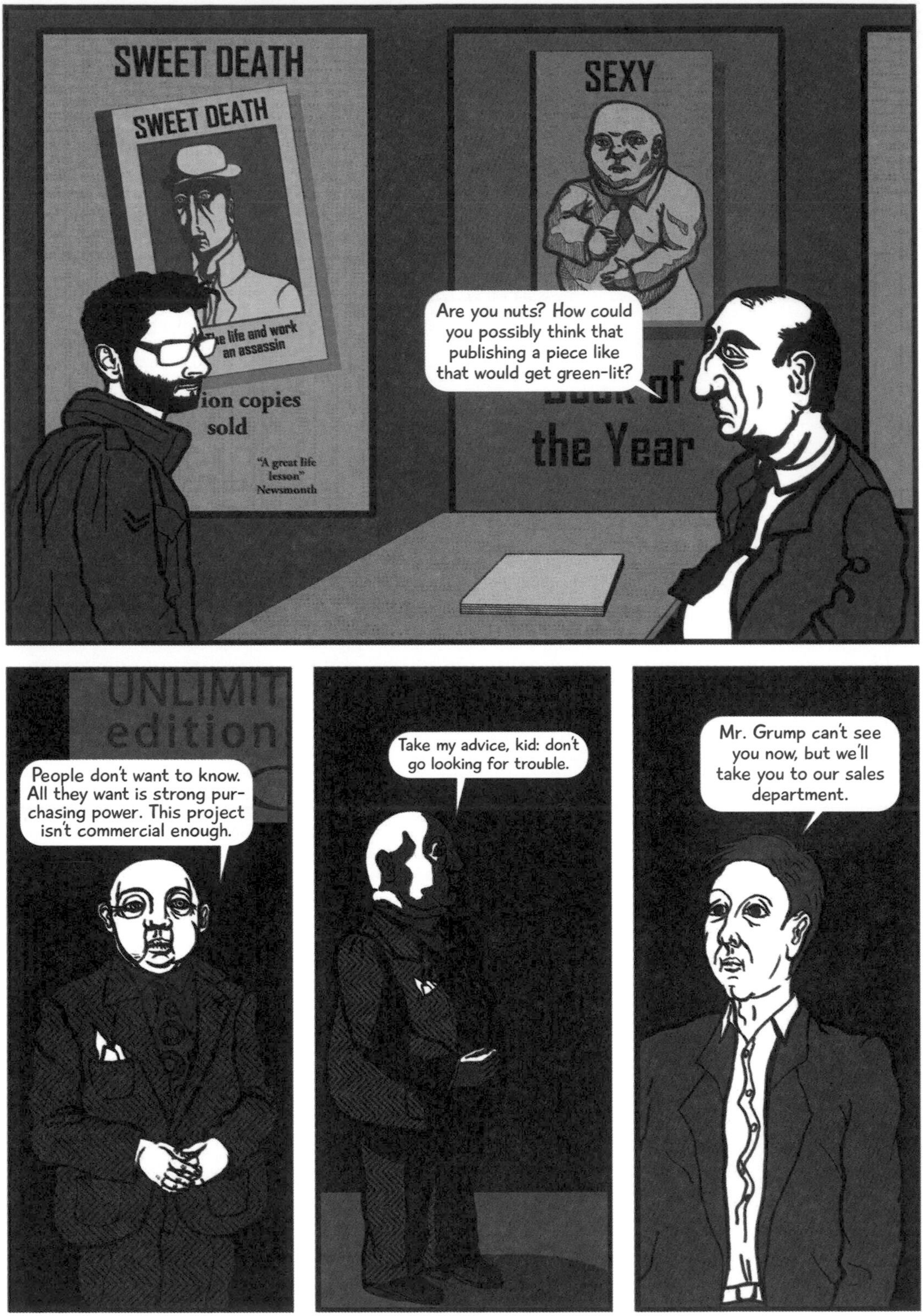
SWEET DEATH
SWEET DEATH
"A great life lesson" Newsmonth
SEXY
the Year
Are you nuts? How could you possibly think that publishing a piece like that would get green-lit?
People don't want to know. All they want is strong pur-chasing power. This project isn't commercial enough.
Take my advice, kid: don't go looking for trouble.
Mr. Grump can't see you now, but we'll take you to our sales department.

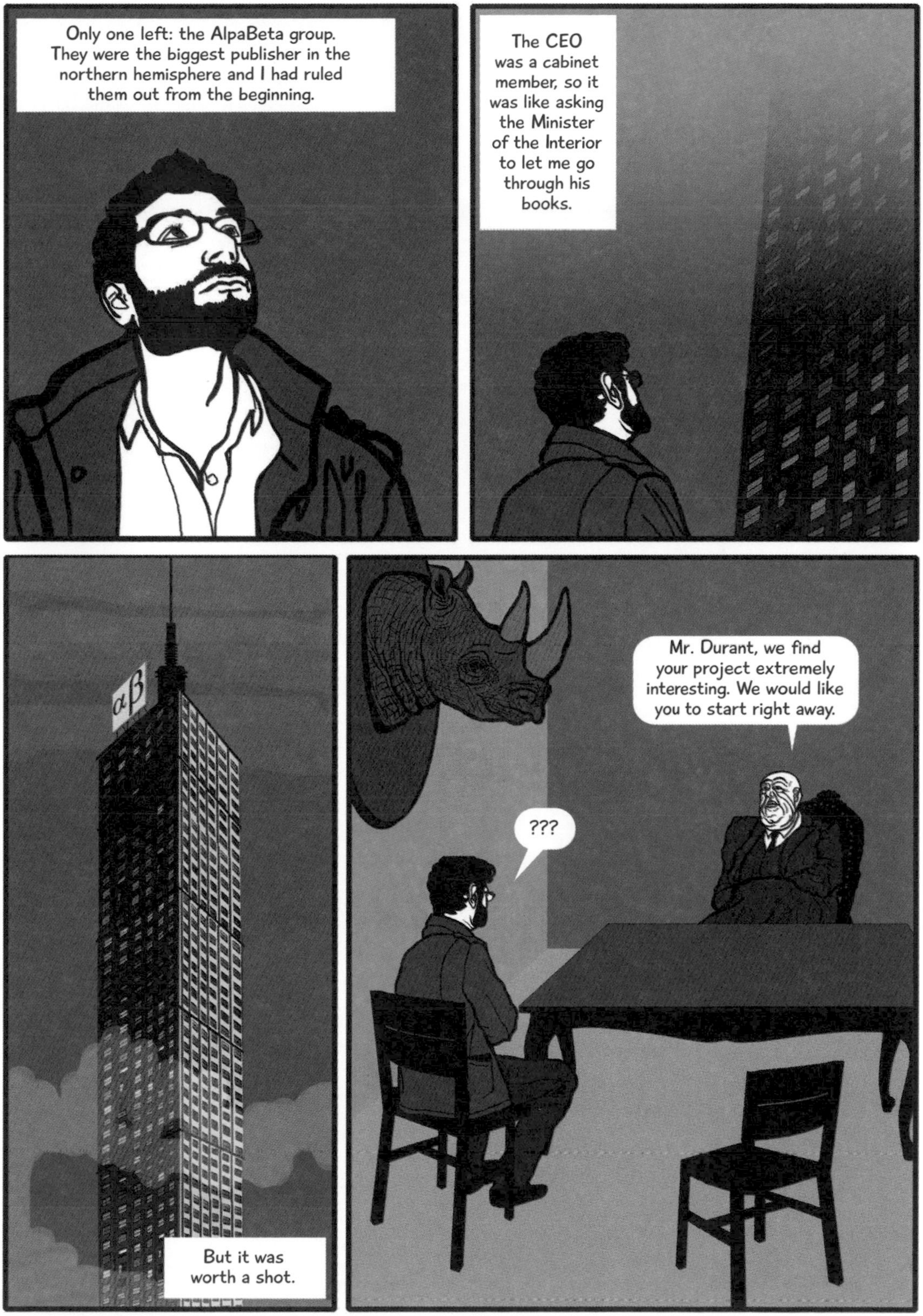
Only one left: the AlpaBeta group. They were the biggest publisher in the northern hemisphere and I had ruled them out from the beginning.
The CEO was a cabinet member, so it was like asking the Minister of the Interior to let me go through his books.
αβ
But it was worth a shot.
Mr. Durant, we find your project extremely interesting. We would like you to start right away.
???

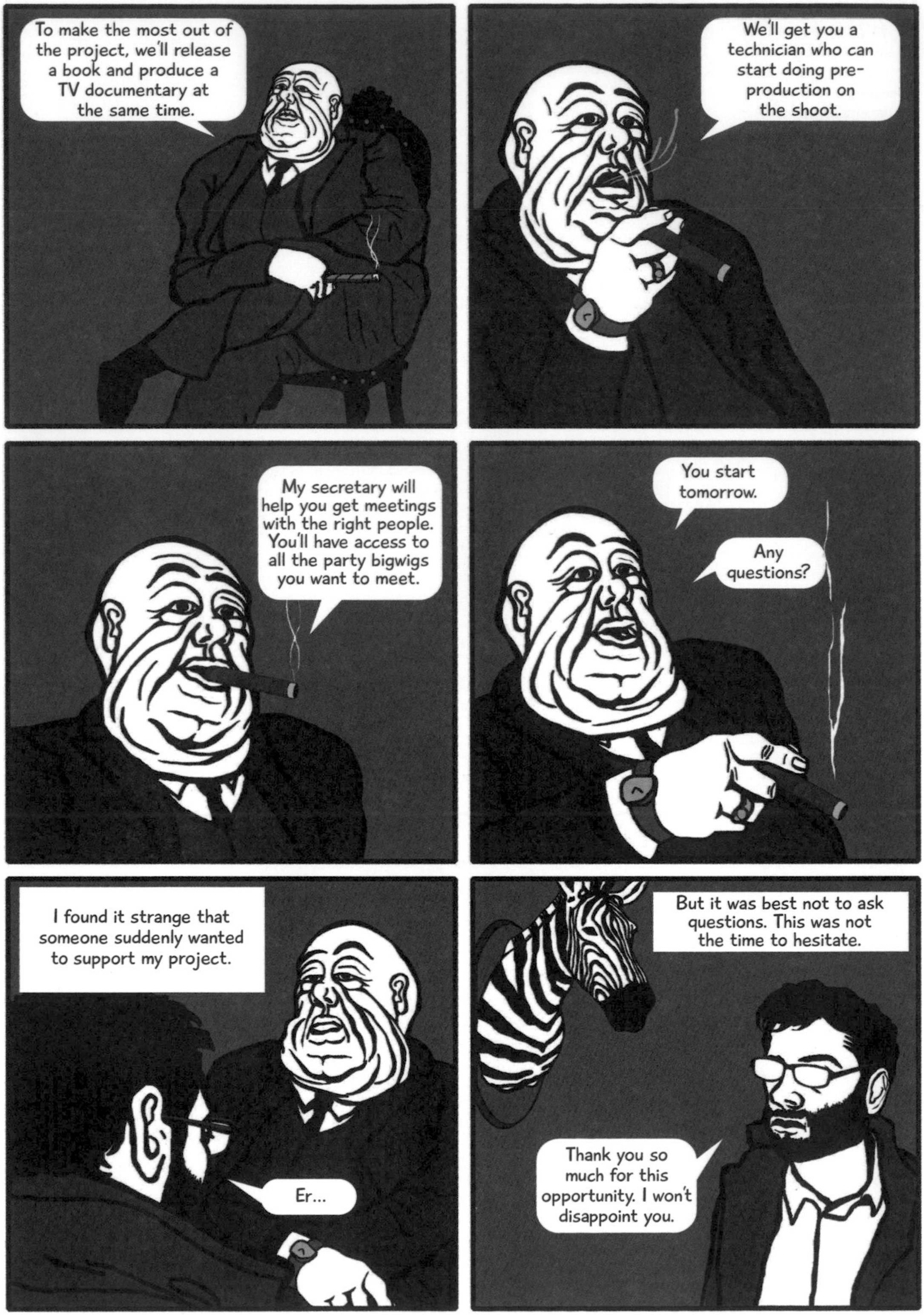
To make the most out of the project, we'll release a book and produce a TV documentary at the same time.
We'll get you a technician who can start doing pre-production on the shoot.
My secretary will help you get meetings with the right people. You'll have access to all the party bigwigs you want to meet.
You start tomorrow.
Any questions?
I found it strange that someone suddenly wanted to support my project.
Er...
But it was best not to ask questions. This was not the time to hesitate.
Thank you so much for this opportunity. I won't disappoint you.

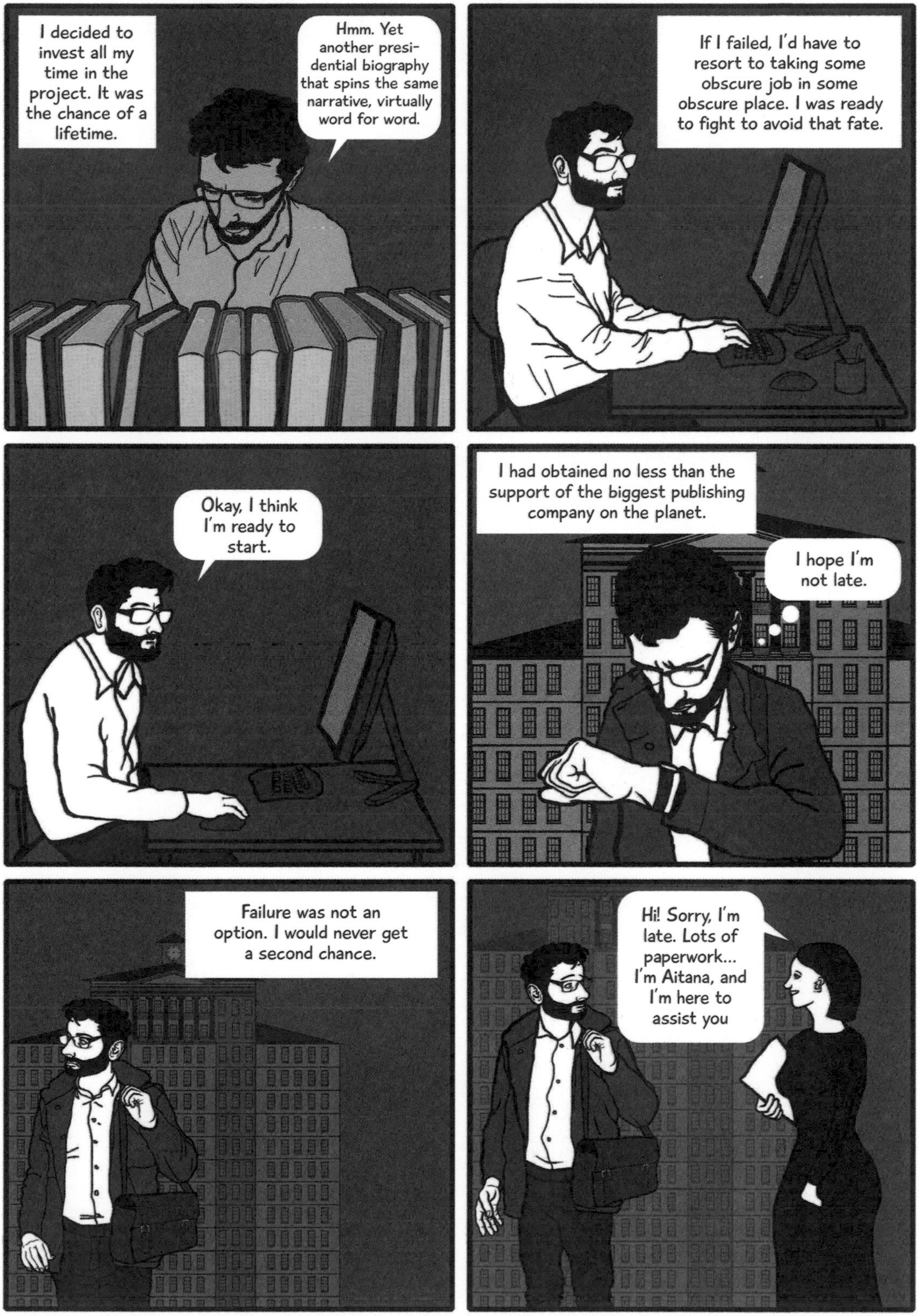
I decided to invest all my time in the project. It was the chance of a lifetime.
Hmm. Yet another presi-dential biography that spins the same narrative, virtually word for word.
If I failed, I'd have to resort to taking some obscure job in some obscure place. I was ready to fight to avoid that fate.
Okay, I think I'm ready to start.
I had obtained no less than the support of the biggest publishing company on the planet.
I hope I'm not late.
Failure was not an option. I would never get a second chance.
Hi! Sorry, I'm late. Lots of paperwork... I'm Aitana, and I'm here to assist you

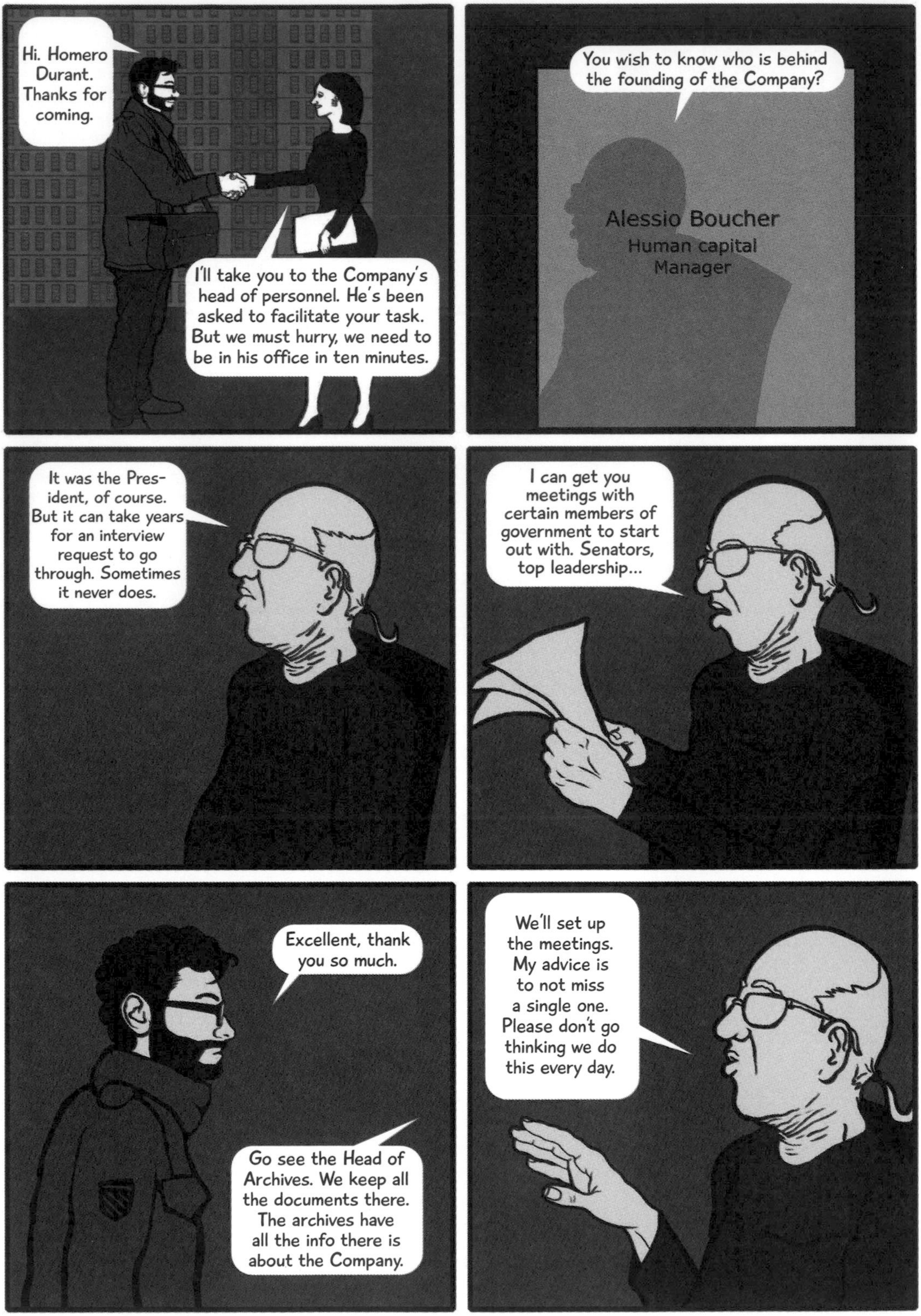

Hi. Homero Durant. Thanks for coming.
I'll take you to the Company's head of personnel. He's been asked to facilitate your task. But we must hurry, we need to be in his office in ten minutes.
You wish to know who is behind the founding of the Company?
Alessio Boucher
Human capital Manager
It was the President, of course. But it can take years for an interview request to go through. Sometimes it never does.
I can get you meetings with certain members of government to start out with. Senators, top leadership...
Excellent, thank you so much.
Go see the Head of Archives. We keep all the documents there. The archives have all the info there is about the Company.
We'll set up the meetings. My advice is to not miss a single one. Please don't go thinking we do this every day.

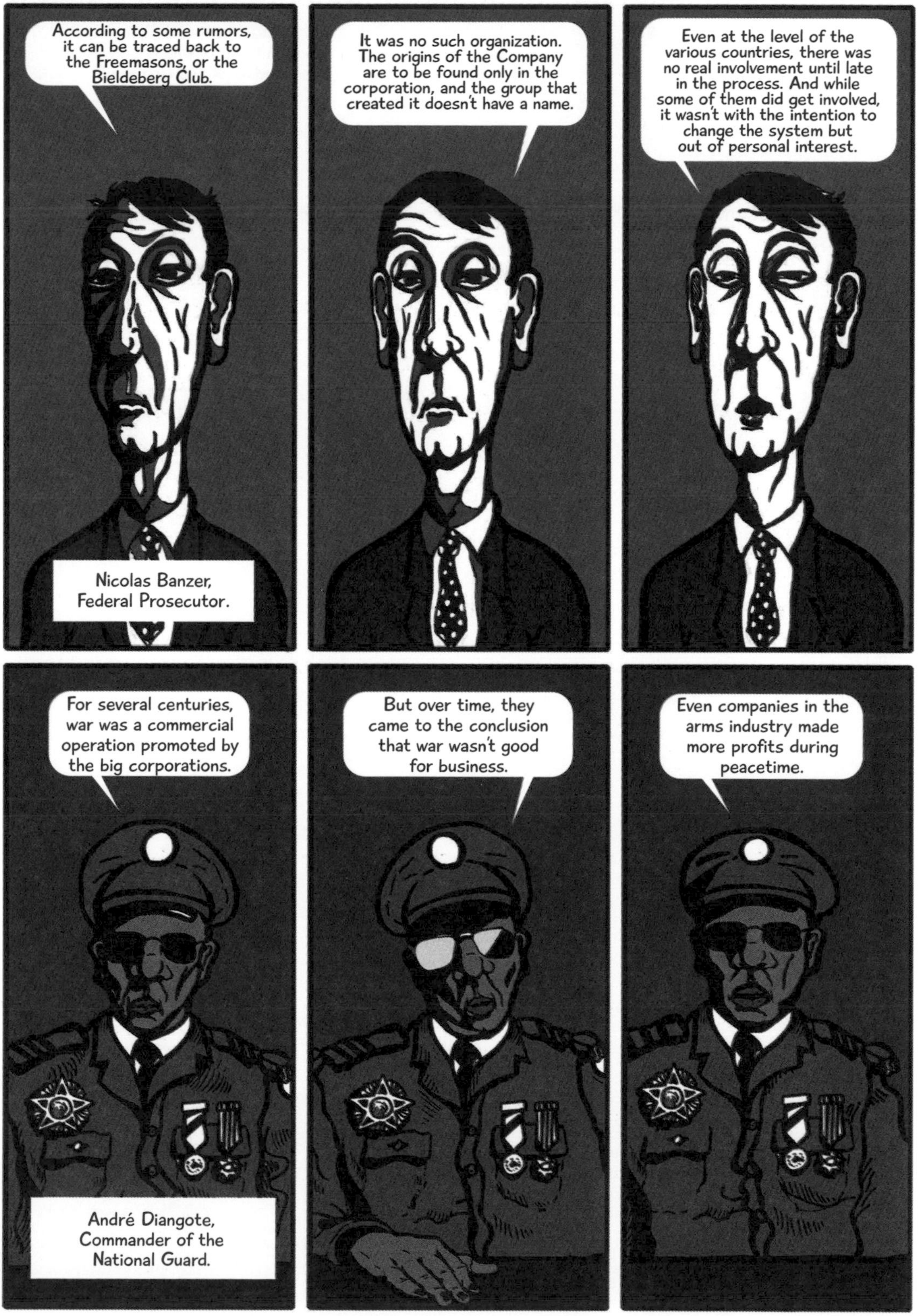
According to some rumors, it can be traced back to the Freemasons, or the Bieldeberg Club.
Nicolas Banzer, Federal Prosecutor.
It was no such organization. The origins of the Company are to be found only in the corporation, and the group that created it doesn't have a name.
Even at the level of the various countries, there was no real involvement until late in the process. And while some of them did get involved, it wasn't with the intention to change the system but out of personal interest.
For several centuries, war was a commercial operation promoted by the big corporations.
André Diangote, Commander of the National Guard.
But over time, they came to the conclusion that war wasn't good for business.
Even companies in the arms industry made more profits during peacetime.

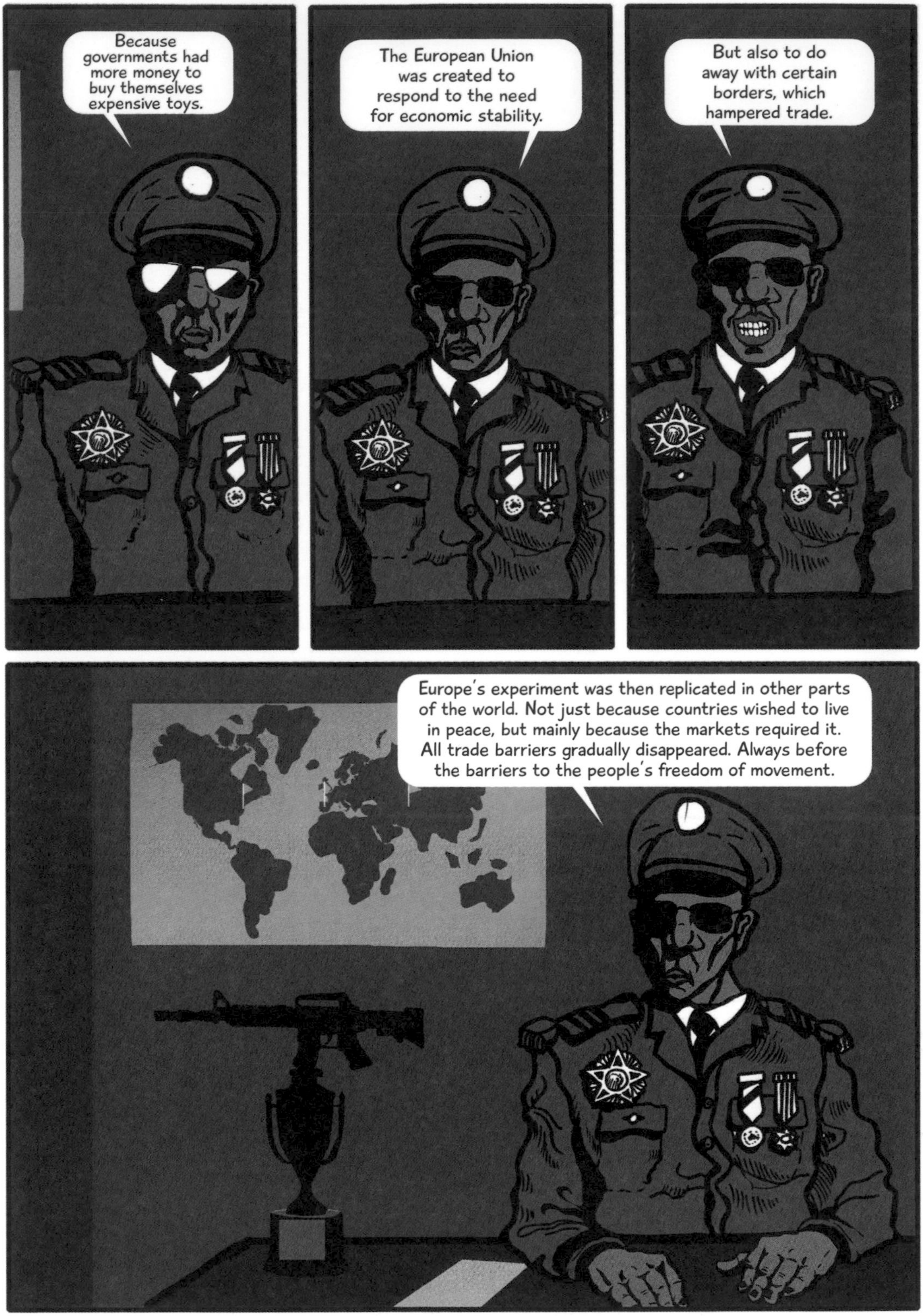
Because governments had more money to buy themselves expensive toys.
The European Union was created to respond to the need for economic stability.
But also to do away with certain borders, which hampered trade.
Europe's experiment was then replicated in other parts of the world. Not just because countries wished to live in peace, but mainly because the markets required it. All trade barriers gradually disappeared. Always before the barriers to the people's freedom of movement.

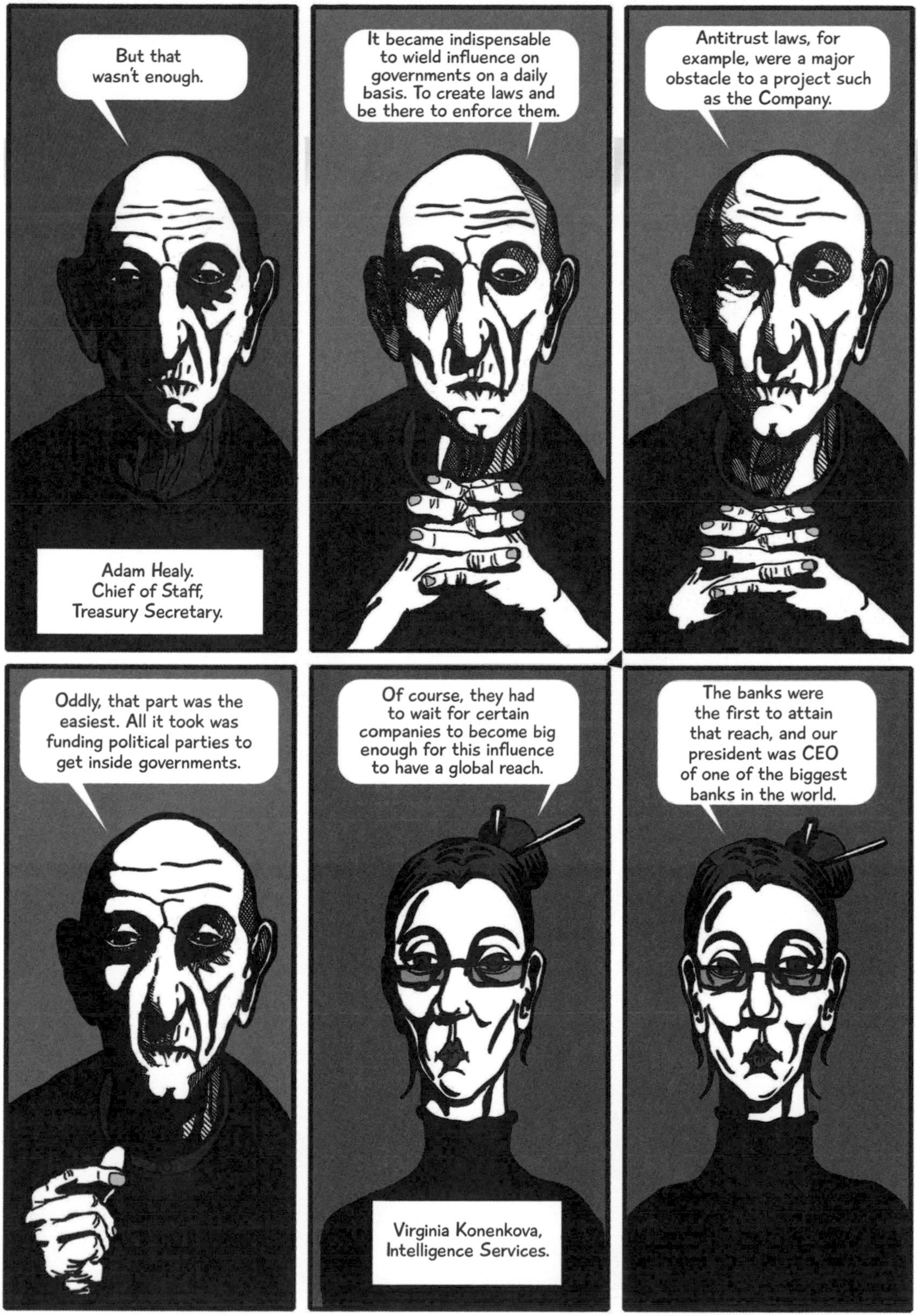
But that wasn't enough.
Adam Healy. Chief of Staff, Treasury Secretary.
It became indispensable to wield influence on governments on a daily basis. To create laws and be there to enforce them.
Antitrust laws, for example, were a major obstacle to a project such as the Company.
Oddly, that part was the easiest. All it took was funding political parties to get inside governments.
Of course, they had to wait for certain companies to become big enough for this influence to have a global reach.
Virginia Konenkova, Intelligence Services.
The banks were the first to attain that reach, and our president was CEO of one of the biggest banks in the world.

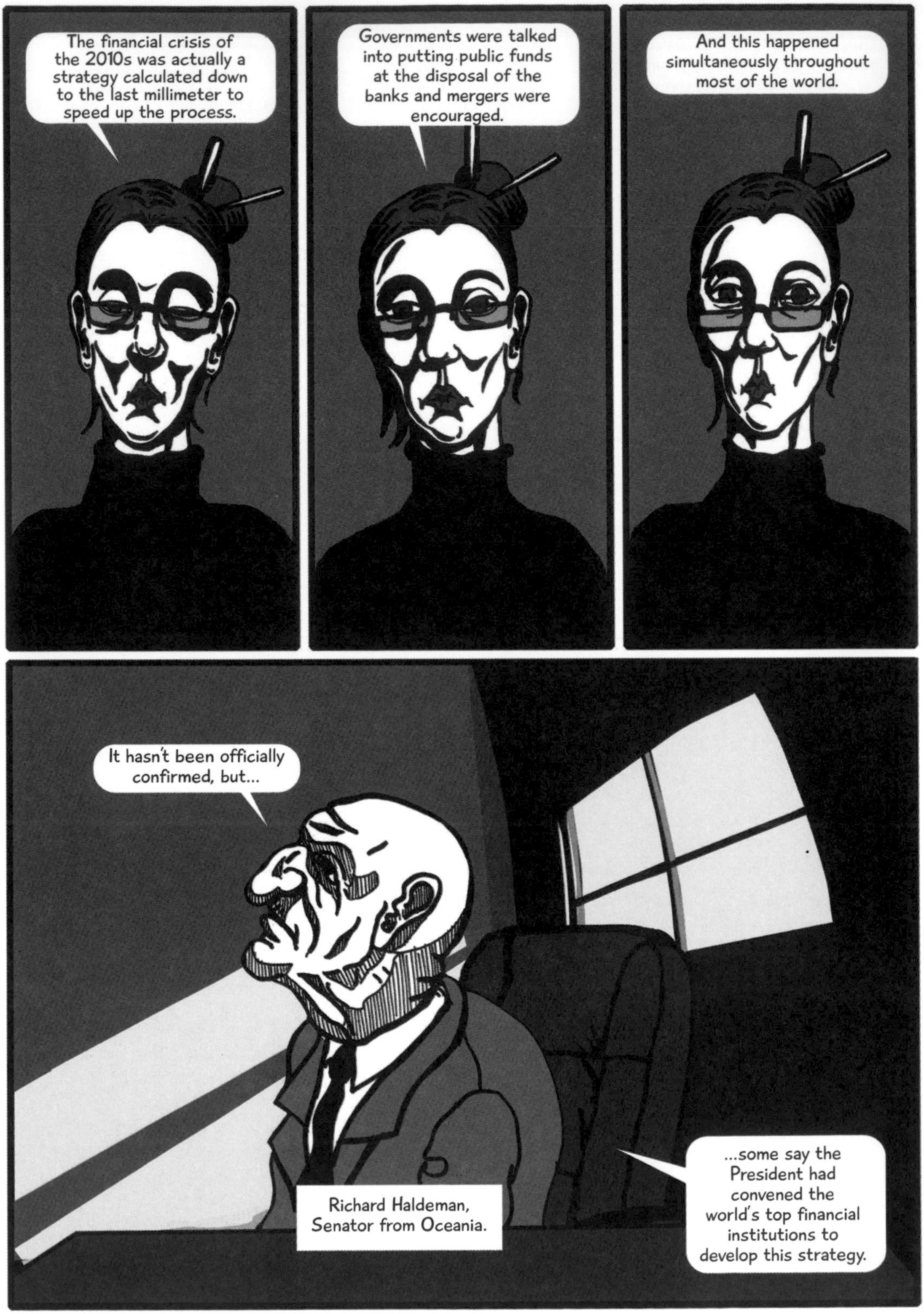

The financial crisis of the 2010s was actually a strategy calculated down to the last millimeter to speed up the process.
Governments were talked into putting public funds at the disposal of the banks and mergers were encouraged.
And this happened simultaneously throughout most of the world.
It hasn't been officially confirmed, but...
Richard Haldeman, Senator from Oceania.
...some say the President had convened the world's top financial institutions to develop this strategy.

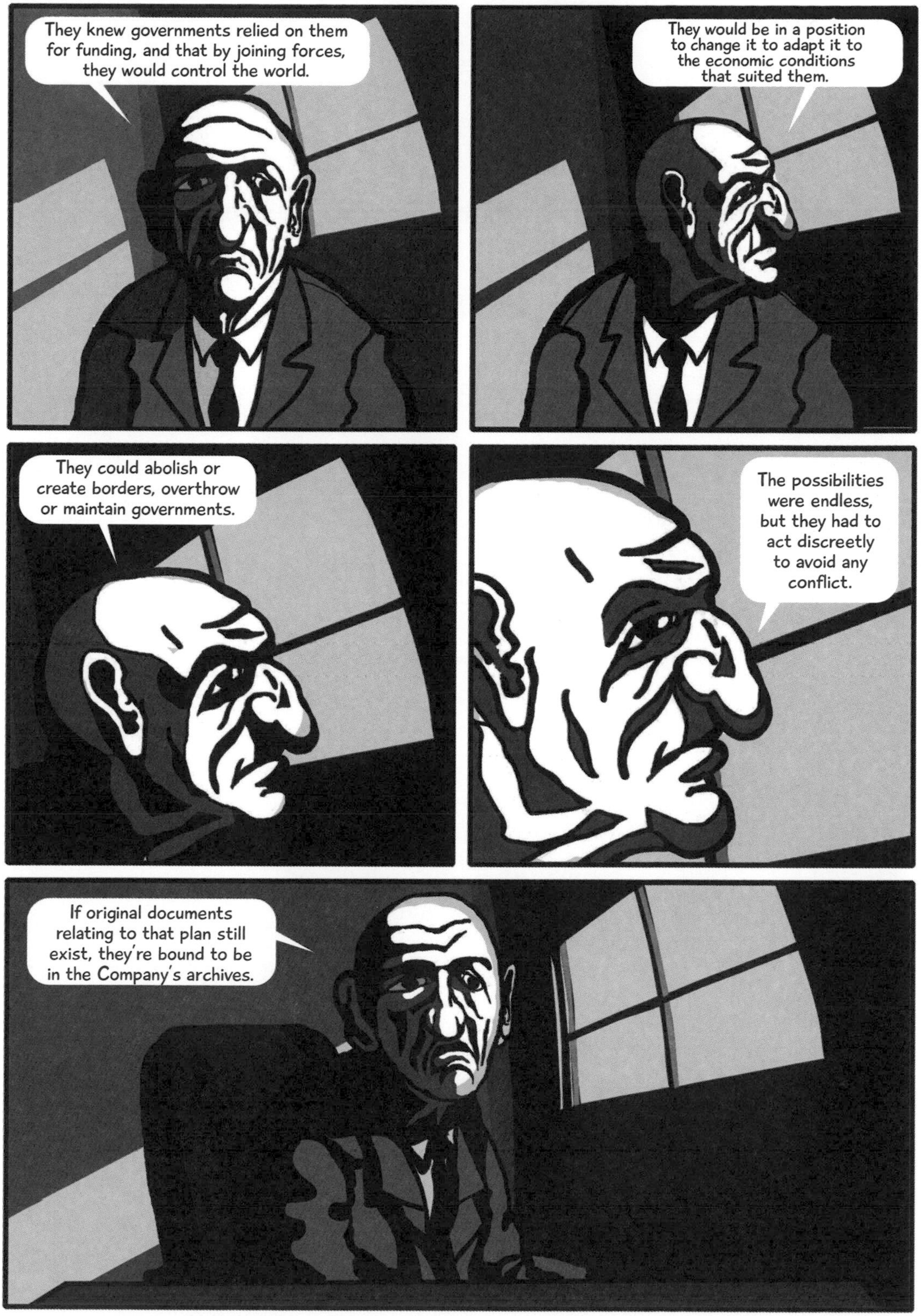
They knew governments relied on them for funding, and that by joining forces, they would control the world.
They would be in a position to change it to adapt it to the economic conditions that suited them.
They could abolish or create borders, overthrow or maintain governments.
The possibilities were endless, but they had to act discreetly to avoid any conflict.
If original documents relating to that plan still exist, they're bound to be in the Company's archives.

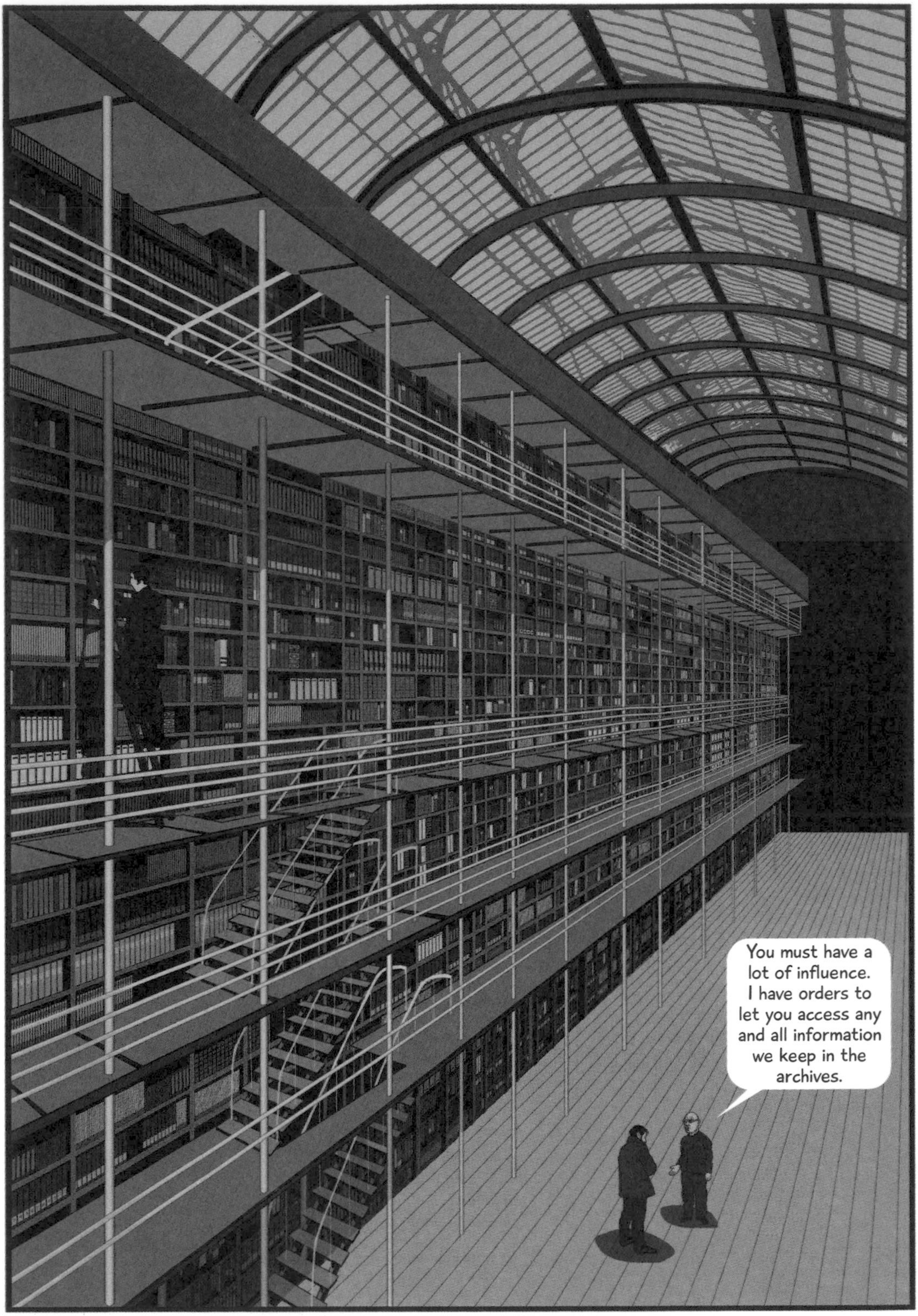
You must have a lot of influence. I have orders to let you access any and all information we keep in the archives.

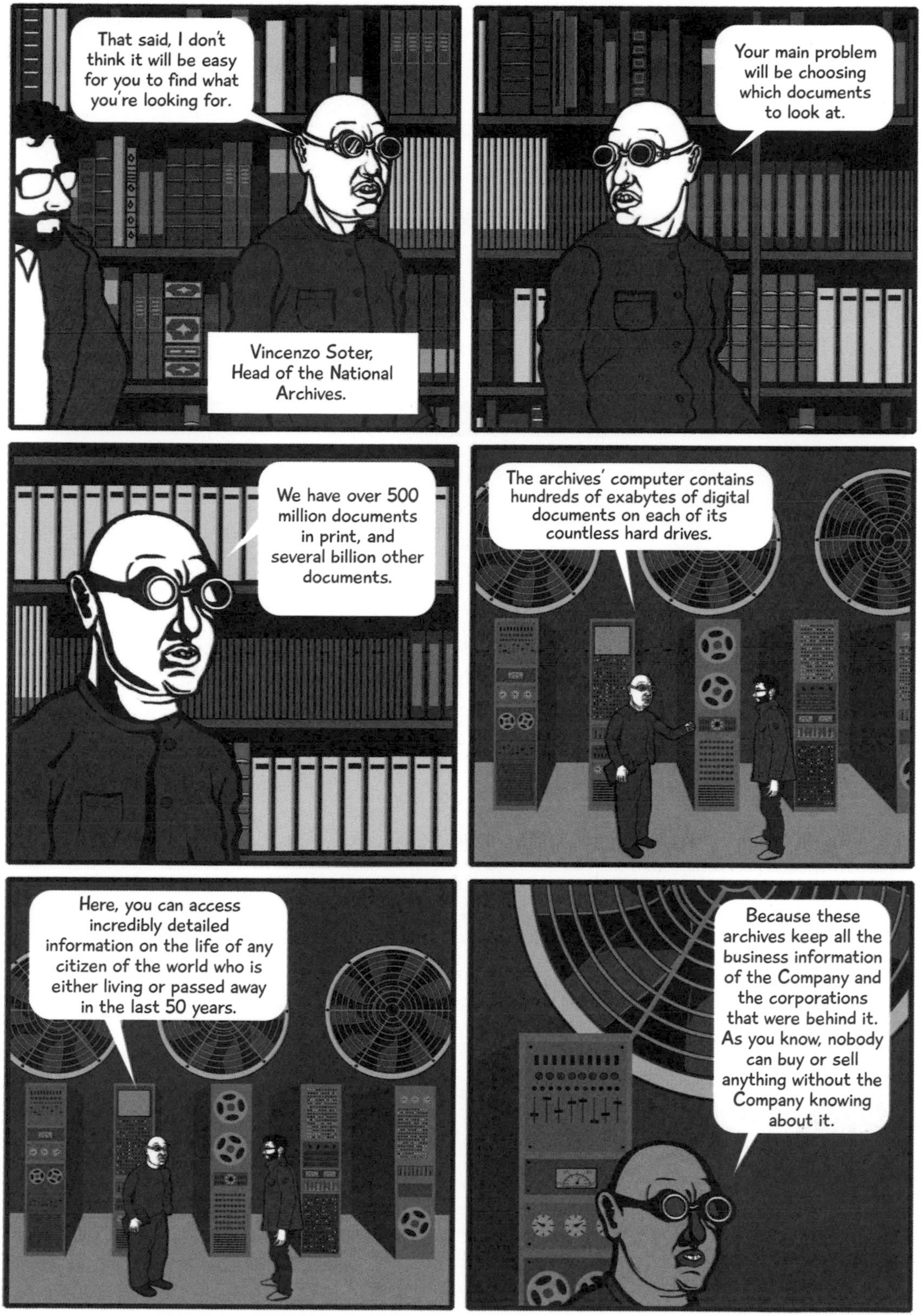
That said, I don't think it will be easy for you to find what you're looking for.
Vincenzo Soter, Head of the National Archives.
Your main problem will be choosing which documents to look at.
We have over 500 million documents in print, and several billion other documents.
The archives' computer contains hundreds of exabytes of digital documents on each of its countless hard drives.
Here, you can access incredibly detailed information on the life of any citizen of the world who is either living or passed away in the last 50 years.
Because these archives keep all the business information of the Company and the corporations that were behind it. As you know, nobody can buy or sell anything without the Company knowing about it.

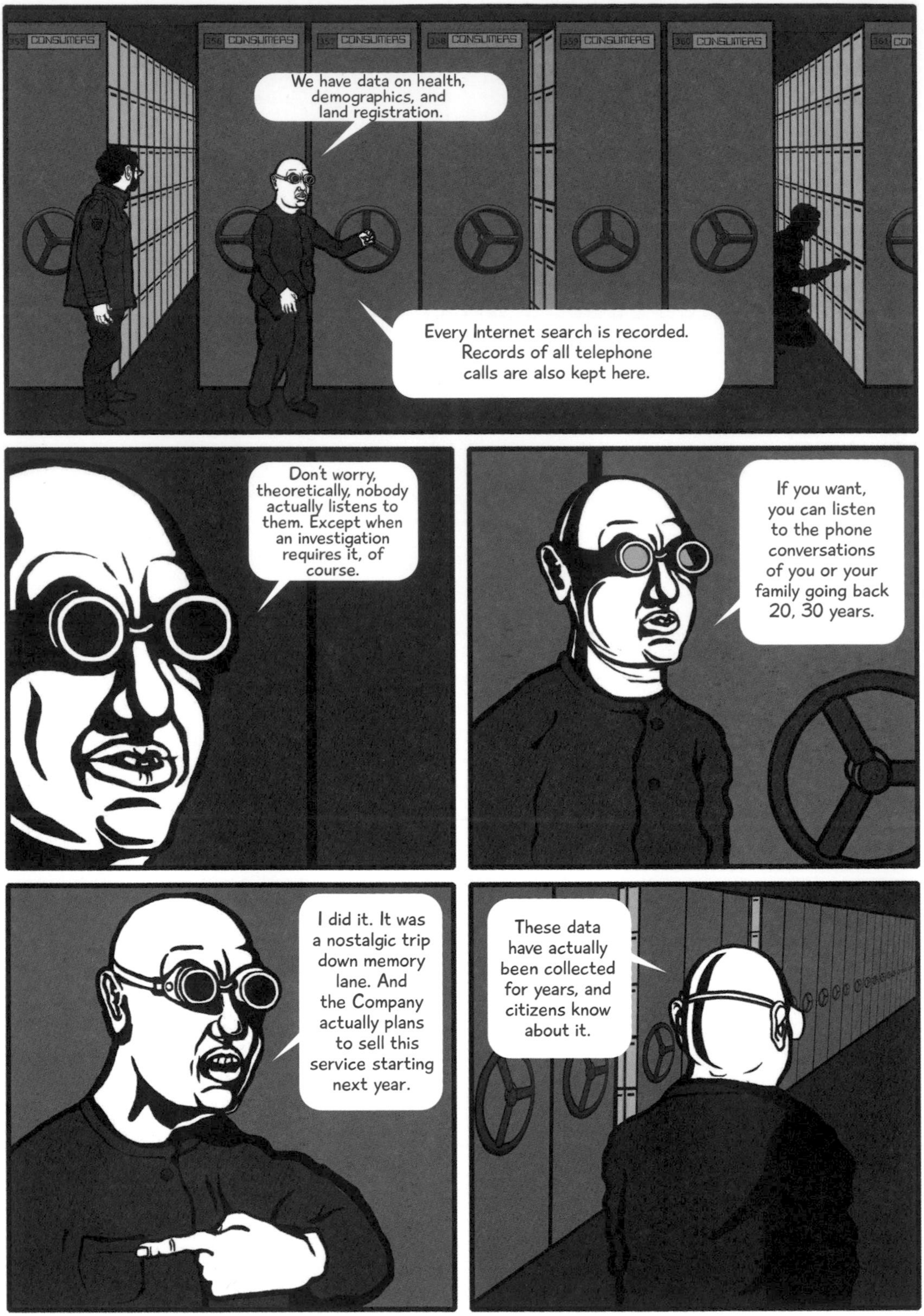
CONSUMERS
We have data on health, demographics, and land registration.
Every Internet search is recorded. Records of all telephone calls are also kept here.
Don't worry, theoretically, nobody actually listens to them. Except when an investigation requires it, of course.
If you want, you can listen to the phone conversations of you or your family going back 20, 30 years.
I did it. It was a nostalgic trip down memory lane. And the Company actually plans to sell this service starting next year.
These data have actually been collected for years, and citizens know about it.

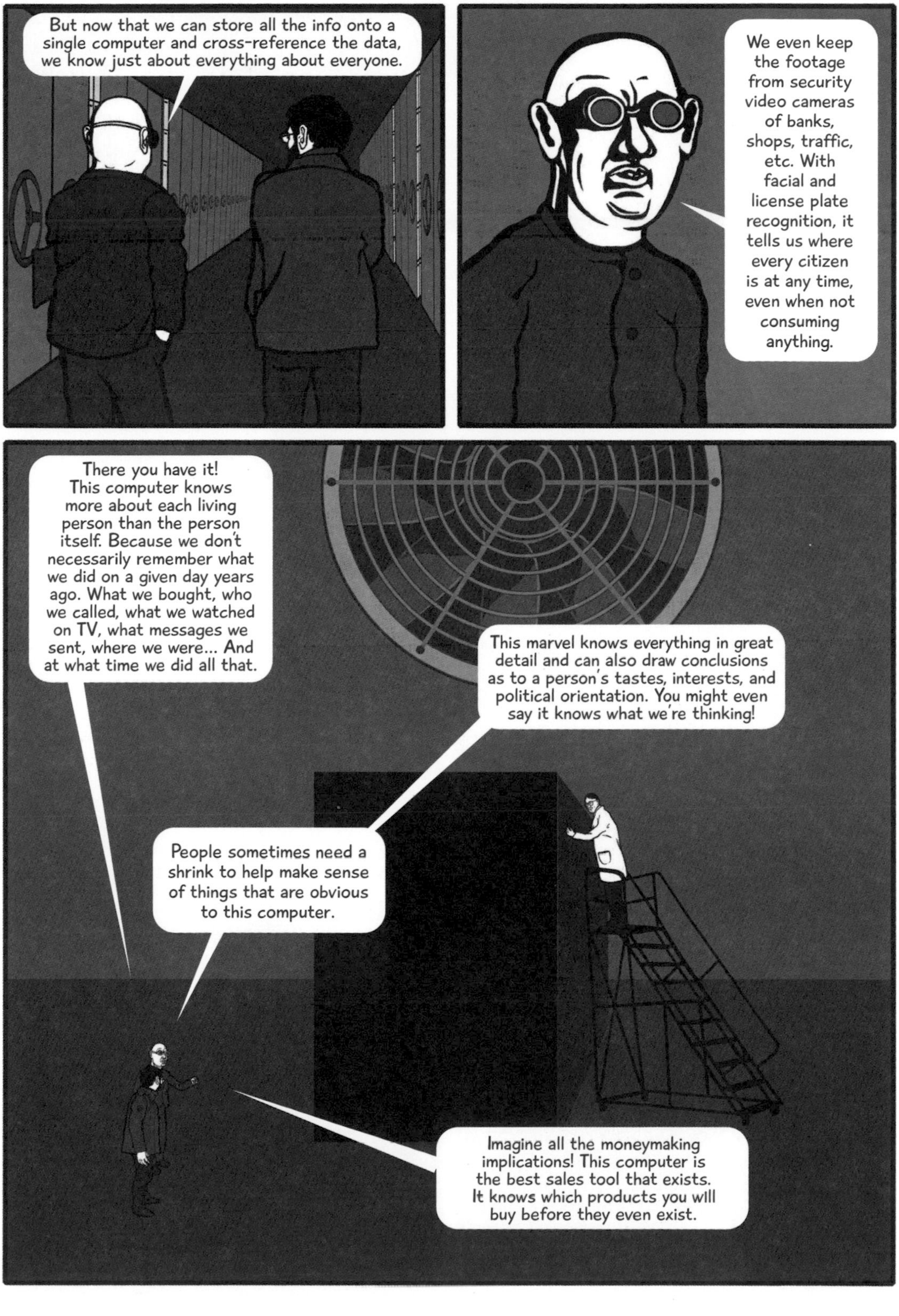
But now that we can store all the info onto a single computer and cross-reference the data, we know just about everything about everyone.
We even keep the footage from security video cameras of banks, shops, traffic, etc. With facial and license plate recognition, it tells us where every citizen is at any time, even when not consuming anything.
There you have it! This computer knows more about each living person than the person itself. Because we don't necessarily remember what we did on a given day years ago. What we bought, who we called, what we watched on TV, what messages we sent, where we were... And at what time we did all that.
This marvel knows everything in great detail and can also draw conclusions as to a person's tastes, interests, and political orientation. You might even say it knows what we're thinking!
People sometimes need a shrink to help make sense of things that are obvious to this computer.
Imagine all the moneymaking implications! This computer is the best sales tool that exists. It knows which products you will buy before they even exist.

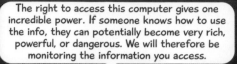

The right to access this computer gives one incredible power. If someone knows how to use the info, they can potentially become very rich, powerful, or dangerous. We will therefore be monitoring the information you access.

Criminal offenses are also stored here. Bribery, theft, murder, and all sorts of illegal services are also recorded by the police or by the Company itself if they are unofficial.

Are you saying that these archives contain evidence of unsolved crimes?

Exactly, my friend. You'll have access to everything and must prepare yourself for what you will find here.

You should know that the one stipulation is that you cannot take anything out of here. You cannot photograph, film, scan or photocopy anything, and no physical or digital file can leave the building

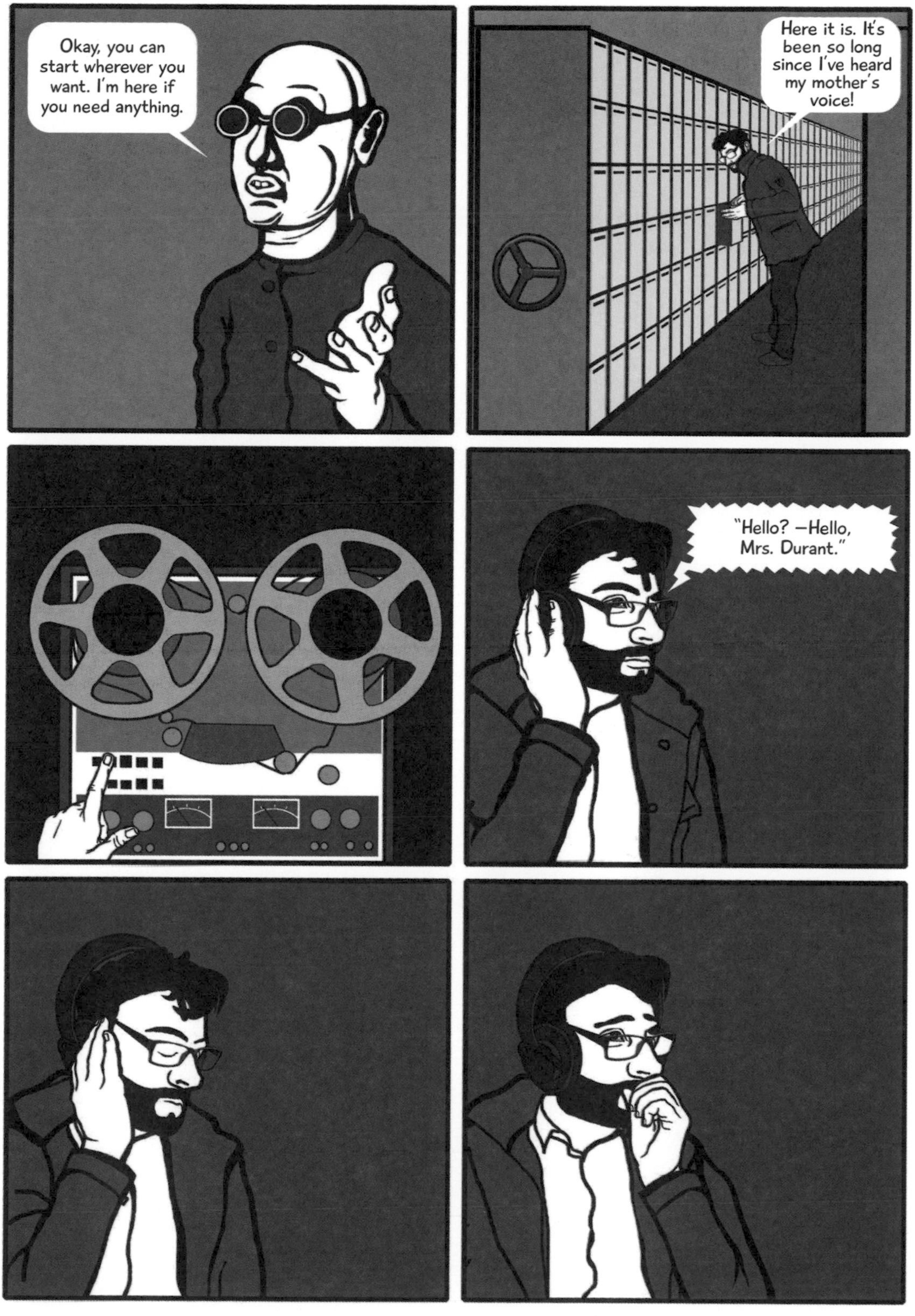
Okay, you can start wherever you want. I'm here if you need anything.
Here it is. It's been so long since I've heard my mother's voice!
"Hello? —Hello, Mrs. Durant."

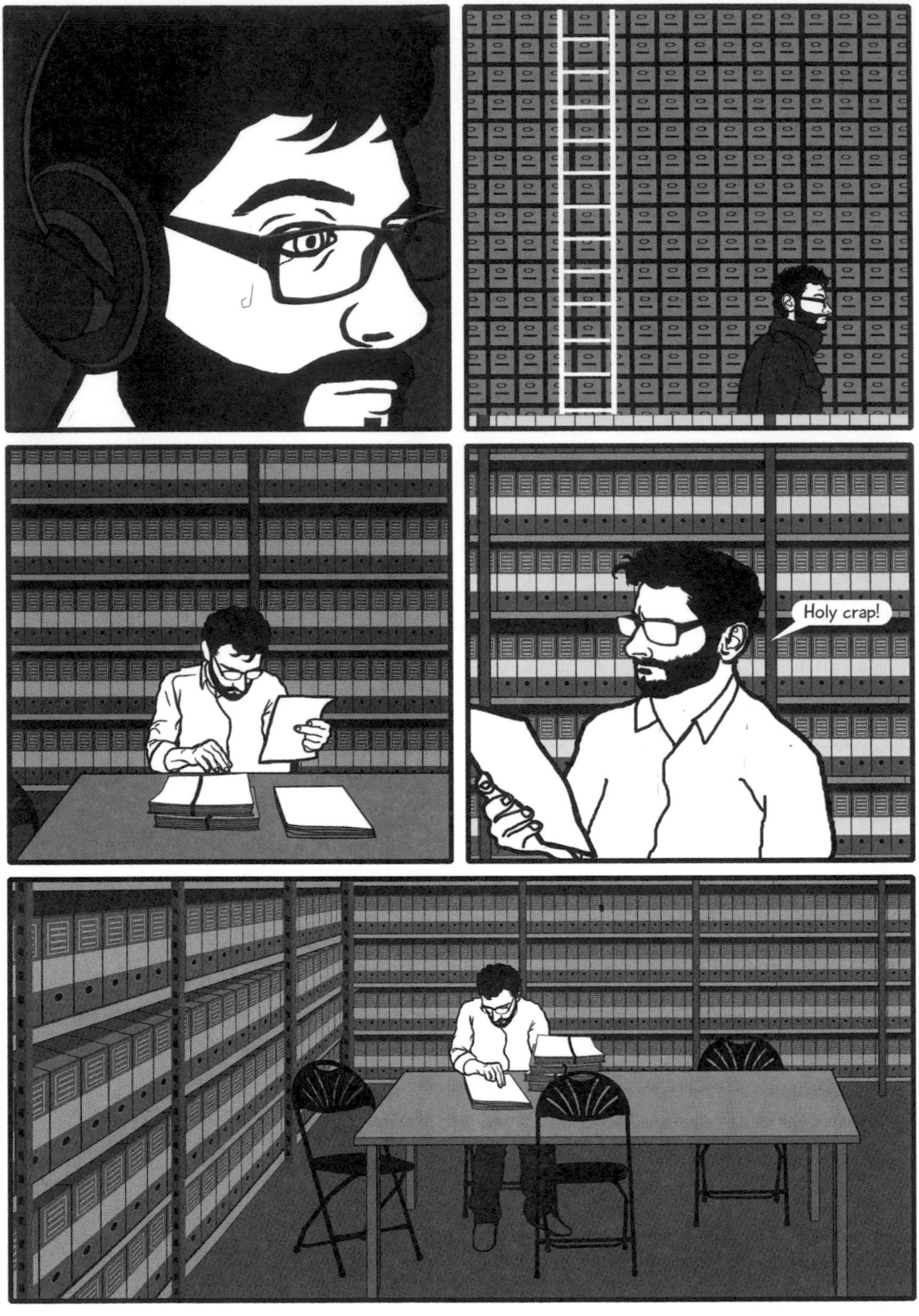
Holy crap!

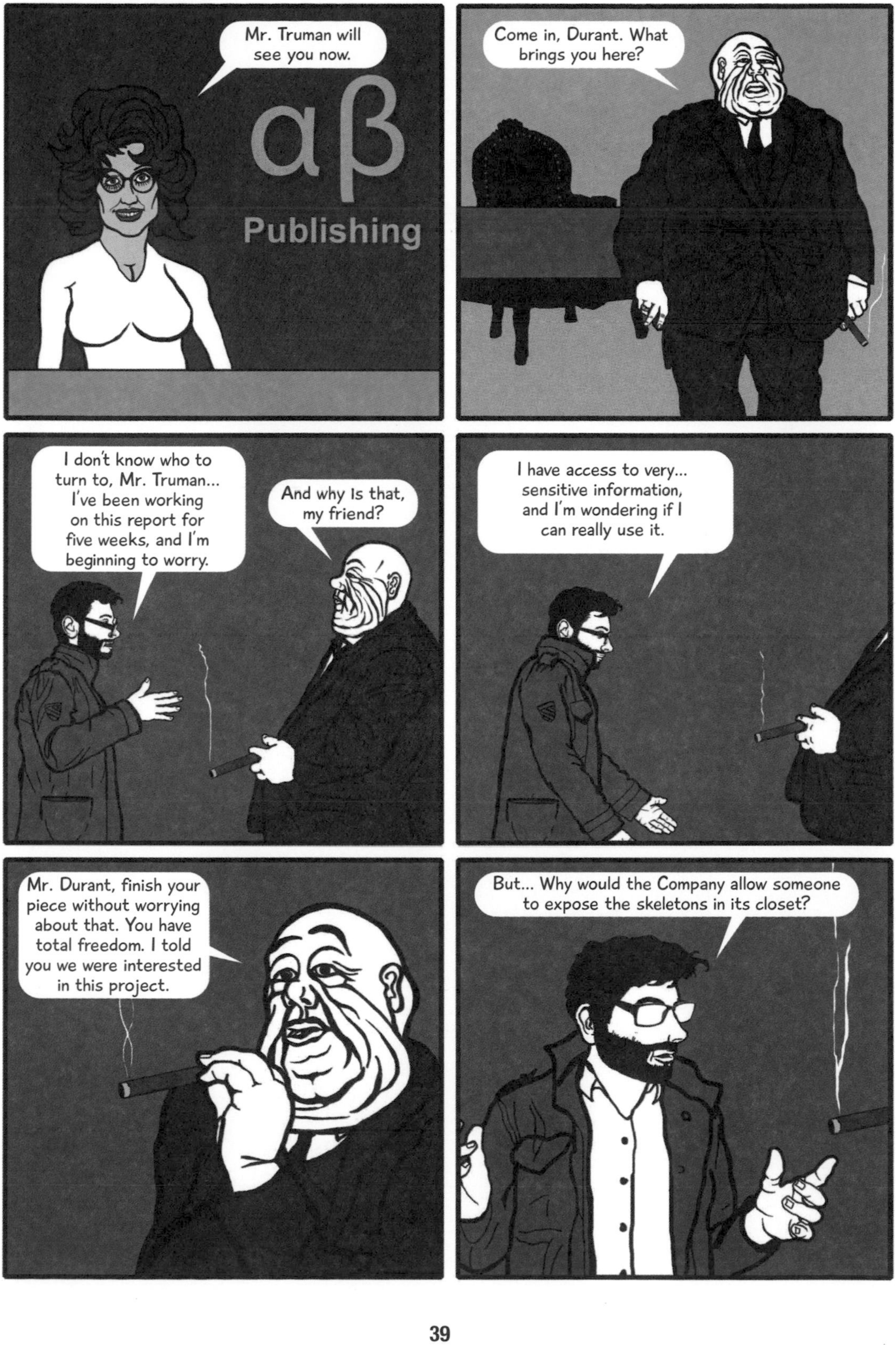
Mr. Truman will see you now.
αβ Publishing
Come in, Durant. What brings you here?
I don't know who to turn to, Mr. Truman... I've been working on this report for five weeks, and I'm beginning to worry.
And why Is that, my friend?
I have access to very... sensitive information, and I'm wondering if I can really use it.
Mr. Durant, finish your piece without worrying about that. You have total freedom. I told you we were interested in this project.
But... Why would the Company allow someone to expose the skeletons in its closet?

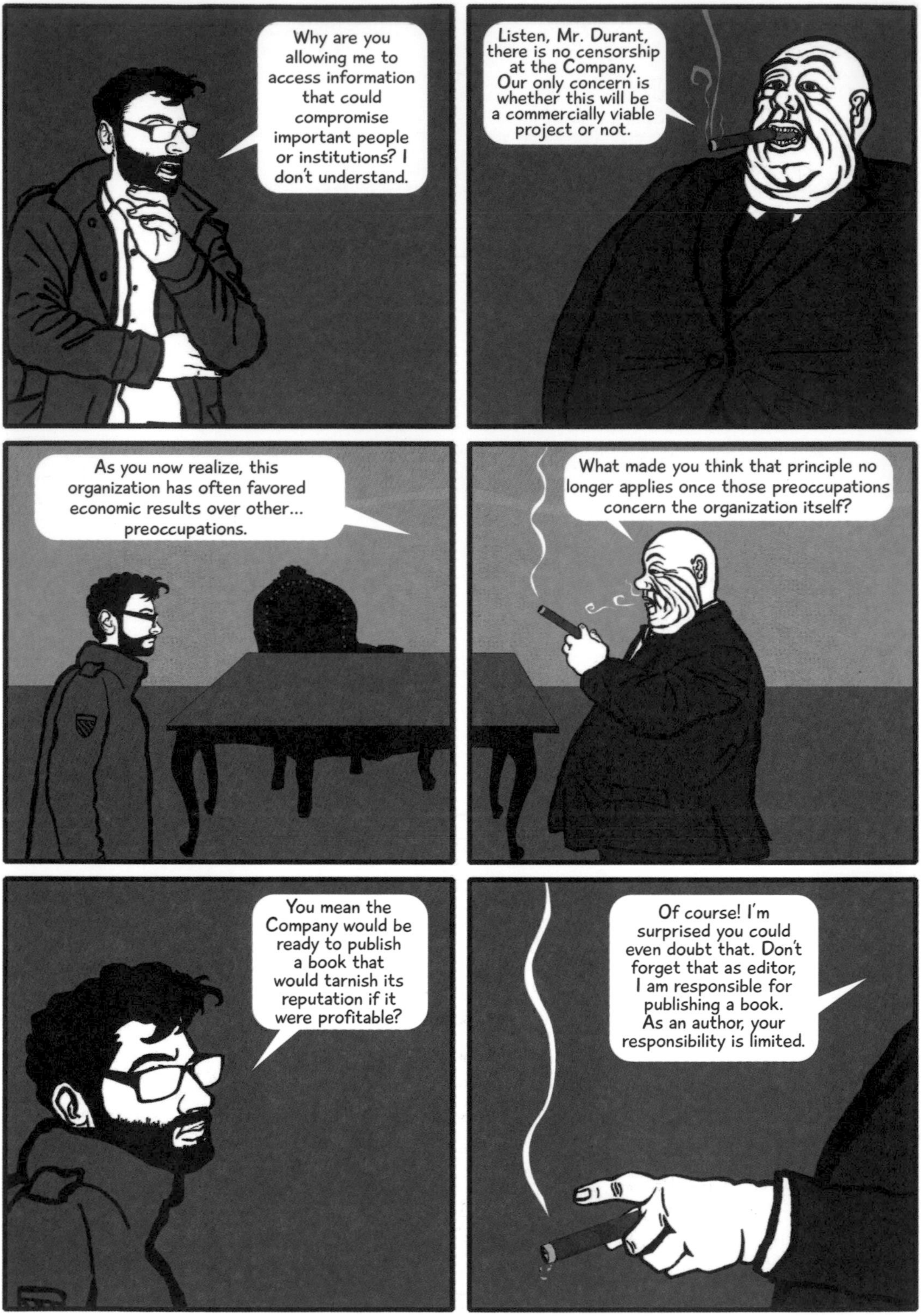
Why are you allowing me to access information that could compromise important people or institutions? I don't understand.
Listen, Mr. Durant, there is no censorship at the Company. Our only concern is whether this will be a commercially viable project or not.
As you now realize, this organization has often favored economic results over other... preoccupations.
What made you think that principle no longer applies once those preoccupations concern the organization itself?
You mean the Company would be ready to publish a book that would tarnish its reputation if it were profitable?
Of course! I'm surprised you could even doubt that. Don't forget that as editor, I am responsible for publishing a book. As an author, your responsibility is limited.

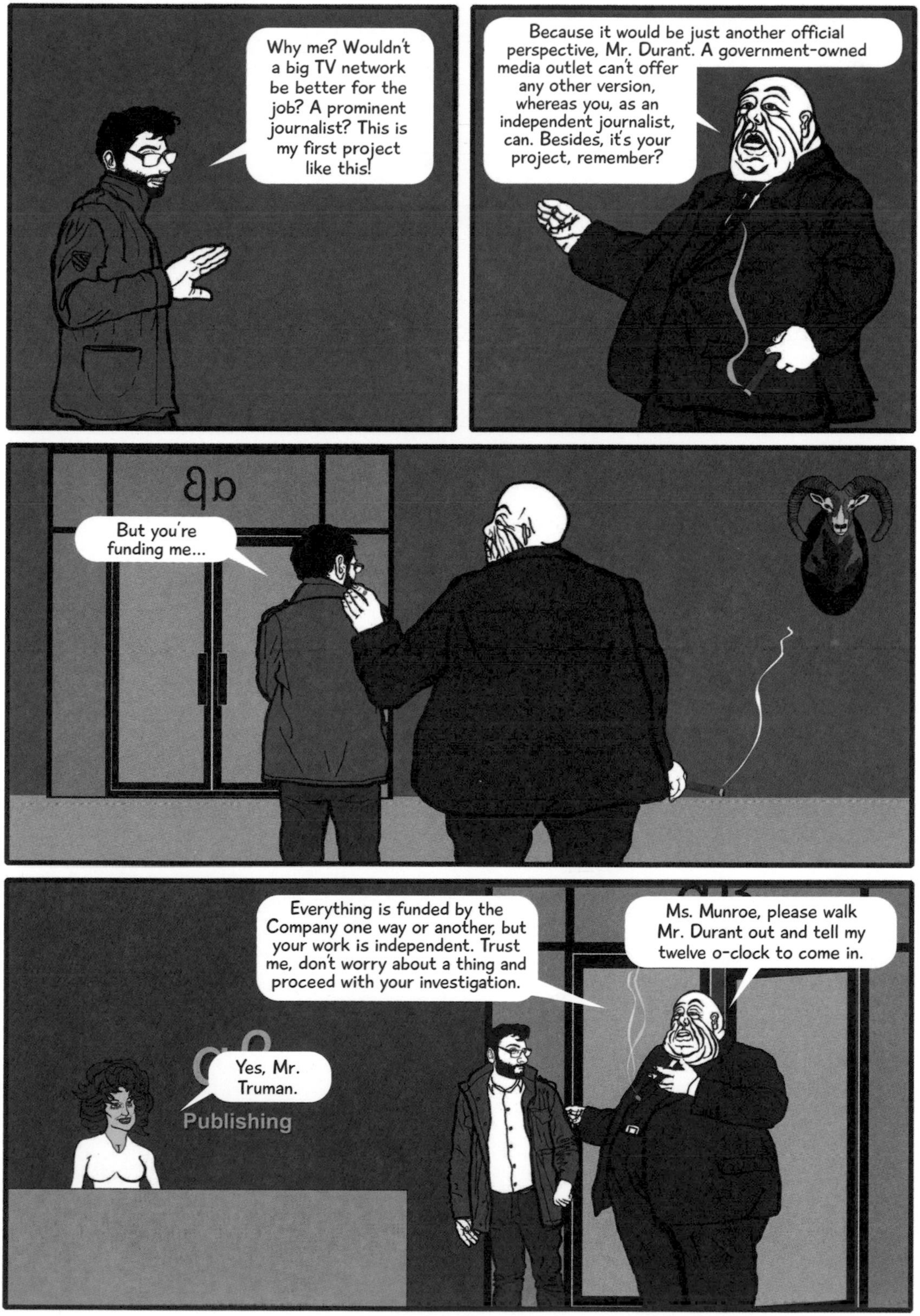

Why me? Wouldn't a big TV network be better for the job? A prominent journalist? This is my first project like this!
Because it would be just another official perspective, Mr. Durant. A government-owned media outlet can't offer any other version, whereas you, as an independent journalist, can. Besides, it's your project, remember?
But you're funding me...
Everything is funded by the Company one way or another, but your work is independent. Trust me, don't worry about a thing and proceed with your investigation.
Ms. Munroe, please walk Mr. Durant out and tell my twelve o-clock to come in.
Yes, Mr. Truman.
Publishing

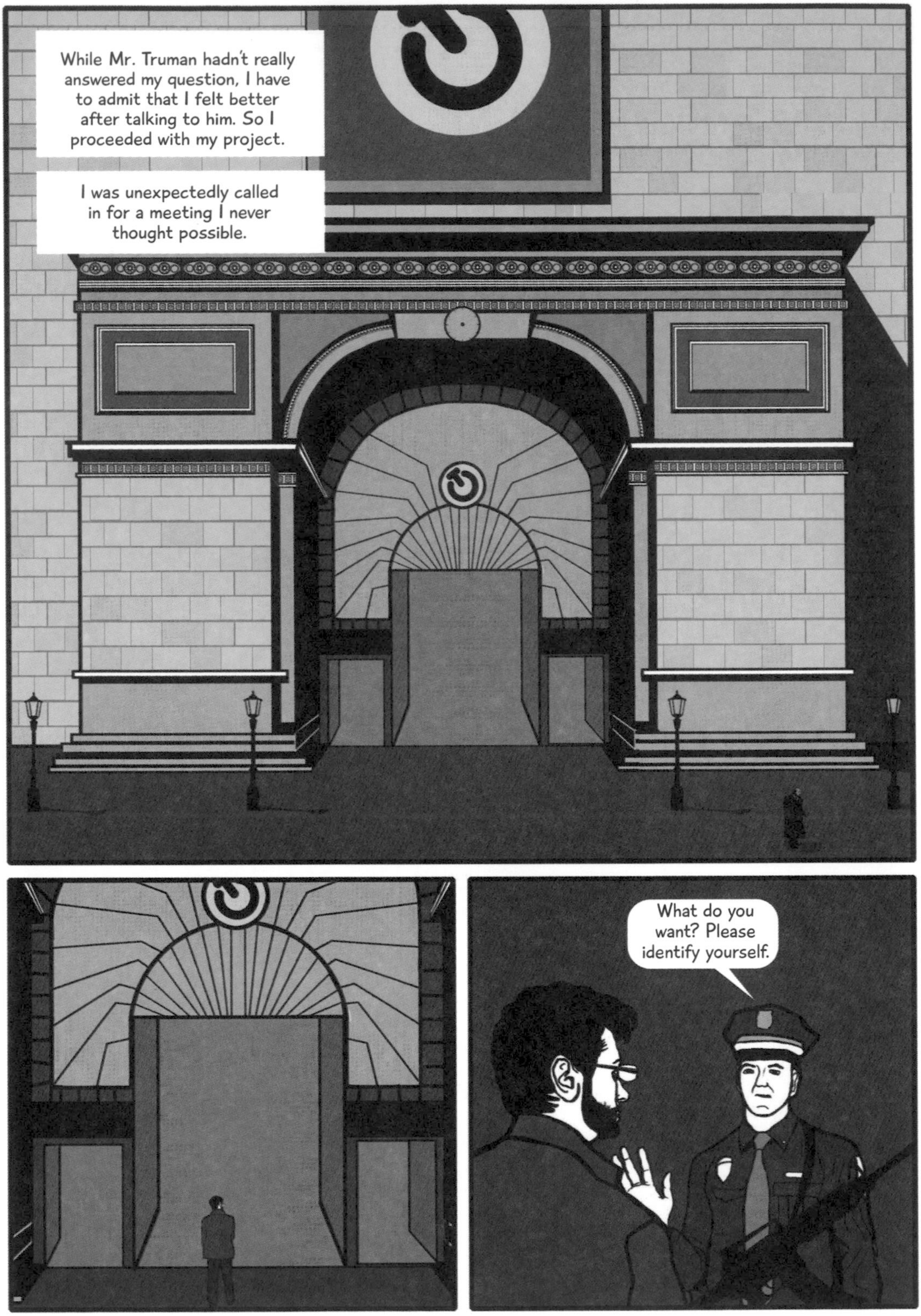
While Mr. Truman hadn't really answered my question, I have to admit that I felt better after talking to him. So I proceeded with my project.
I was unexpectedly called in for a meeting I never thought possible.
What do you want? Please identify yourself.

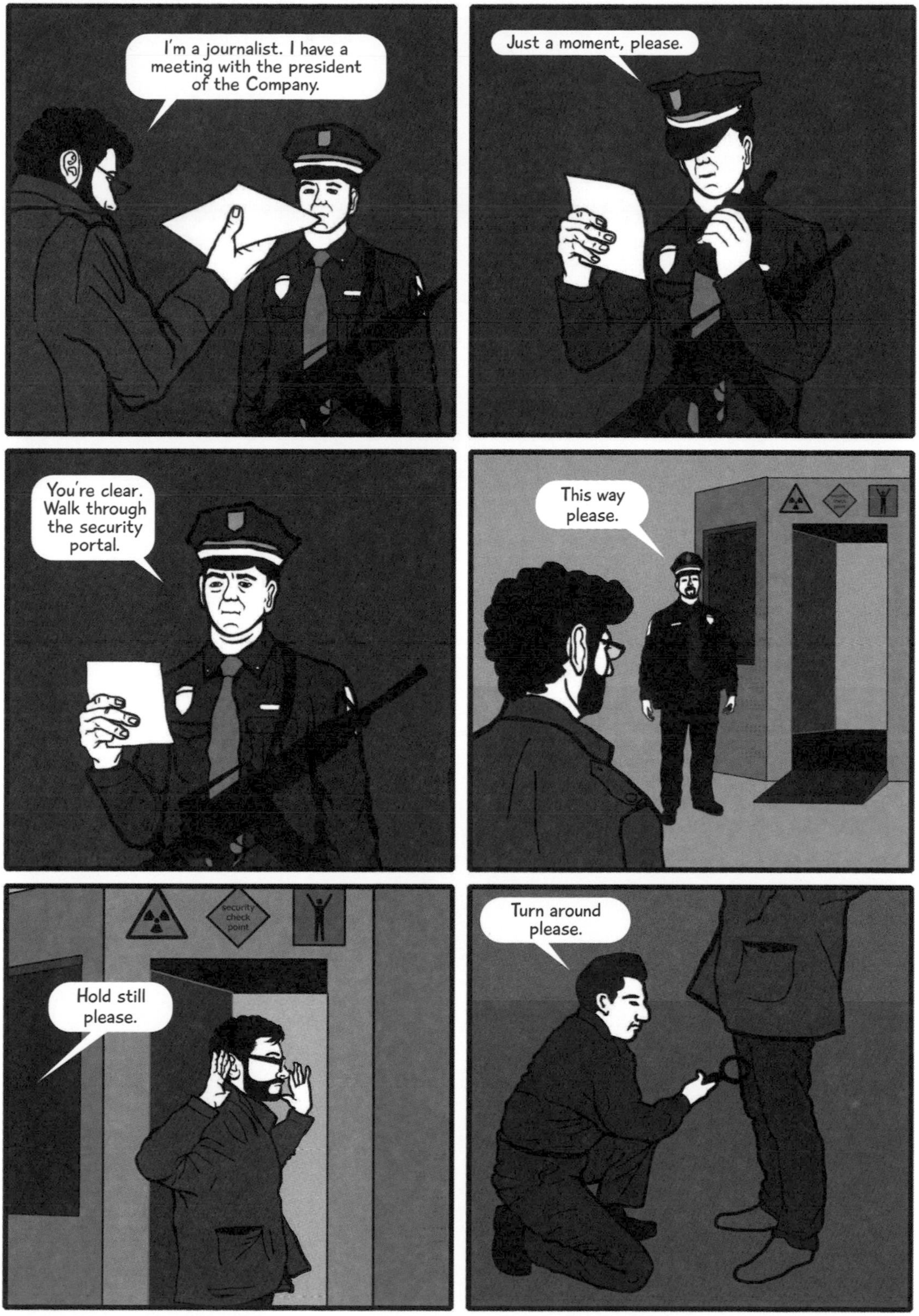
I'm a journalist. I have a meeting with the president of the Company.
Just a moment, please.
You're clear. Walk through the security portal.
This way please.
security check point
Hold still please.
Turn around please.

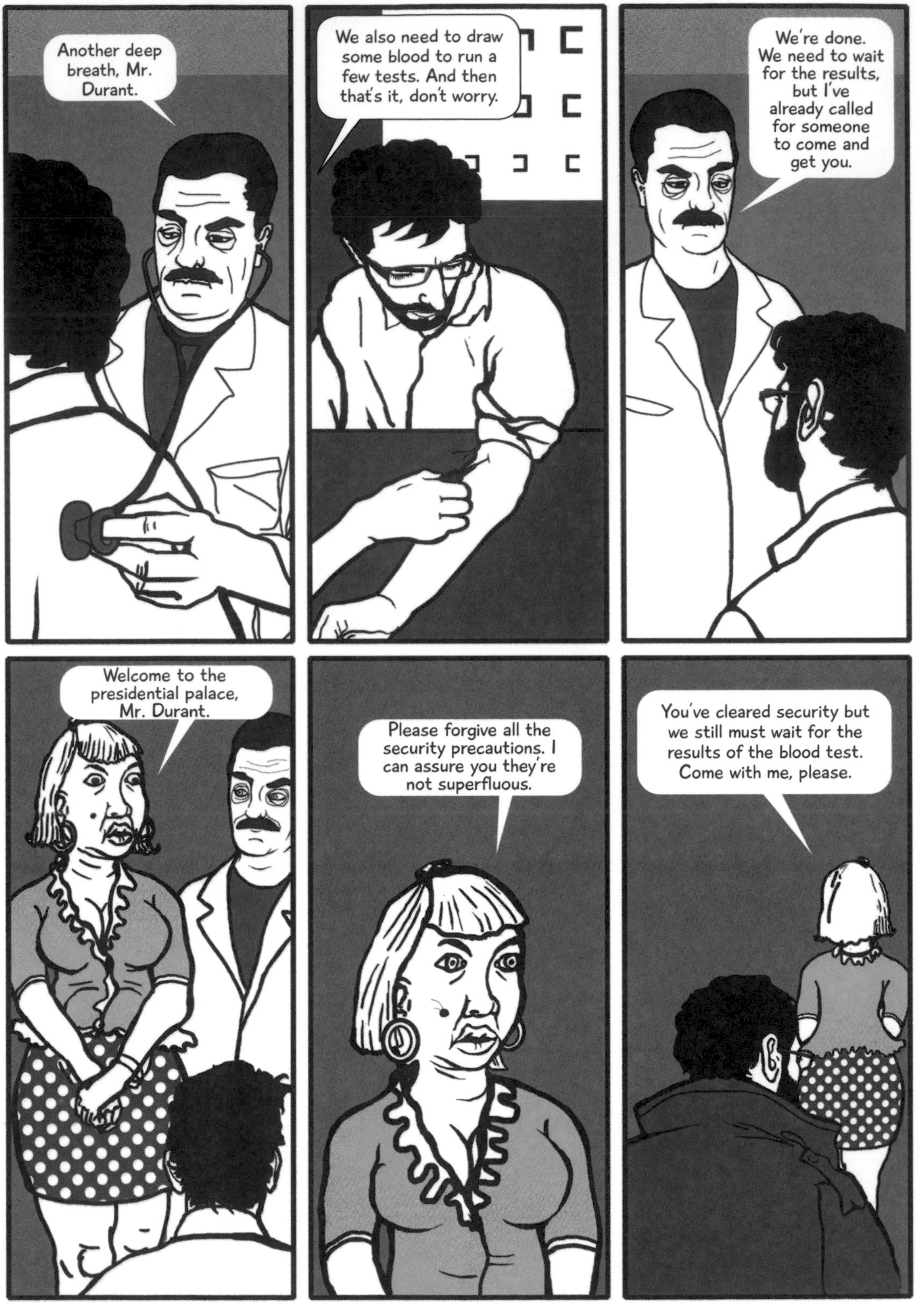
Another deep breath, Mr. Durant.
We also need to draw some blood to run a few tests. And then that's it, don't worry.
We're done. We need to wait for the results, but I've already called for someone to come and get you.
Welcome to the presidential palace, Mr. Durant.
Please forgive all the security precautions. I can assure you they're not superfluous.
You've cleared security but we still must wait for the results of the blood test. Come with me, please.

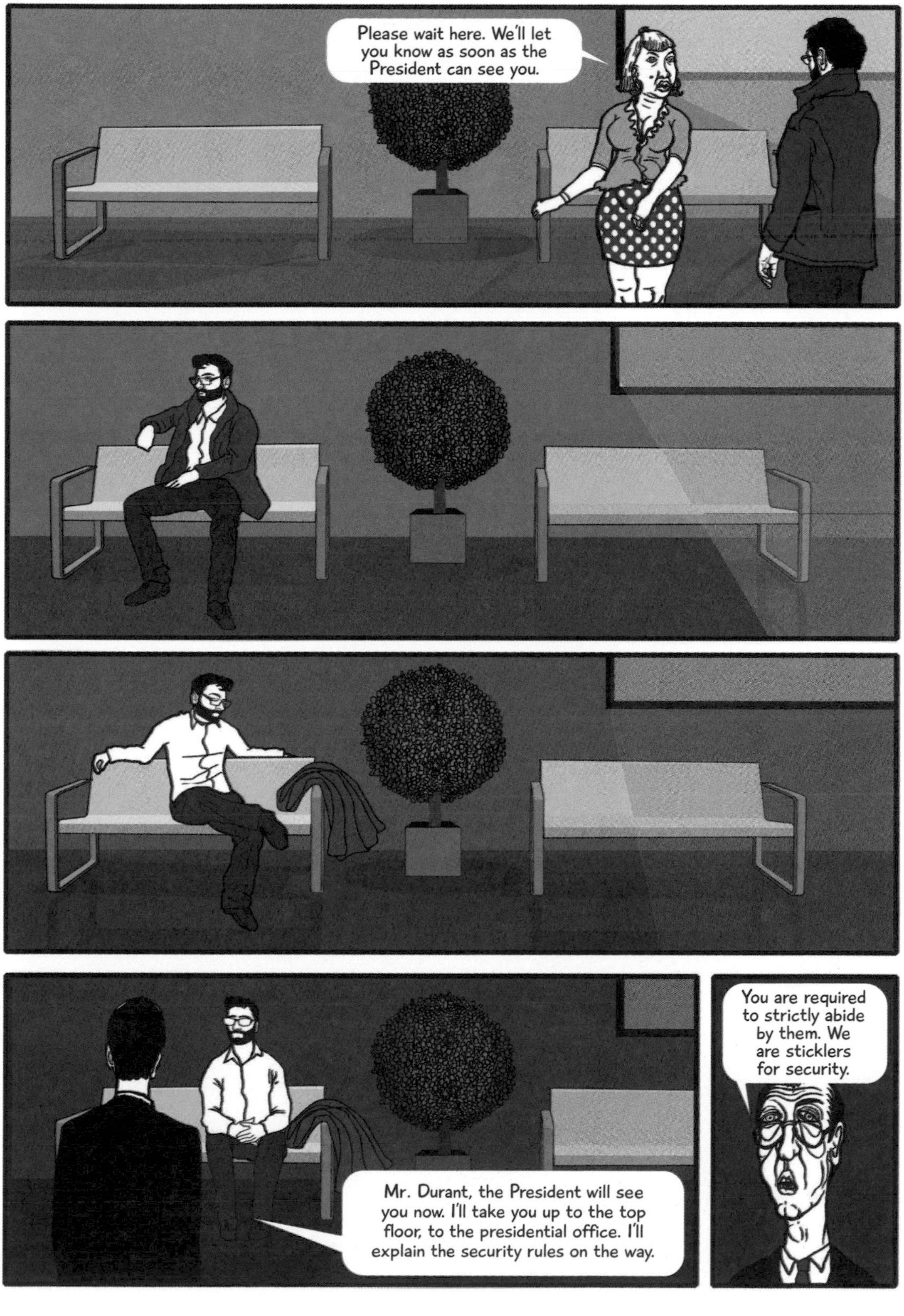
Please wait here. We'll let you know as soon as the President can see you.
Mr. Durant, the President will see you now. I'll take you up to the top floor, to the presidential office. I'll explain the security rules on the way.
You are required to strictly abide by them. We are sticklers for security.

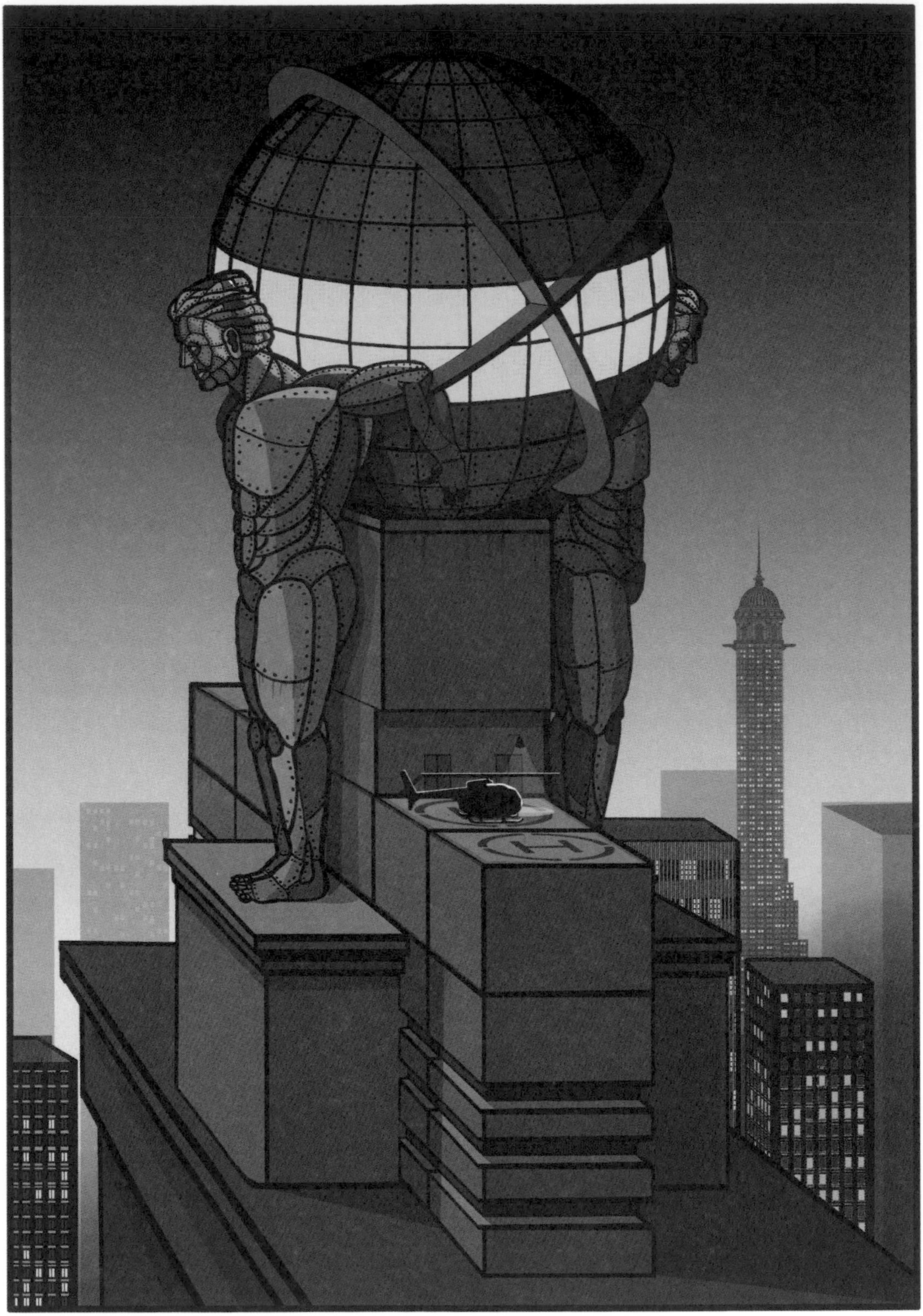

This way
please.

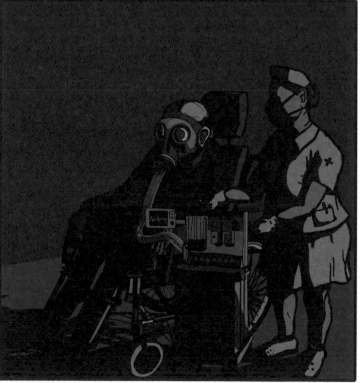

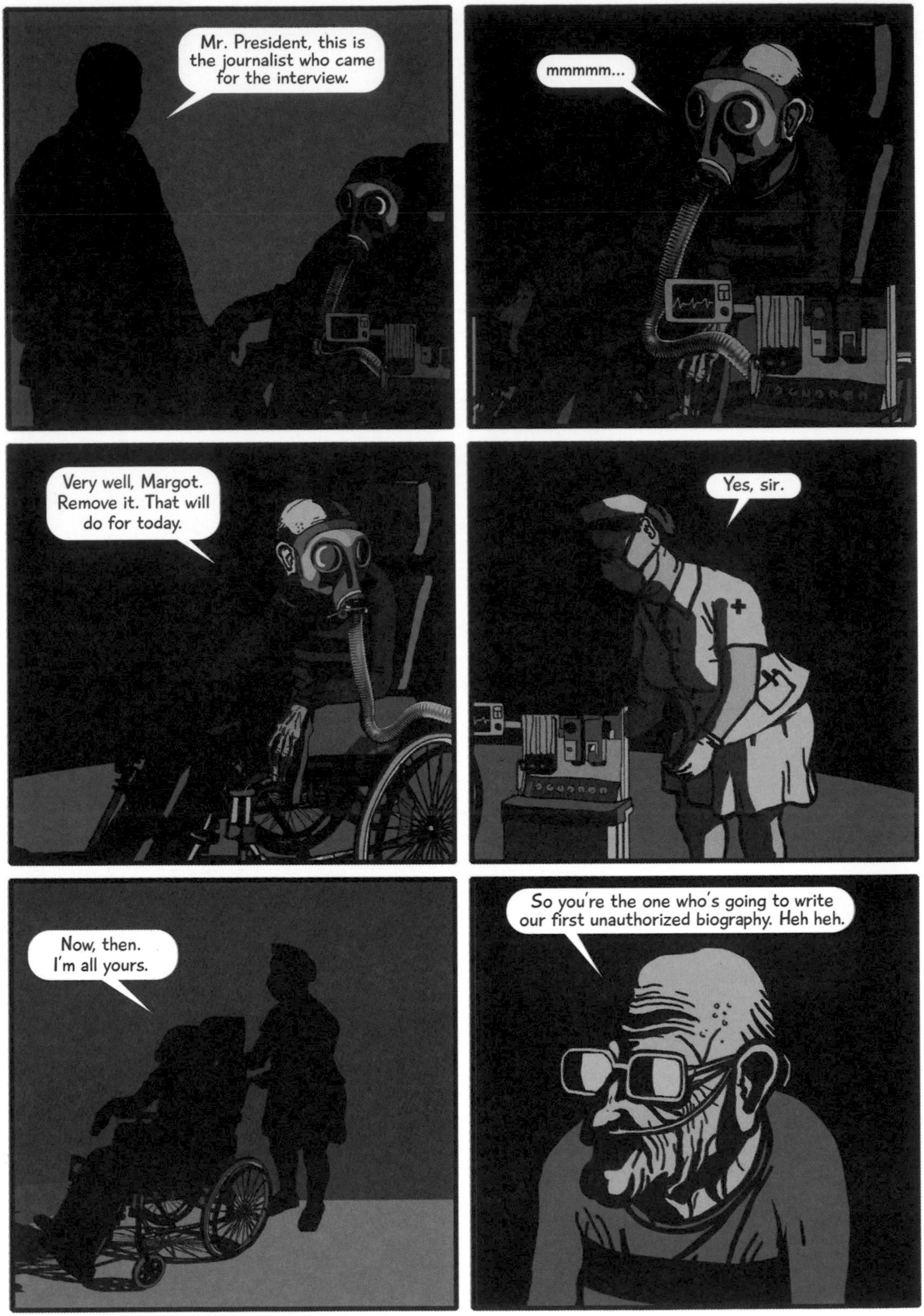

Mr. President, this is the journalist who came for the interview.
mmmmm...
Very well, Margot. Remove it. That will do for today.
Yes, sir.
Now, then. I'm all yours.
So you're the one who's going to write our first unauthorized biography. Heh heh.

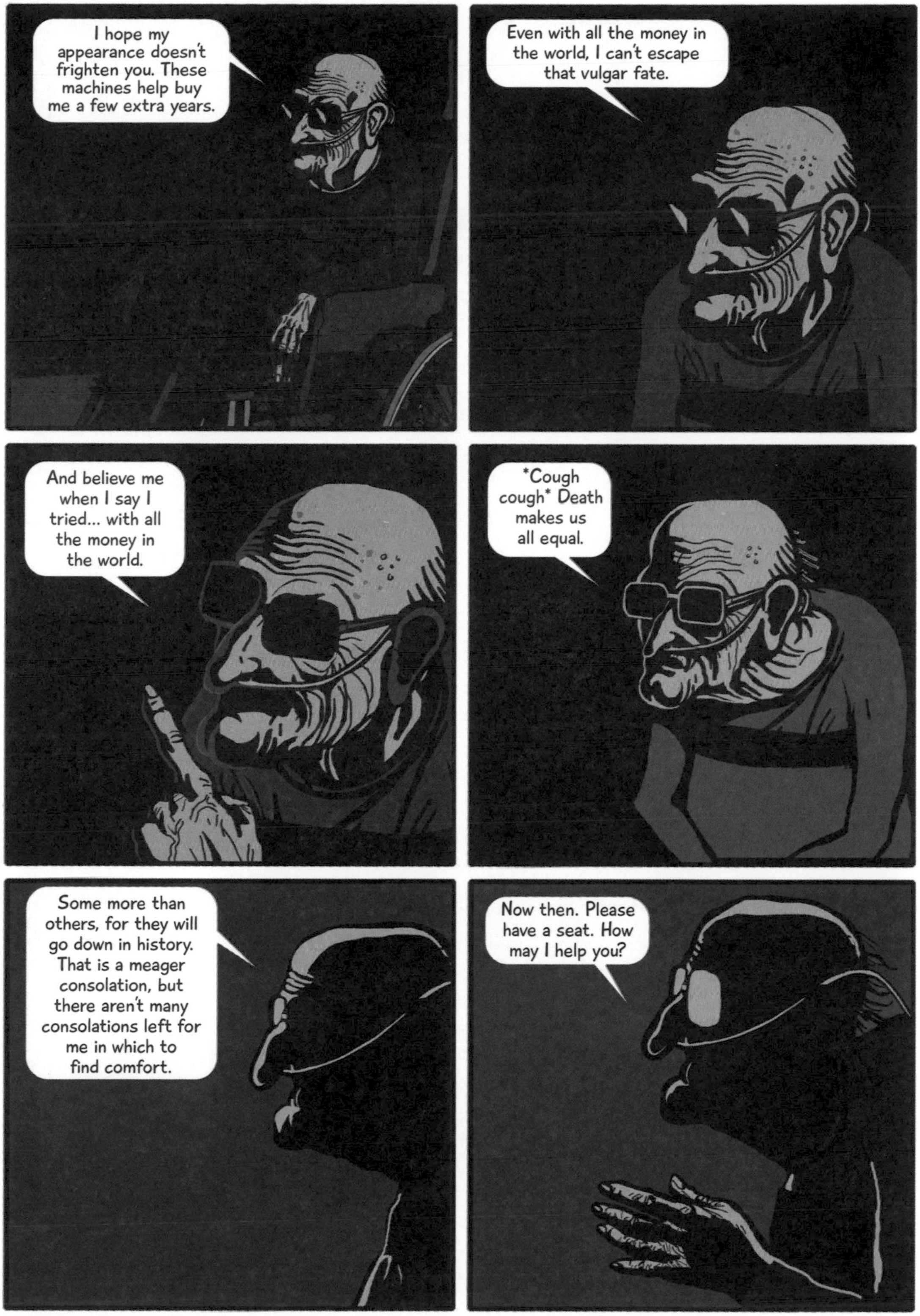
I hope my appearance doesn't frighten you. These machines help buy me a few extra years.
Even with all the money in the world, I can't escape that vulgar fate.
And believe me when I say I tried... with all the money in the world.
Cough cough Death makes us all equal.
Some more than others, for they will go down in history. That is a meager consolation, but there aren't many consolations left for me in which to find comfort.
Now then. Please have a seat. How may I help you?

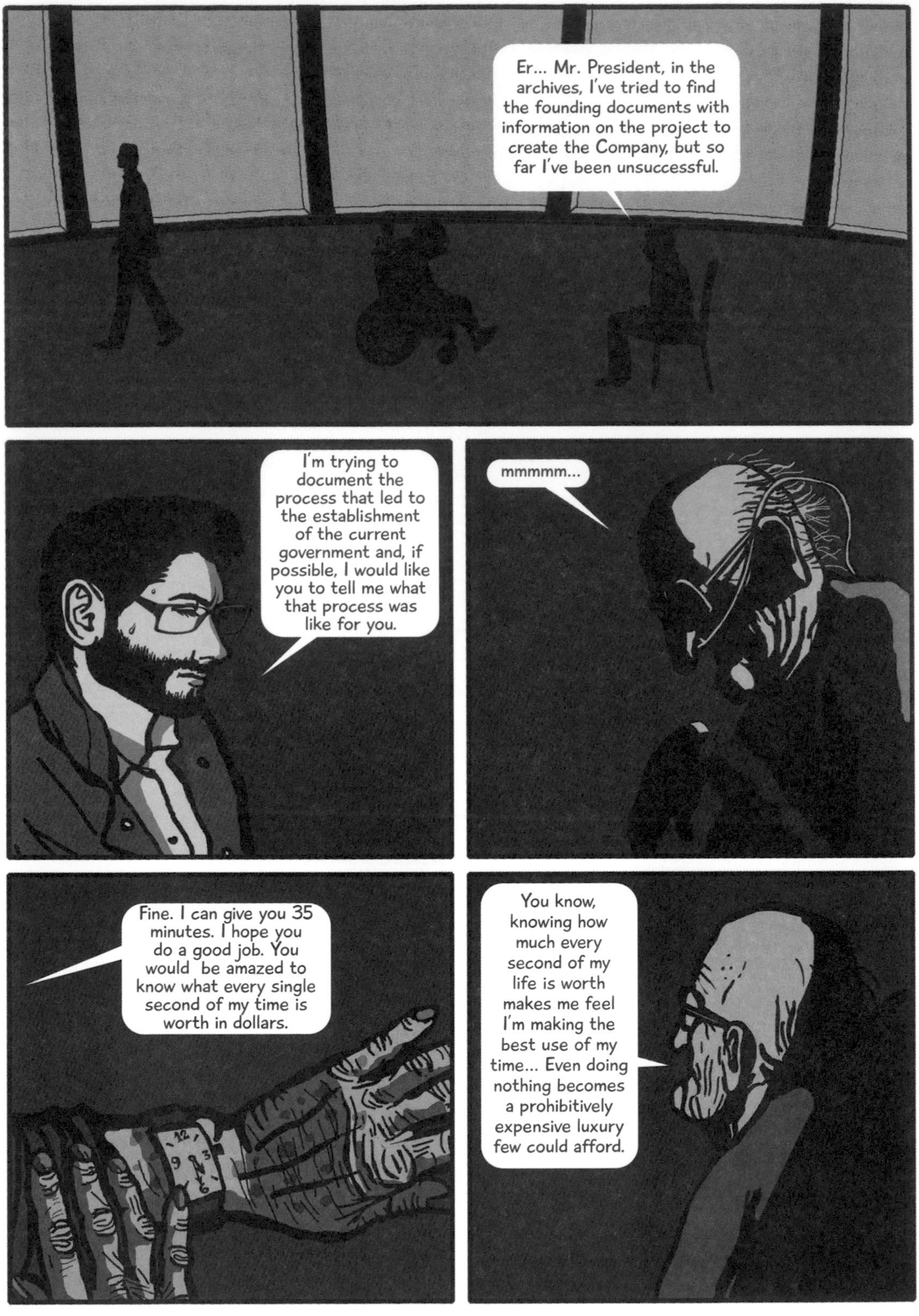
Er... Mr. President, in the archives, I've tried to find the founding documents with information on the project to create the Company, but so far I've been unsuccessful.
I'm trying to document the process that led to the establishment of the current government and, if possible, I would like you to tell me what that process was like for you.
mmmmm...
Fine. I can give you 35 minutes. I hope you do a good job. You would be amazed to know what every single second of my time is worth in dollars.
You know, knowing how much every second of my life is worth makes me feel I'm making the best use of my time... Even doing nothing becomes a prohibitively expensive luxury few could afford.

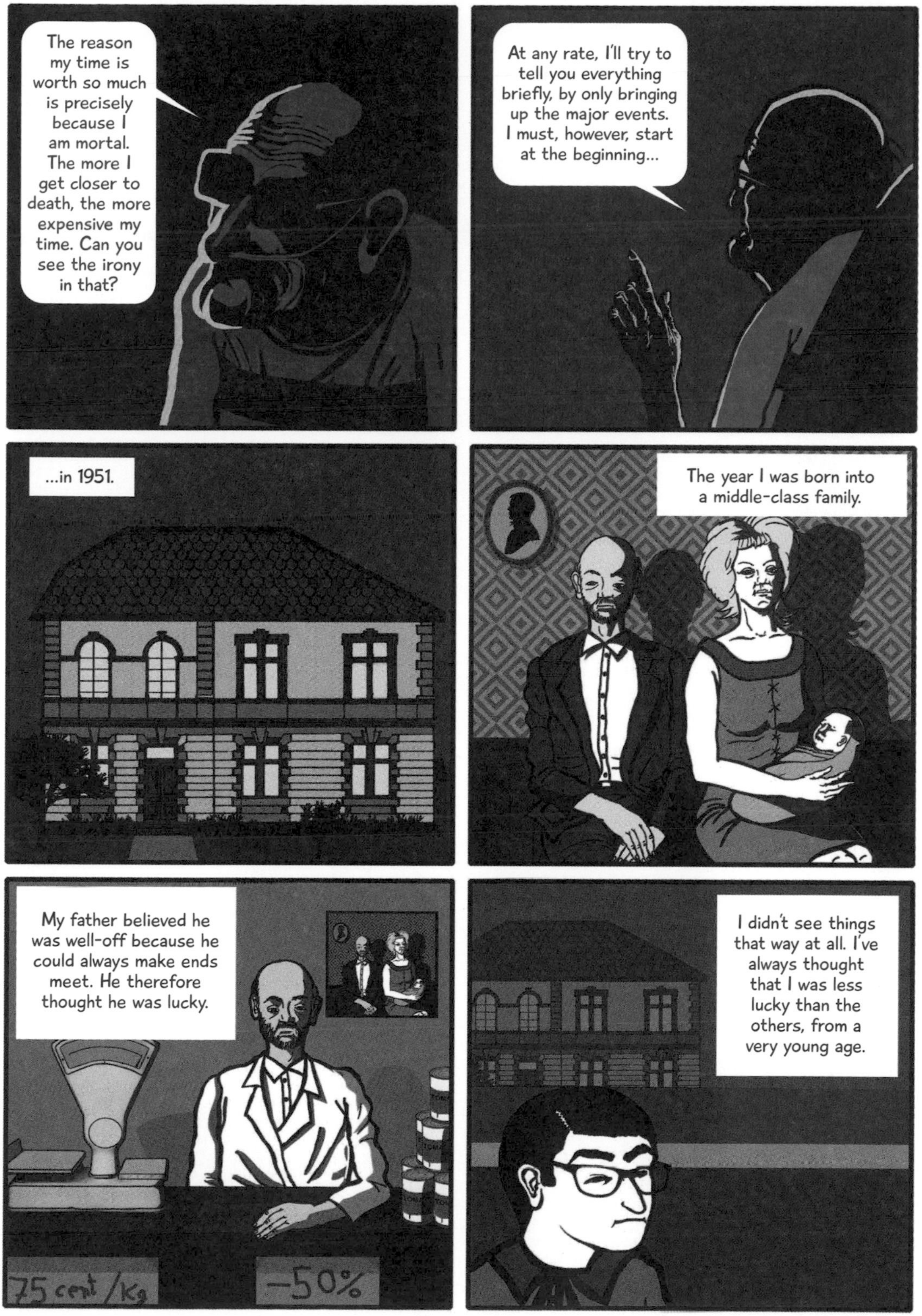
The reason my time is worth so much is precisely because I am mortal. The more I get closer to death, the more expensive my time. Can you see the irony in that?
At any rate, I'll try to tell you everything briefly, by only bringing up the major events. I must, however, start at the beginning...
...in 1951.
The year I was born into a middle-class family.
My father believed he was well-off because he could always make ends meet. He therefore thought he was lucky.
75 cent /Kg
-50%
I didn't see things that way at all. I've always thought that I was less lucky than the others, from a very young age.

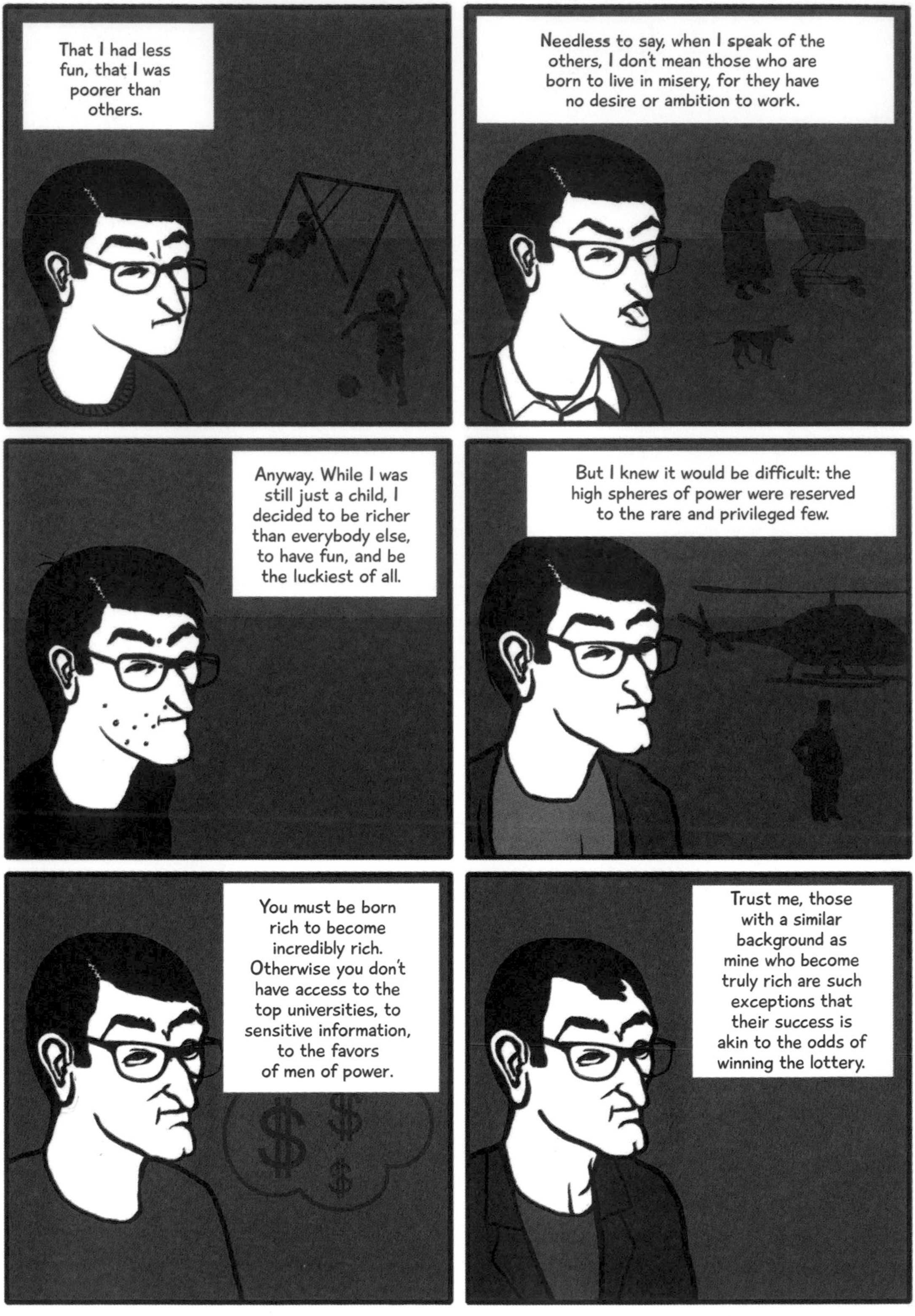
That I had less fun, that I was poorer than others.
Needless to say, when I speak of the others, I don't mean those who are born to live in misery, for they have no desire or ambition to work.
Anyway. While I was still just a child, I decided to be richer than everybody else, to have fun, and be the luckiest of all.
But I knew it would be difficult: the high spheres of power were reserved to the rare and privileged few.
You must be born rich to become incredibly rich. Otherwise you don't have access to the top universities, to sensitive information, to the favors of men of power.
$ $ $
Trust me, those with a similar background as mine who become truly rich are such exceptions that their success is akin to the odds of winning the lottery.

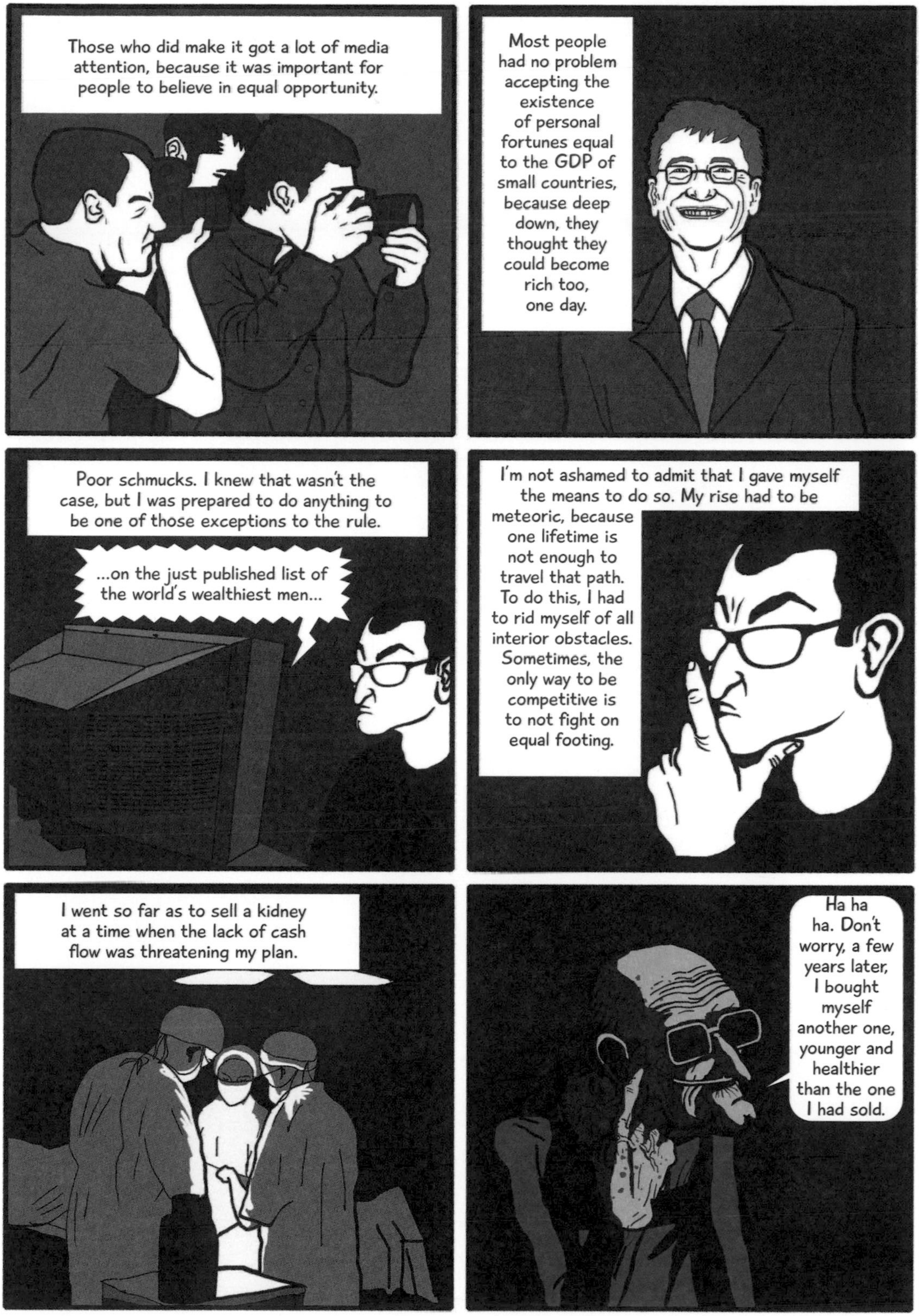
Those who did make it got a lot of media attention, because it was important for people to believe in equal opportunity.
Most people had no problem accepting the existence of personal fortunes equal to the GDP of small countries, because deep down, they thought they could become rich too, one day.
Poor schmucks. I knew that wasn't the case, but I was prepared to do anything to be one of those exceptions to the rule.
...on the just published list of the world's wealthiest men...
I'm not ashamed to admit that I gave myself the means to do so. My rise had to be meteoric, because one lifetime is not enough to travel that path. To do this, I had to rid myself of all interior obstacles. Sometimes, the only way to be competitive is to not fight on equal footing.
I went so far as to sell a kidney at a time when the lack of cash flow was threatening my plan.
Ha ha ha. Don't worry, a few years later, I bought myself another one, younger and healthier than the one I had sold.

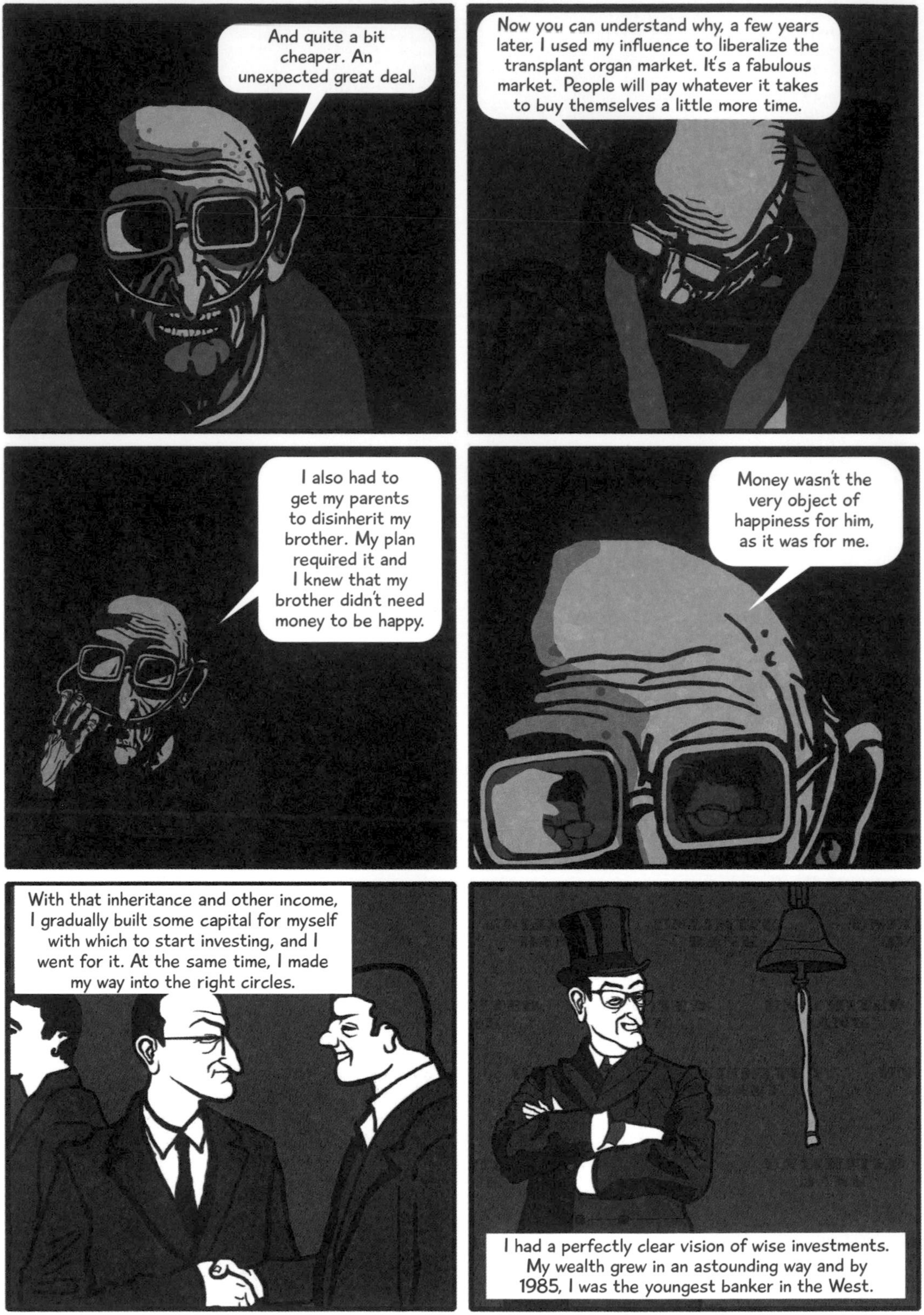
And quite a bit cheaper. An unexpected great deal.
Now you can understand why, a few years later, I used my influence to liberalize the transplant organ market. It's a fabulous market. People will pay whatever it takes to buy themselves a little more time.
I also had to get my parents to disinherit my brother. My plan required it and I knew that my brother didn't need money to be happy.
Money wasn't the very object of happiness for him, as it was for me.
With that inheritance and other income, I gradually built some capital for myself with which to start investing, and I went for it. At the same time, I made my way into the right circles.
I had a perfectly clear vision of wise investments. My wealth grew in an astounding way and by 1985, I was the youngest banker in the West.

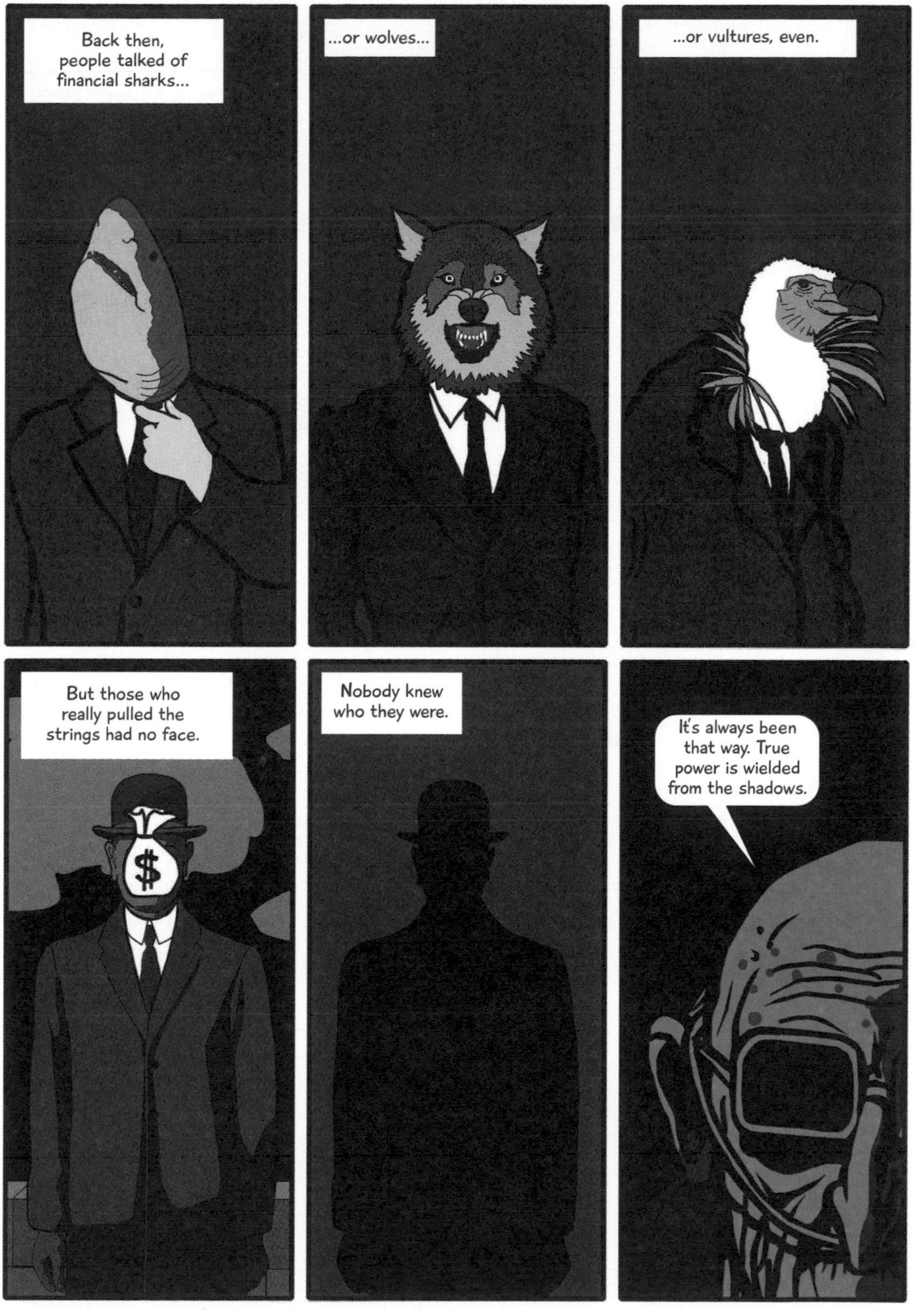
Back then, people talked of financial sharks...
...or wolves...
...or vultures, even.
But those who really pulled the strings had no face.
Nobody knew who they were.
It's always been that way. True power is wielded from the shadows.

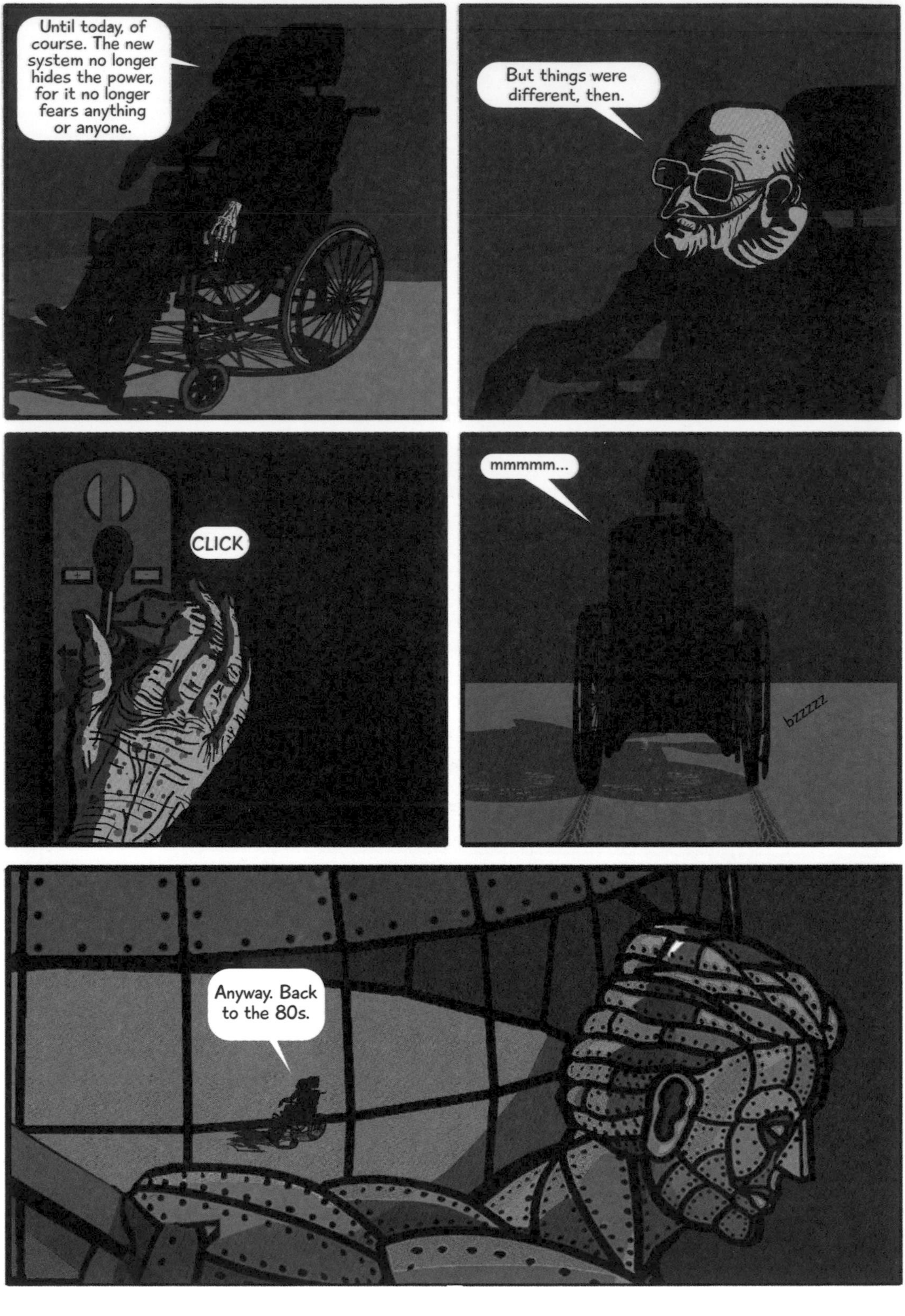
Until today, of course. The new system no longer hides the power, for it no longer fears anything or anyone.
But things were different, then.
CLICK
mmmmm...
bzzzzz
Anyway. Back to the 80s.

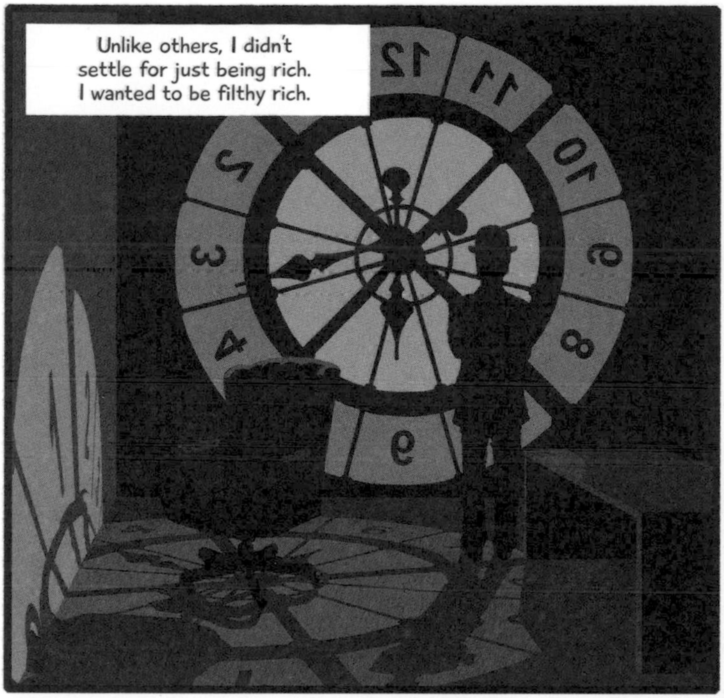
Unlike others, I didn't settle for just being rich. I wanted to be filthy rich.

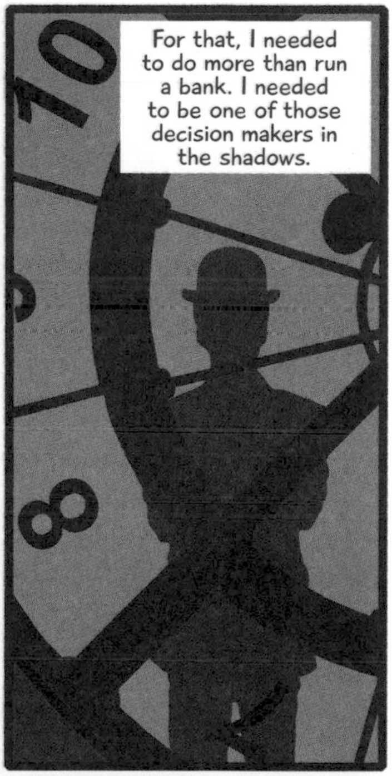
For that, I needed to do more than run a bank. I needed to be one of those decision makers in the shadows.

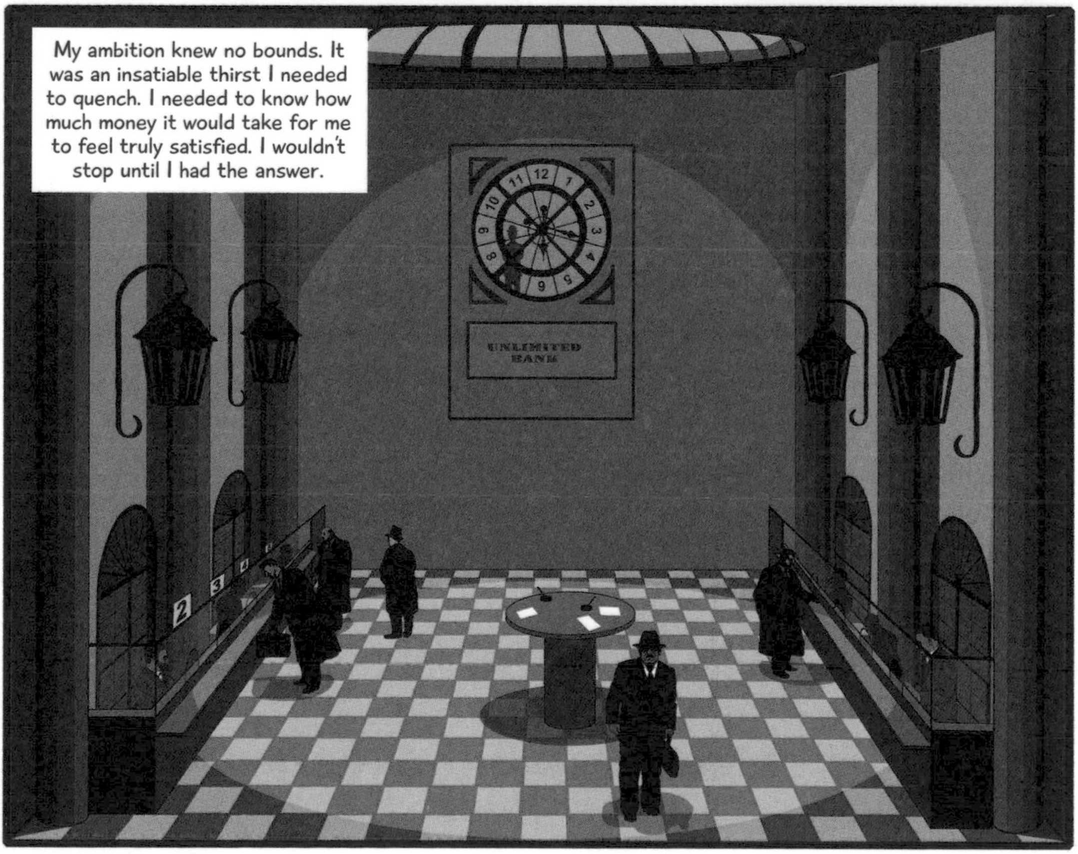
My ambition knew no bounds. It was an insatiable thirst I needed to quench. I needed to know how much money it would take for me to feel truly satisfied. I wouldn't stop until I had the answer.
UNLIMITED BANK

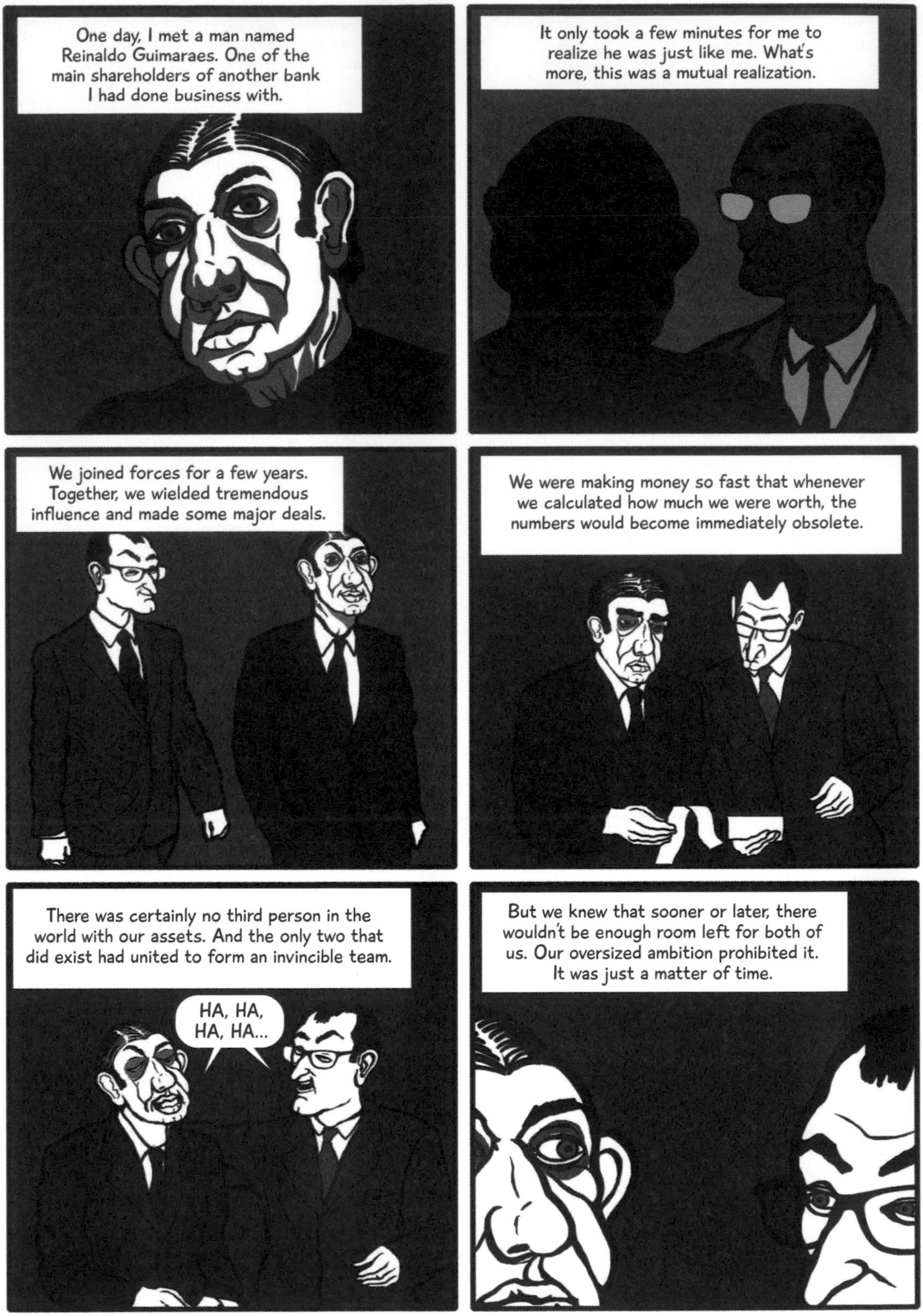
One day, I met a man named Reinaldo Guimaraes. One of the main shareholders of another bank I had done business with.
It only took a few minutes for me to realize he was just like me. What's more, this was a mutual realization.
We joined forces for a few years. Together, we wielded tremendous influence and made some major deals.
We were making money so fast that whenever we calculated how much we were worth, the numbers would become immediately obsolete.
There was certainly no third person in the world with our assets. And the only two that did exist had united to form an invincible team.
HA, HA, HA, HA...
But we knew that sooner or later, there wouldn't be enough room left for both of us. Our oversized ambition prohibited it. It was just a matter of time.

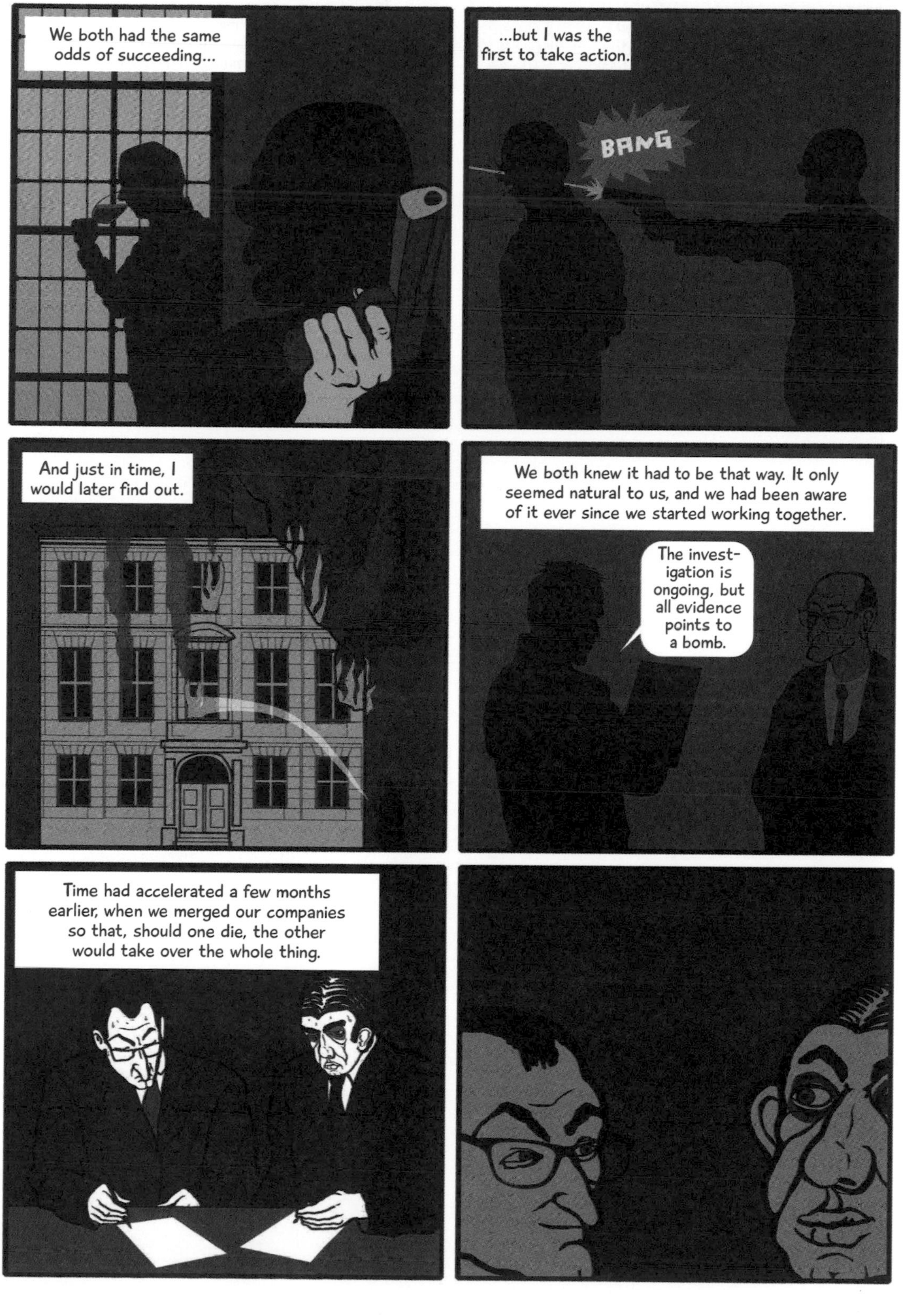
We both had the same odds of succeeding...
...but I was the first to take action.
BANG
And just in time, I would later find out.
We both knew it had to be that way. It only seemed natural to us, and we had been aware of it ever since we started working together.
The investigation is ongoing, but all evidence points to a bomb.
Time had accelerated a few months earlier, when we merged our companies so that, should one die, the other would take over the whole thing.

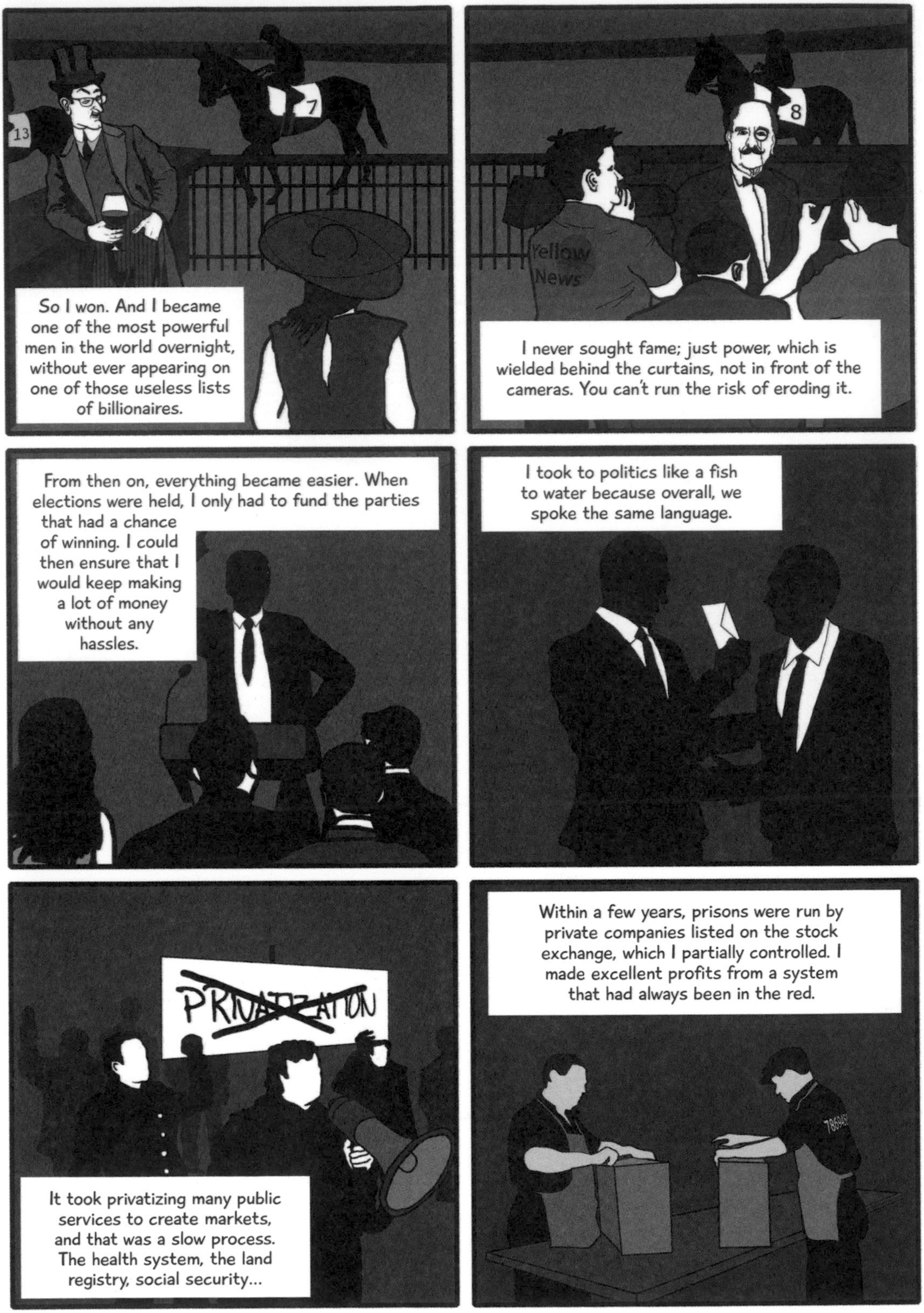
13
7
So I won. And I became one of the most powerful men in the world overnight, without ever appearing on one of those useless lists of billionaires.
8
Yellow News
I never sought fame; just power, which is wielded behind the curtains, not in front of the cameras. You can't run the risk of eroding it.
From then on, everything became easier. When elections were held, I only had to fund the parties that had a chance of winning. I could then ensure that I would keep making a lot of money without any hassles.
I took to politics like a fish to water because overall, we spoke the same language.
PRIVATIZATION
It took privatizing many public services to create markets, and that was a slow process. The health system, the land registry, social security...
Within a few years, prisons were run by private companies listed on the stock exchange, which I partially controlled. I made excellent profits from a system that had always been in the red.

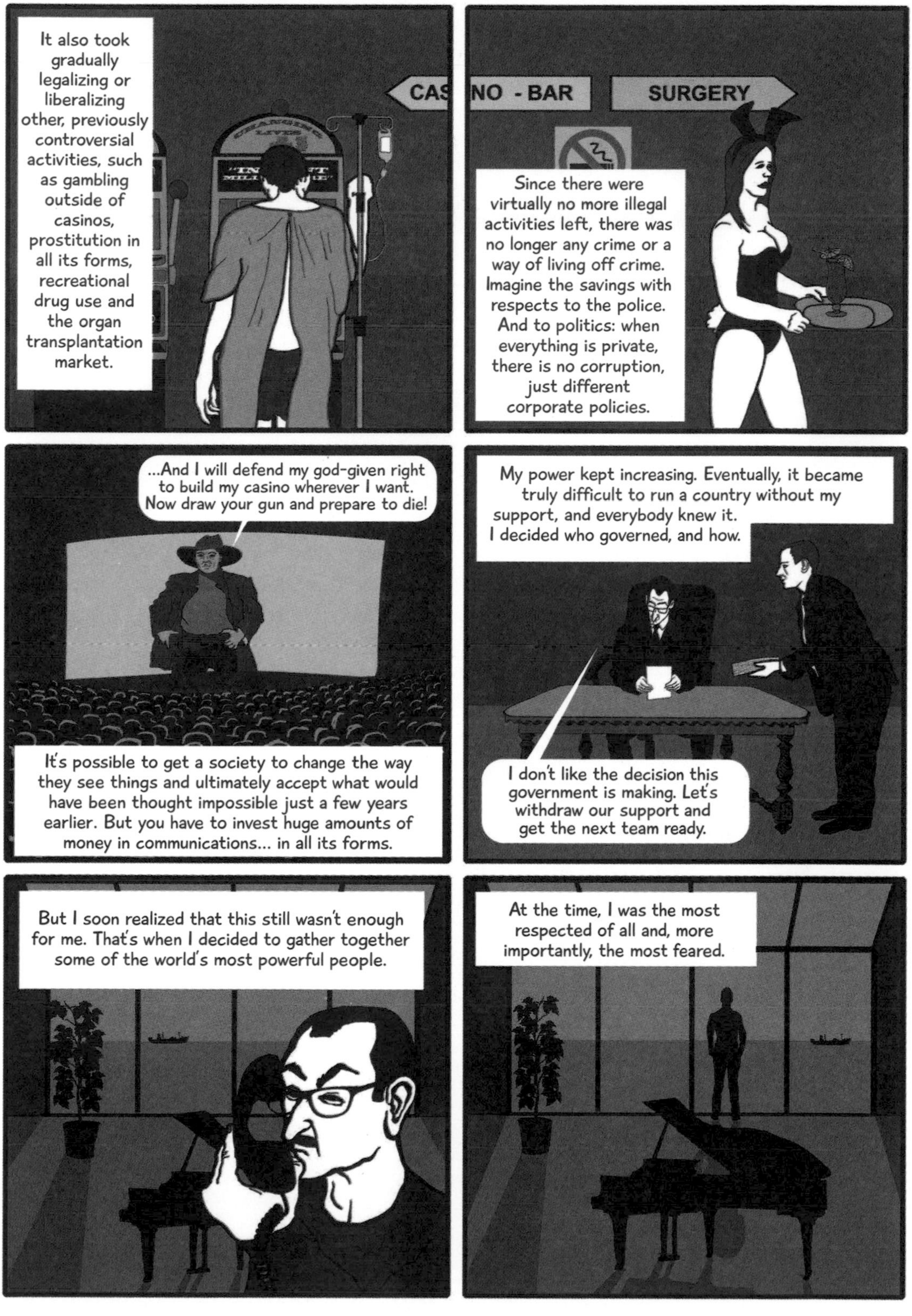
It also took gradually legalizing or liberalizing other, previously controversial activities, such as gambling outside of casinos, prostitution in all its forms, recreational drug use and the organ transplantation market.
CAS NO - BAR
SURGERY
Since there were virtually no more illegal activities left, there was no longer any crime or a way of living off crime. Imagine the savings with respects to the police. And to politics: when everything is private, there is no corruption, just different corporate policies.
...And I will defend my god-given right to build my casino wherever I want. Now draw your gun and prepare to die!
It's possible to get a society to change the way they see things and ultimately accept what would have been thought impossible just a few years earlier. But you have to invest huge amounts of money in communications... in all its forms.
My power kept increasing. Eventually, it became truly difficult to run a country without my support, and everybody knew it. I decided who governed, and how.
I don't like the decision this government is making. Let's withdraw our support and get the next team ready.
But I soon realized that this still wasn't enough for me. That's when I decided to gather together some of the world's most powerful people.
At the time, I was the most respected of all and, more importantly, the most feared.

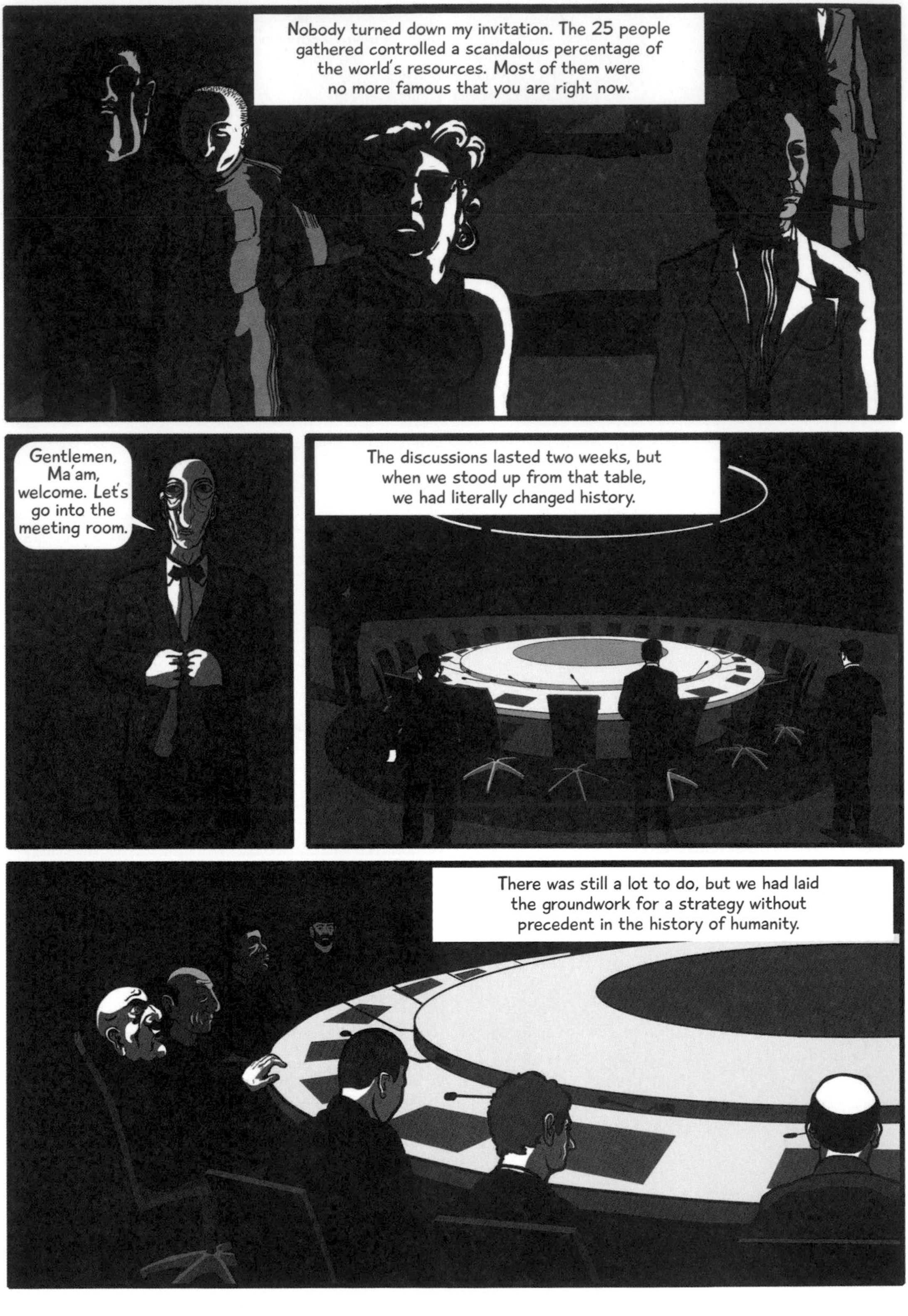
Nobody turned down my invitation. The 25 people gathered controlled a scandalous percentage of the world's resources. Most of them were no more famous that you are right now.
Gentlemen, Ma'am, welcome. Let's go into the meeting room.
The discussions lasted two weeks, but when we stood up from that table, we had literally changed history.
There was still a lot to do, but we had laid the groundwork for a strategy without precedent in the history of humanity.

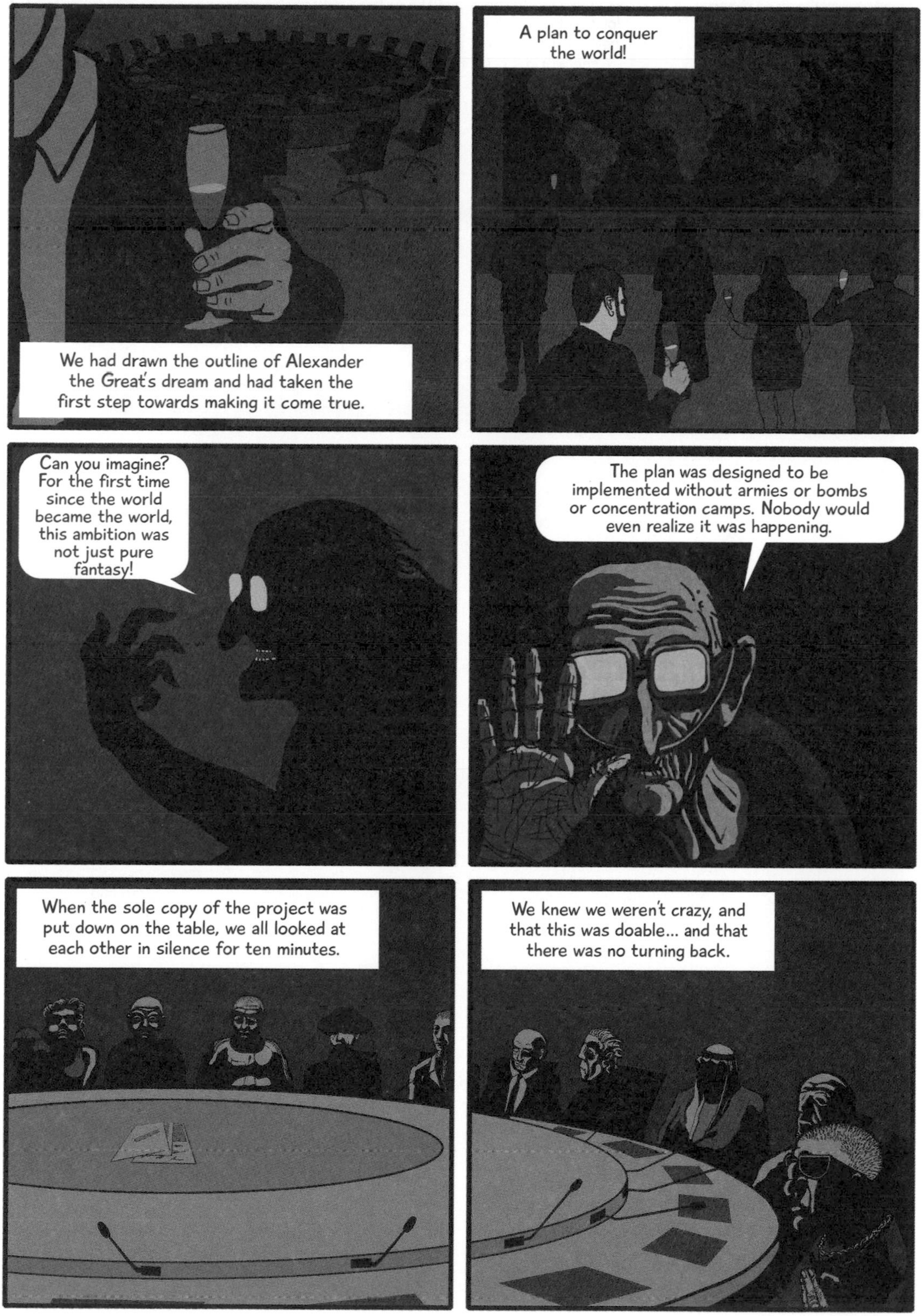
We had drawn the outline of Alexander the Great's dream and had taken the first step towards making it come true.
A plan to conquer the world!
Can you imagine? For the first time since the world became the world, this ambition was not just pure fantasy!
The plan was designed to be implemented without armies or bombs or concentration camps. Nobody would even realize it was happening.
When the sole copy of the project was put down on the table, we all looked at each other in silence for ten minutes.
We knew we weren't crazy, and that this was doable... and that there was no turning back.

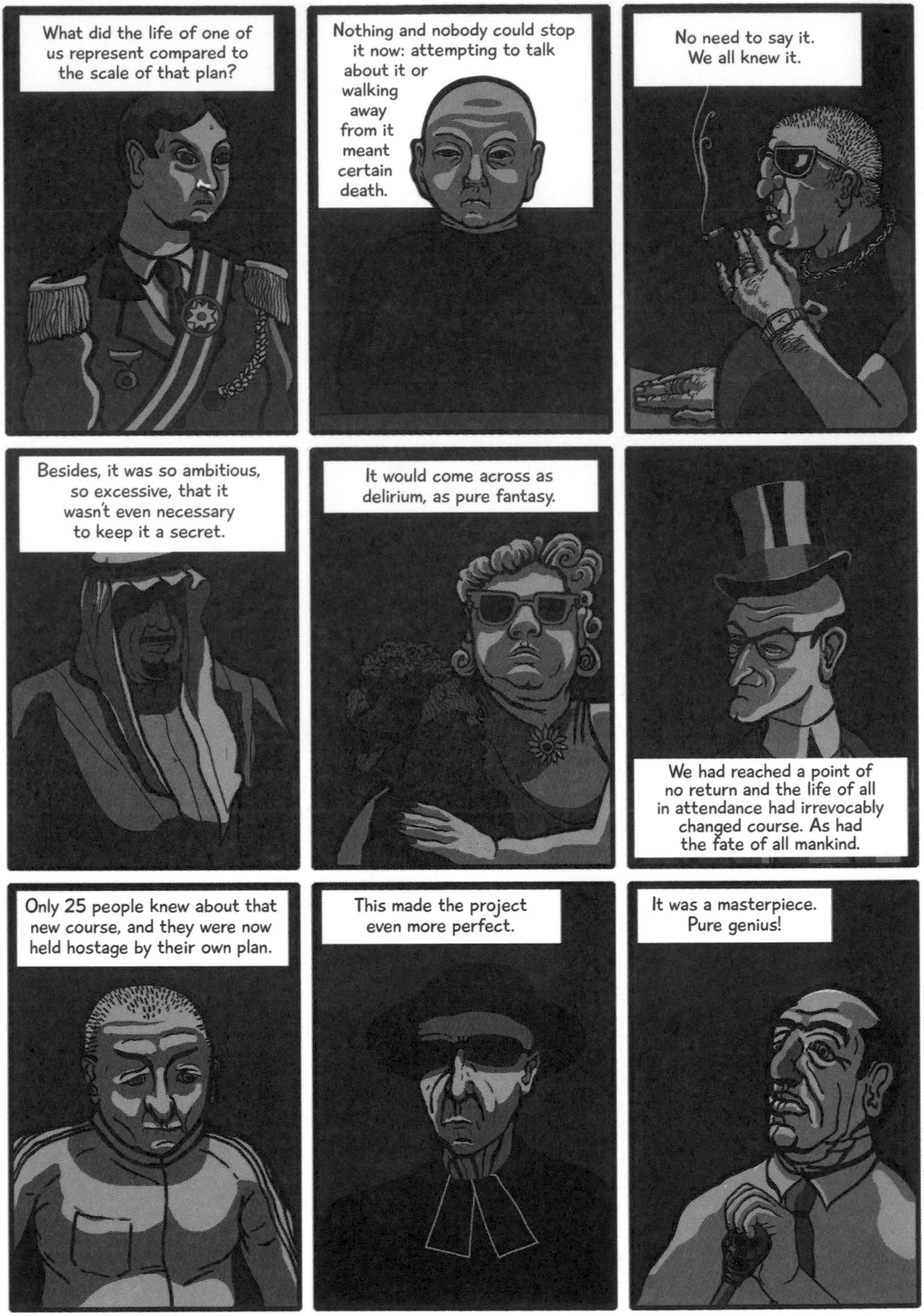
What did the life of one of us represent compared to the scale of that plan?
Nothing and nobody could stop it now: attempting to talk about it or walking away from it meant certain death.
No need to say it. We all knew it.
Besides, it was so ambitious, so excessive, that it wasn't even necessary to keep it a secret.
It would come across as delirium, as pure fantasy.
We had reached a point of no return and the life of all in attendance had irrevocably changed course. As had the fate of all mankind.
Only 25 people knew about that new course, and they were now held hostage by their own plan.
This made the project even more perfect.
It was a masterpiece. Pure genius!

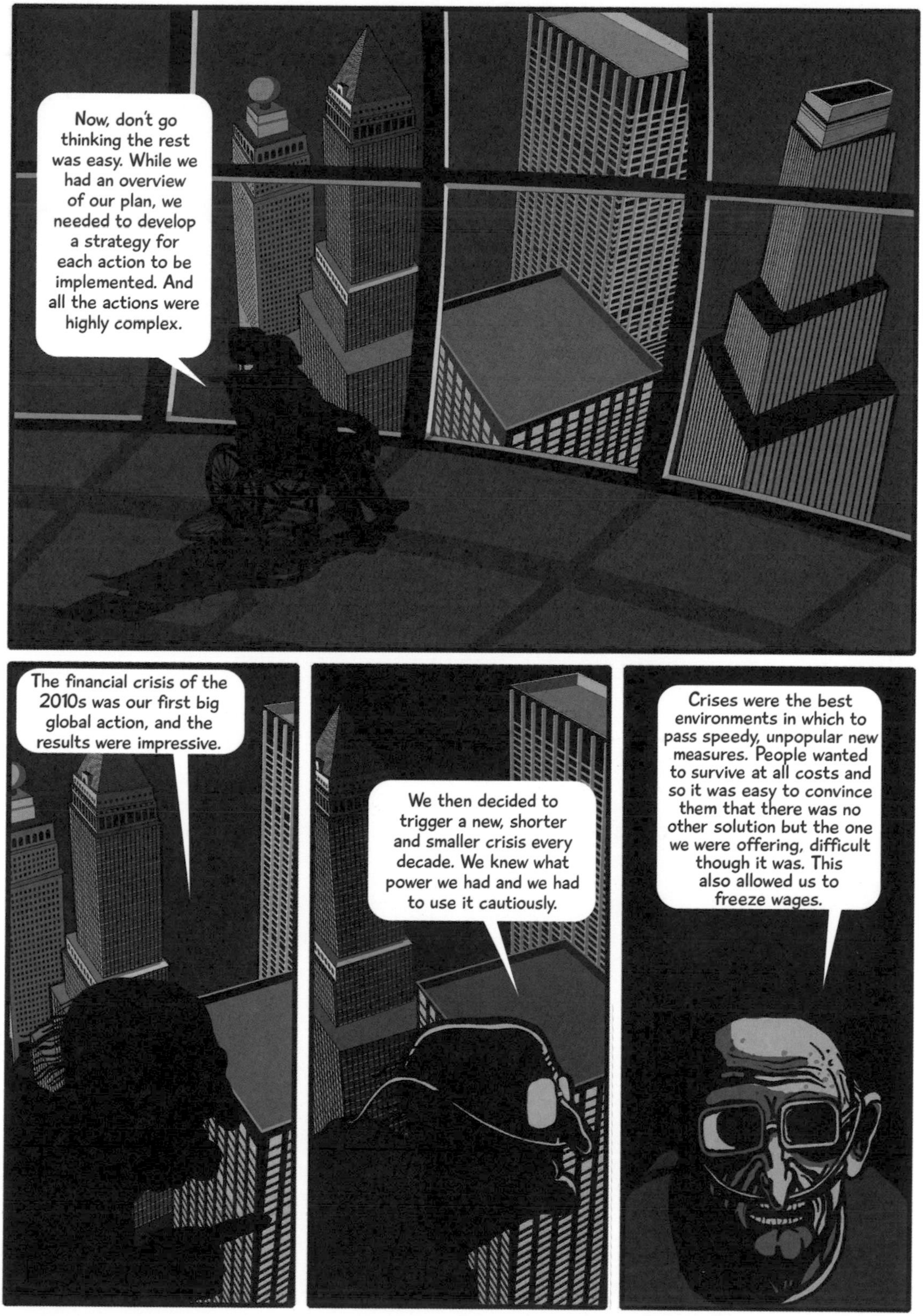
Now, don't go thinking the rest was easy. While we had an overview of our plan, we needed to develop a strategy for each action to be implemented. And all the actions were highly complex.
The financial crisis of the 2010s was our first big global action, and the results were impressive.
We then decided to trigger a new, shorter and smaller crisis every decade. We knew what power we had and we had to use it cautiously.
Crises were the best environments in which to pass speedy, unpopular new measures. People wanted to survive at all costs and so it was easy to convince them that there was no other solution but the one we were offering, difficult though it was. This also allowed us to freeze wages.

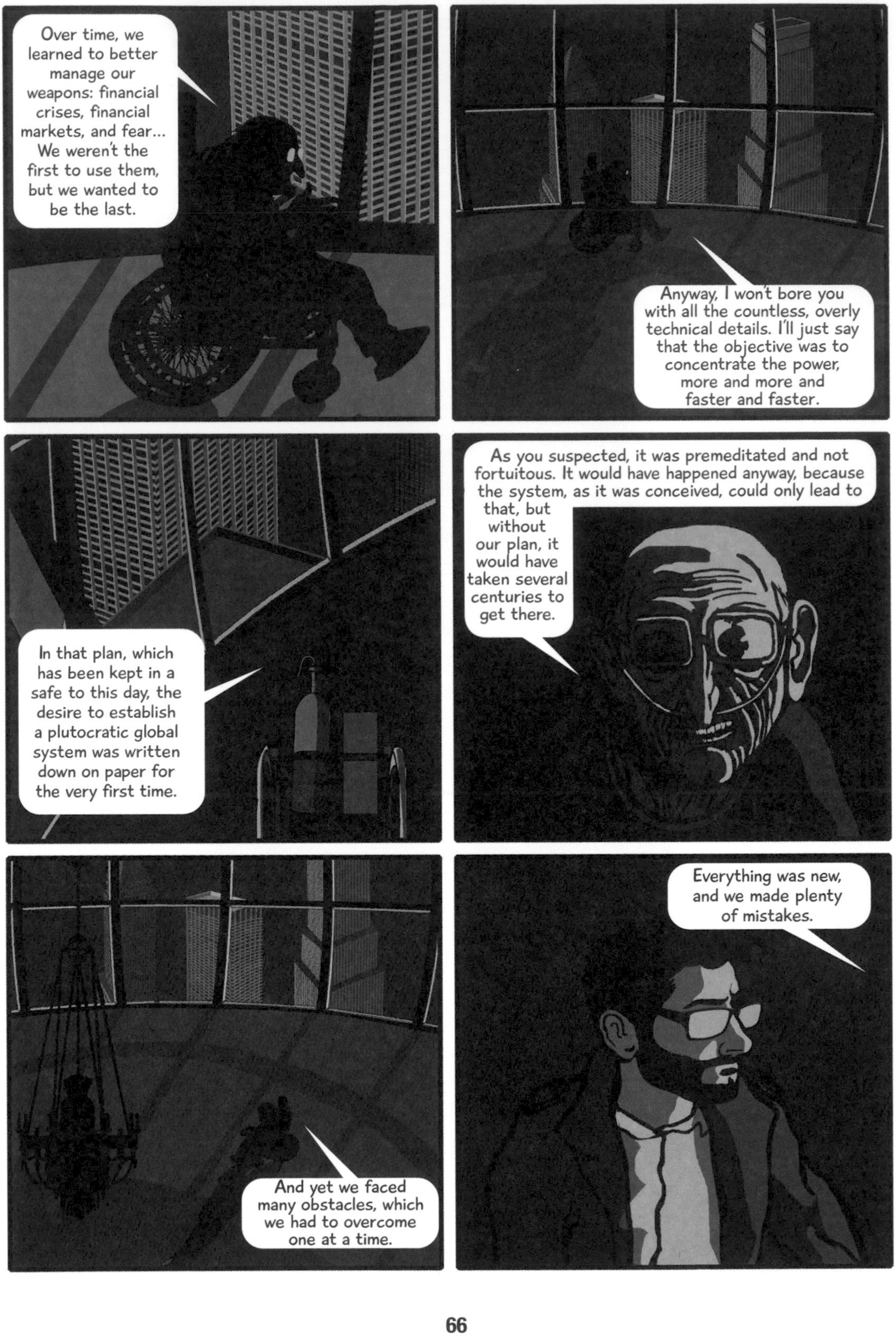
Over time, we learned to better manage our weapons: financial crises, financial markets, and fear... We weren't the first to use them, but we wanted to be the last.
Anyway, I won't bore you with all the countless, overly technical details. I'll just say that the objective was to concentrate the power, more and more and faster and faster.
In that plan, which has been kept in a safe to this day, the desire to establish a plutocratic global system was written down on paper for the very first time.
As you suspected, it was premeditated and not fortuitous. It would have happened anyway, because the system, as it was conceived, could only lead to that, but without our plan, it would have taken several centuries to get there.
And yet we faced many obstacles, which we had to overcome one at a time.
Everything was new, and we made plenty of mistakes.

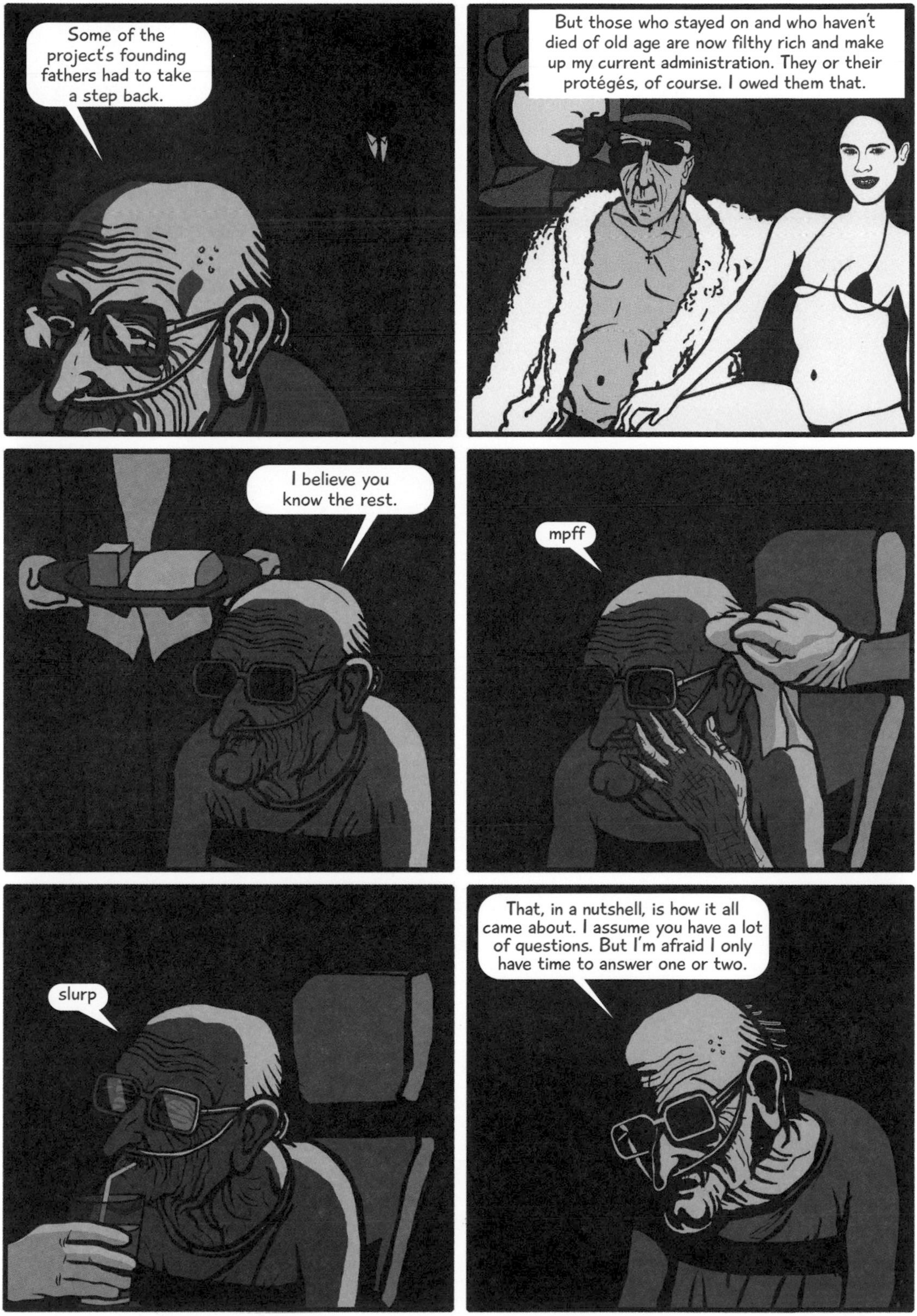
Some of the project's founding fathers had to take a step back.
But those who stayed on and who haven't died of old age are now filthy rich and make up my current administration. They or their protégés, of course. I owed them that.
I believe you know the rest.
mpff
slurp
That, in a nutshell, is how it all came about. I assume you have a lot of questions. But I'm afraid I only have time to answer one or two.

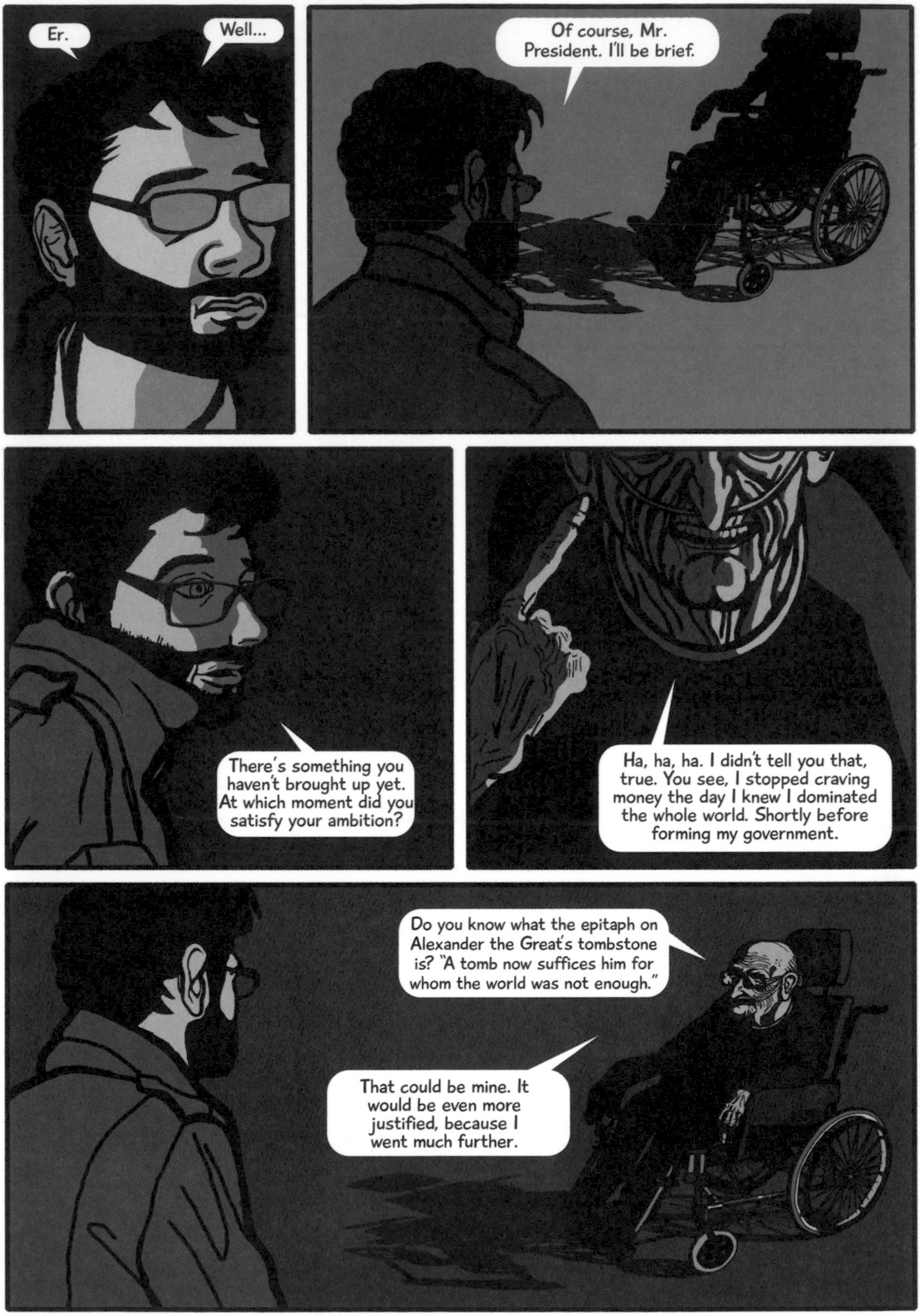
Er.
Well...
Of course, Mr. President. I'll be brief.
There's something you haven't brought up yet. At which moment did you satisfy your ambition?
Ha, ha, ha. I didn't tell you that, true. You see, I stopped craving money the day I knew I dominated the whole world. Shortly before forming my government.
Do you know what the epitaph on Alexander the Great's tombstone is? "A tomb now suffices him for whom the world was not enough."
That could be mine. It would be even more justified, because I went much further.

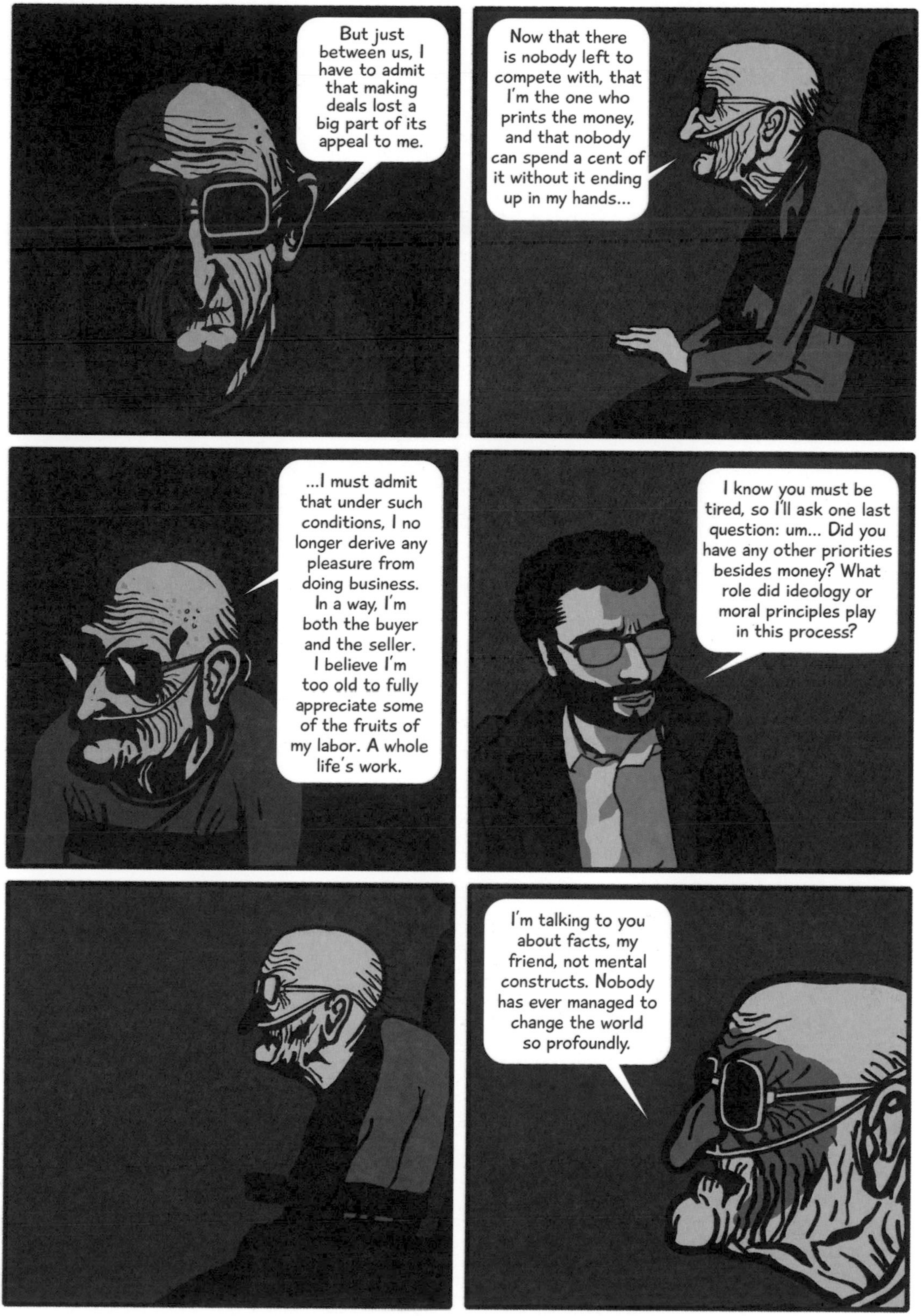
But just between us, I have to admit that making deals lost a big part of its appeal to me.
Now that there is nobody left to compete with, that I'm the one who prints the money, and that nobody can spend a cent of it without it ending up in my hands...
...I must admit that under such conditions, I no longer derive any pleasure from doing business. In a way, I'm both the buyer and the seller. I believe I'm too old to fully appreciate some of the fruits of my labor. A whole life's work.
I know you must be tired, so I'll ask one last question: um... Did you have any other priorities besides money? What role did ideology or moral principles play in this process?
I'm talking to you about facts, my friend, not mental constructs. Nobody has ever managed to change the world so profoundly.

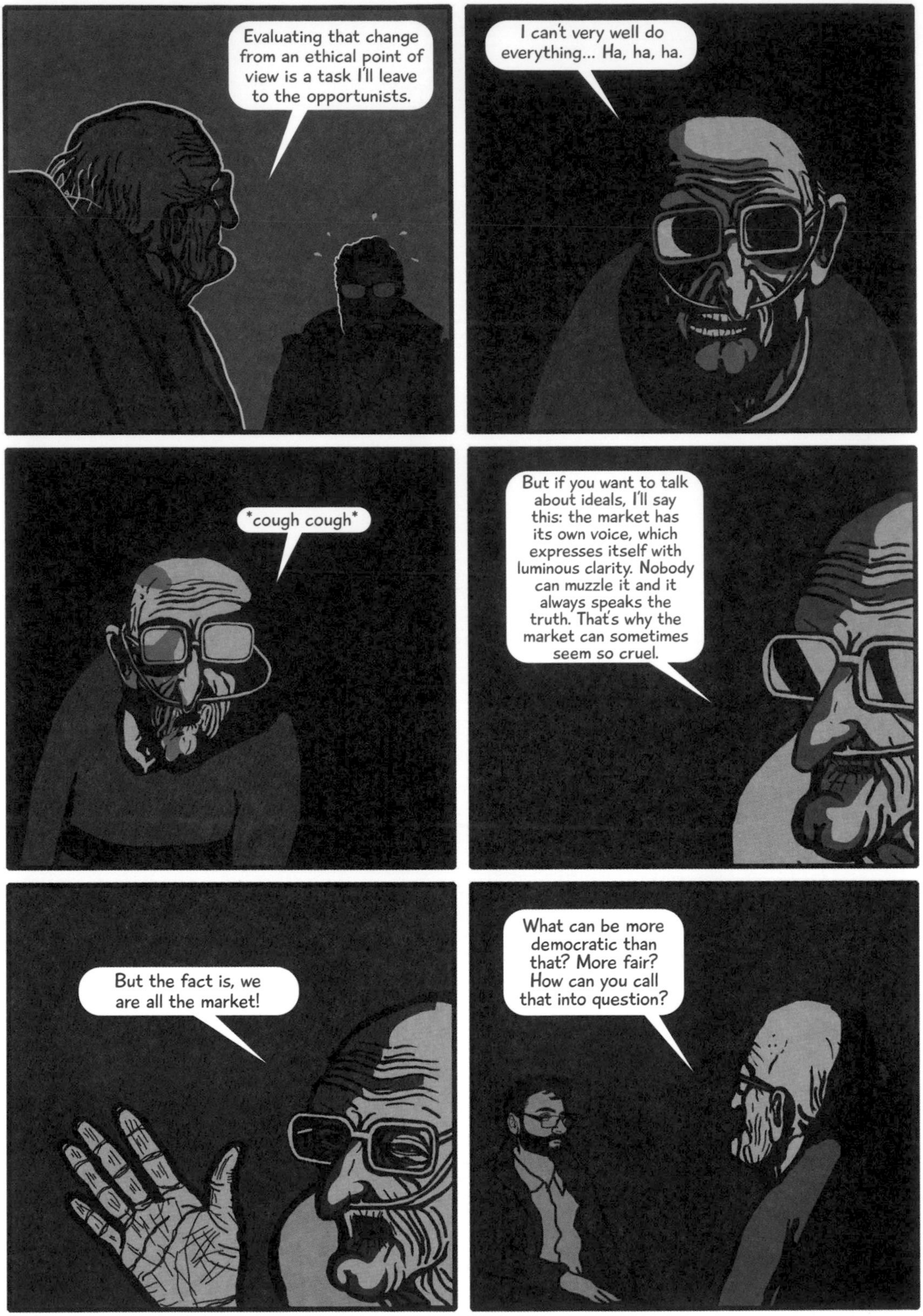
Evaluating that change from an ethical point of view is a task I'll leave to the opportunists.
I can't very well do everything... Ha, ha, ha.
cough cough
But if you want to talk about ideals, I'll say this: the market has its own voice, which expresses itself with luminous clarity. Nobody can muzzle it and it always speaks the truth. That's why the market can sometimes seem so cruel.
But the fact is, we are all the market!
What can be more democratic than that? More fair? How can you call that into question?

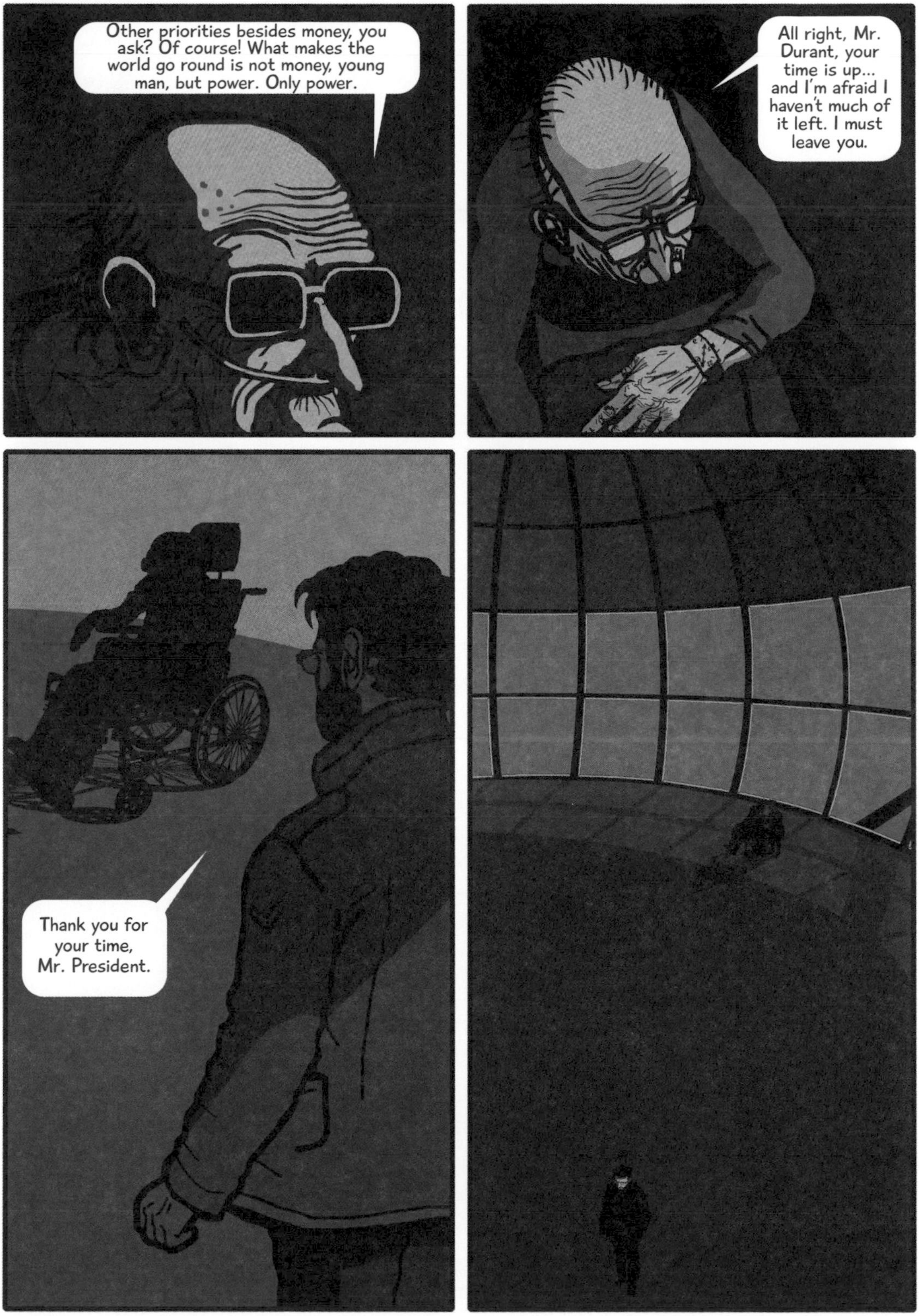
Other priorities besides money, you ask? Of course! What makes the world go round is not money, young man, but power. Only power.
All right, Mr. Durant, your time is up... and I'm afraid I haven't much of it left. I must leave you.
Thank you for your time, Mr. President.

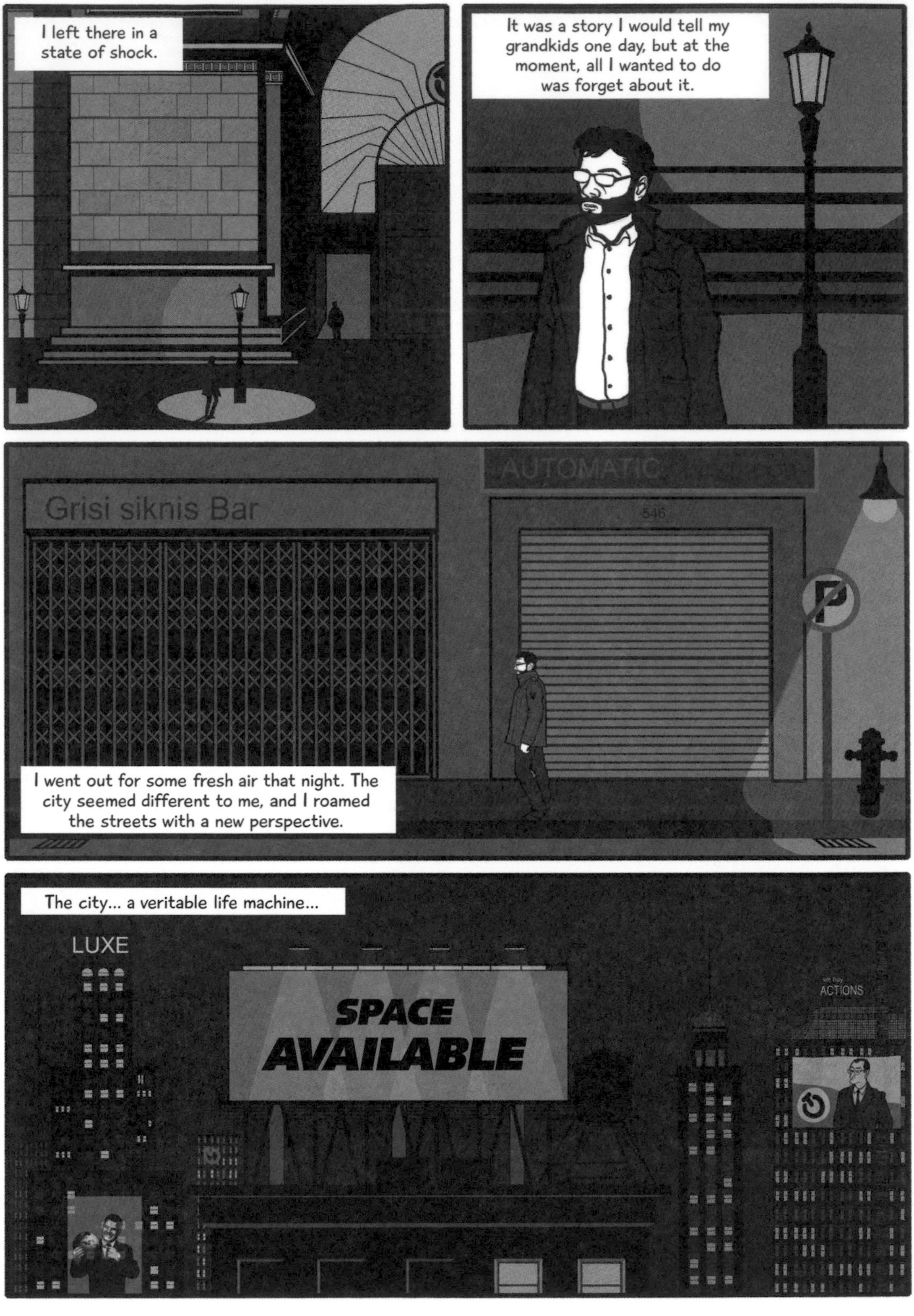
I left there in a state of shock.
It was a story I would tell my grandkids one day, but at the moment, all I wanted to do was forget about it.
Grisi siknis Bar
AUTOMATIC
546
I went out for some fresh air that night. The city seemed different to me, and I roamed the streets with a new perspective.
The city... a veritable life machine...
LUXE
SPACE AVAILABLE
ACTIONS

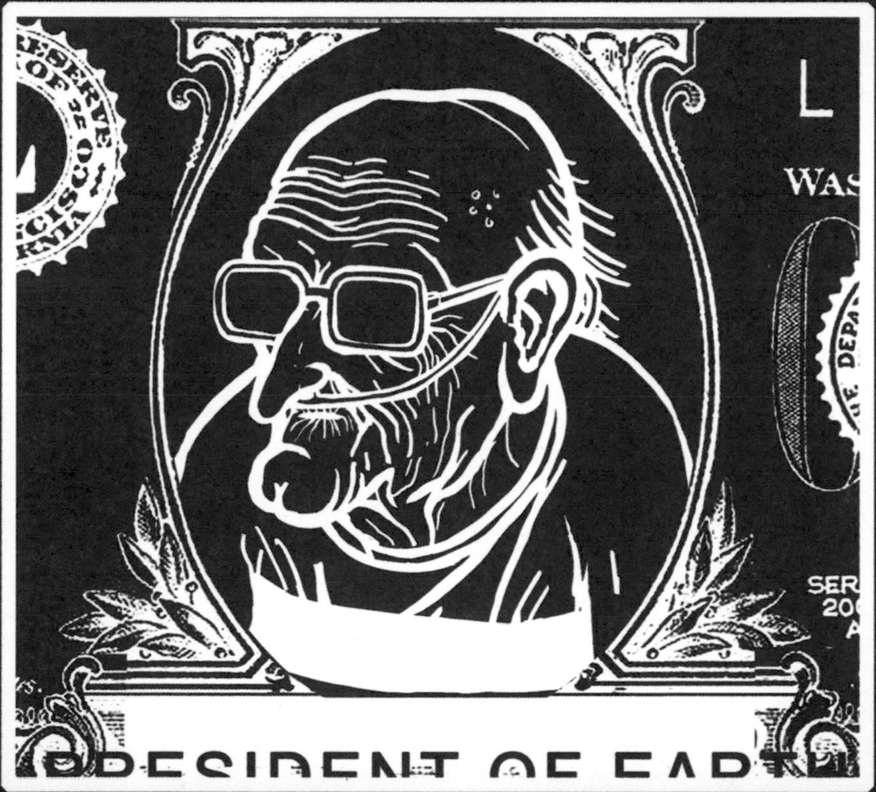
PRESIDENT OF EARTH

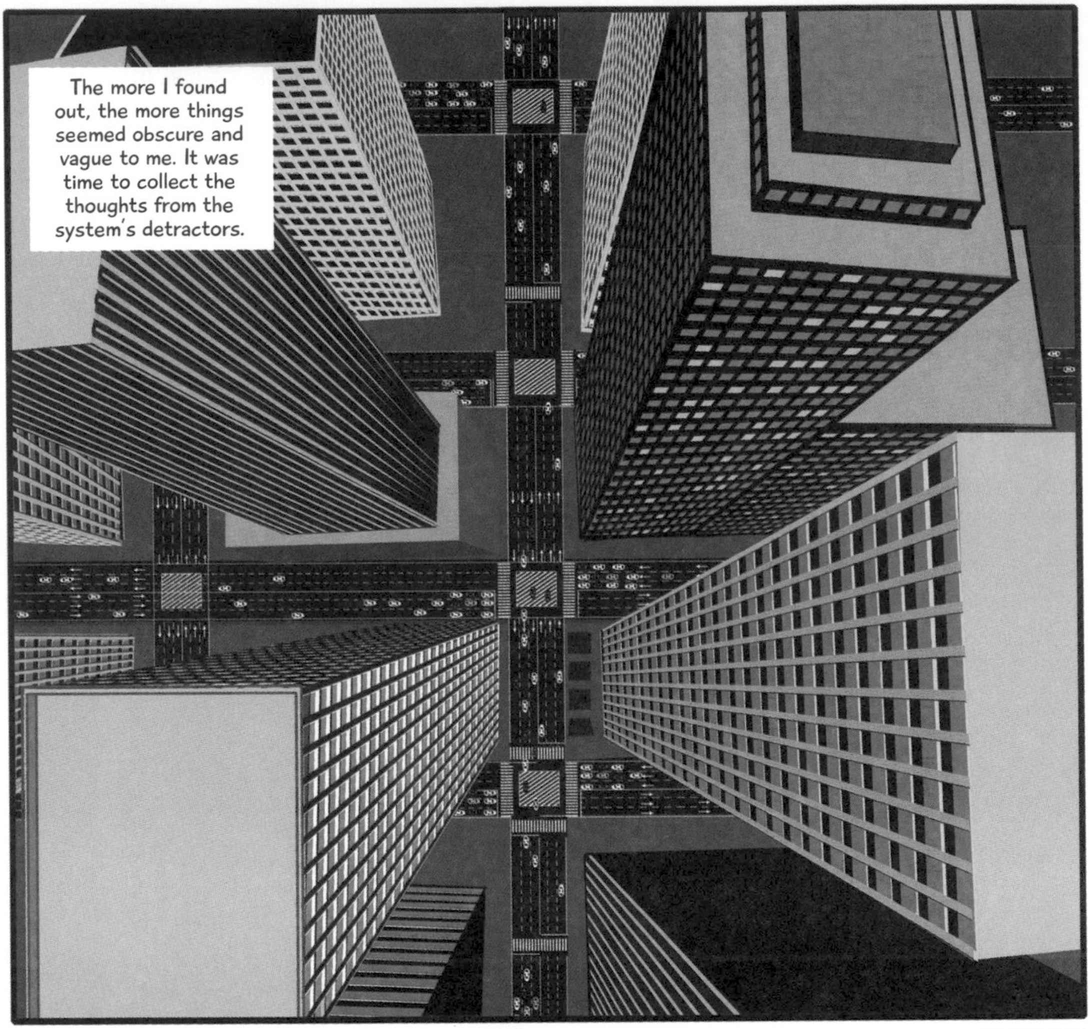
The more I found out, the more things seemed obscure and vague to me. It was time to collect the thoughts from the system's detractors.

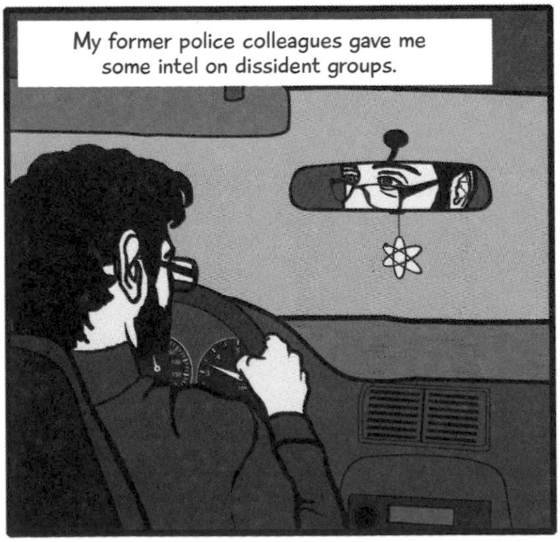
My former police colleagues gave me some intel on dissident groups.

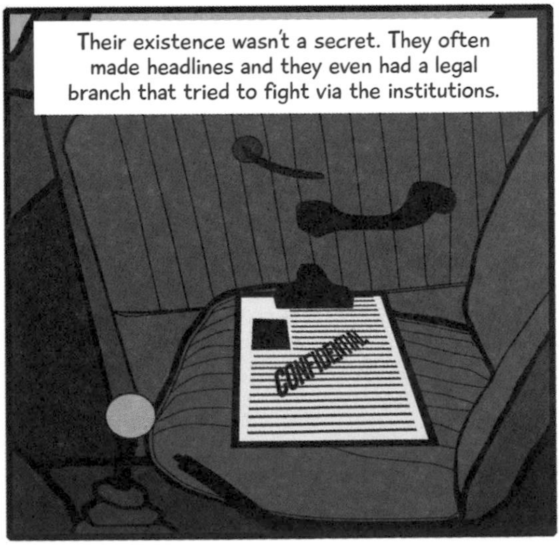
Their existence wasn't a secret. They often made headlines and they even had a legal branch that tried to fight via the institutions.
CONFIDENTIAL

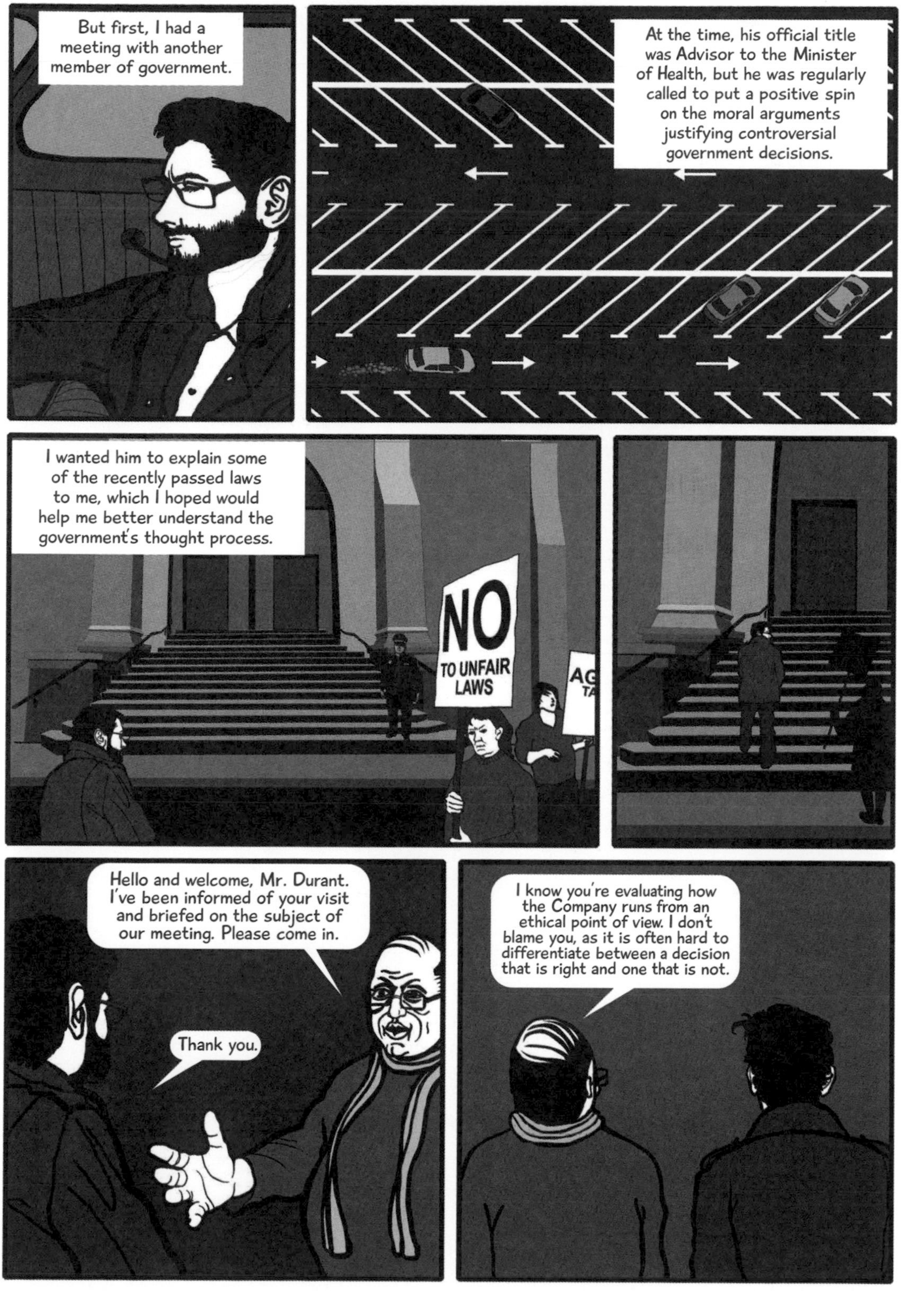

But first, I had a meeting with another member of government.
At the time, his official title was Advisor to the Minister of Health, but he was regularly called to put a positive spin on the moral arguments justifying controversial government decisions.
I wanted him to explain some of the recently passed laws to me, which I hoped would help me better understand the government's thought process.
NO TO UNFAIR LAWS
Hello and welcome, Mr. Durant. I've been informed of your visit and briefed on the subject of our meeting. Please come in.
Thank you.
I know you're evaluating how the Company runs from an ethical point of view. I don't blame you, as it is often hard to differentiate between a decision that is right and one that is not.

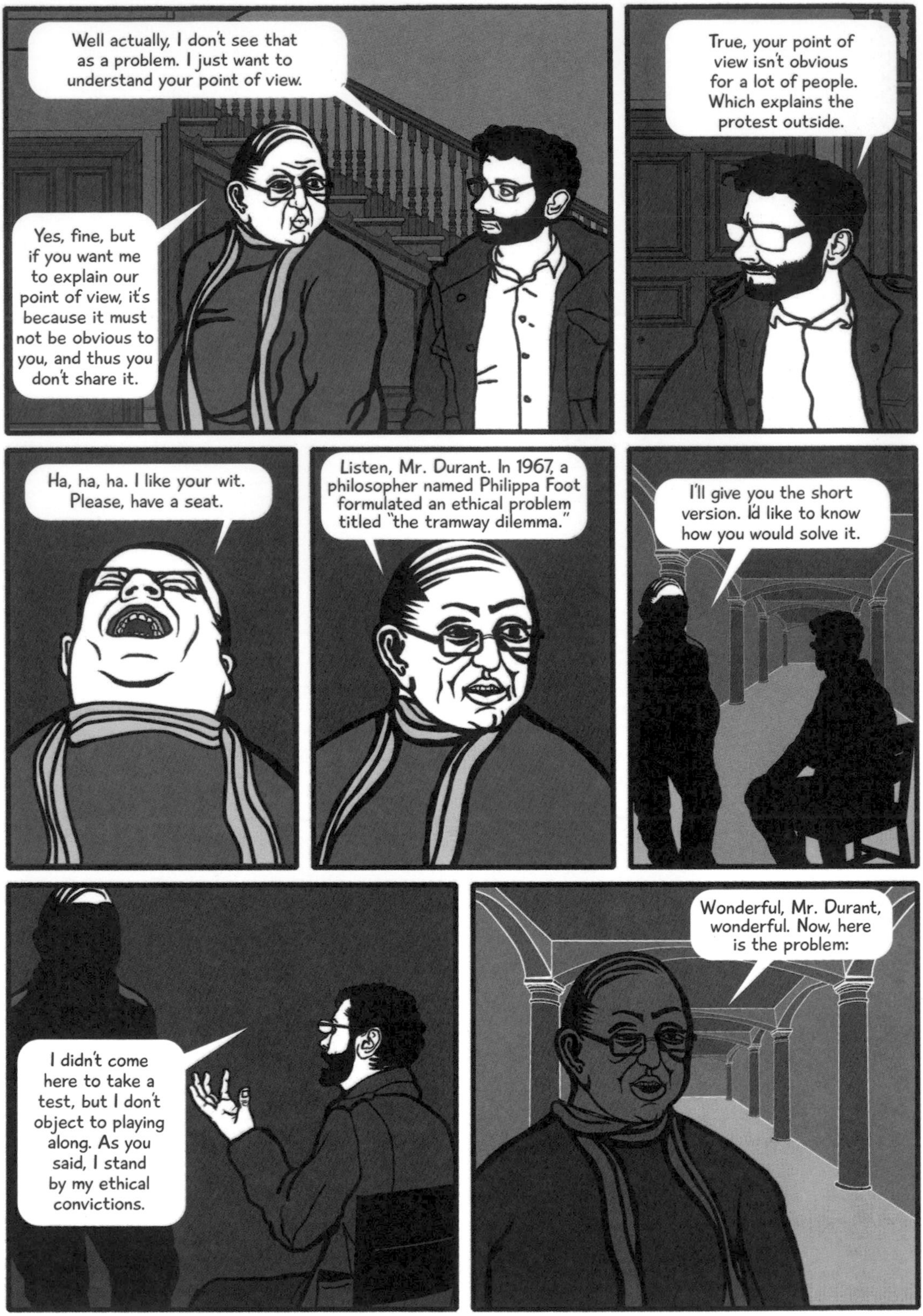
Well actually, I don't see that as a problem. I just want to understand your point of view.
Yes, fine, but if you want me to explain our point of view, it's because it must not be obvious to you, and thus you don't share it.
True, your point of view isn't obvious for a lot of people. Which explains the protest outside.
Ha, ha, ha. I like your wit. Please, have a seat.
Listen, Mr. Durant. In 1967, a philosopher named Philippa Foot formulated an ethical problem titled "the tramway dilemma."
I'll give you the short version. I'd like to know how you would solve it.
I didn't come here to take a test, but I don't object to playing along. As you said, I stand by my ethical convictions.
Wonderful, Mr. Durant, wonderful. Now, here is the problem:

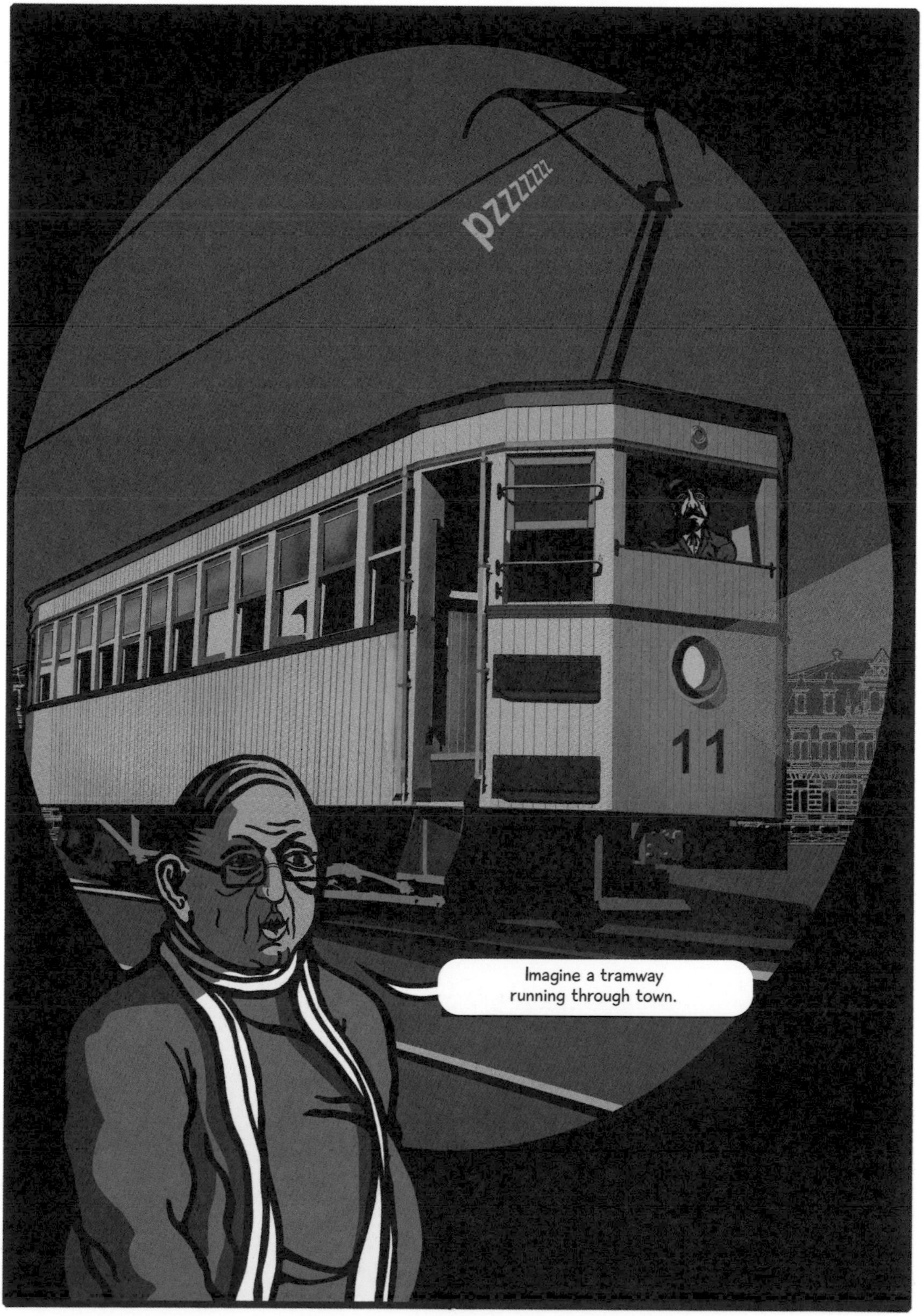
pzzzzzz
11
Imagine a tramway running through town.

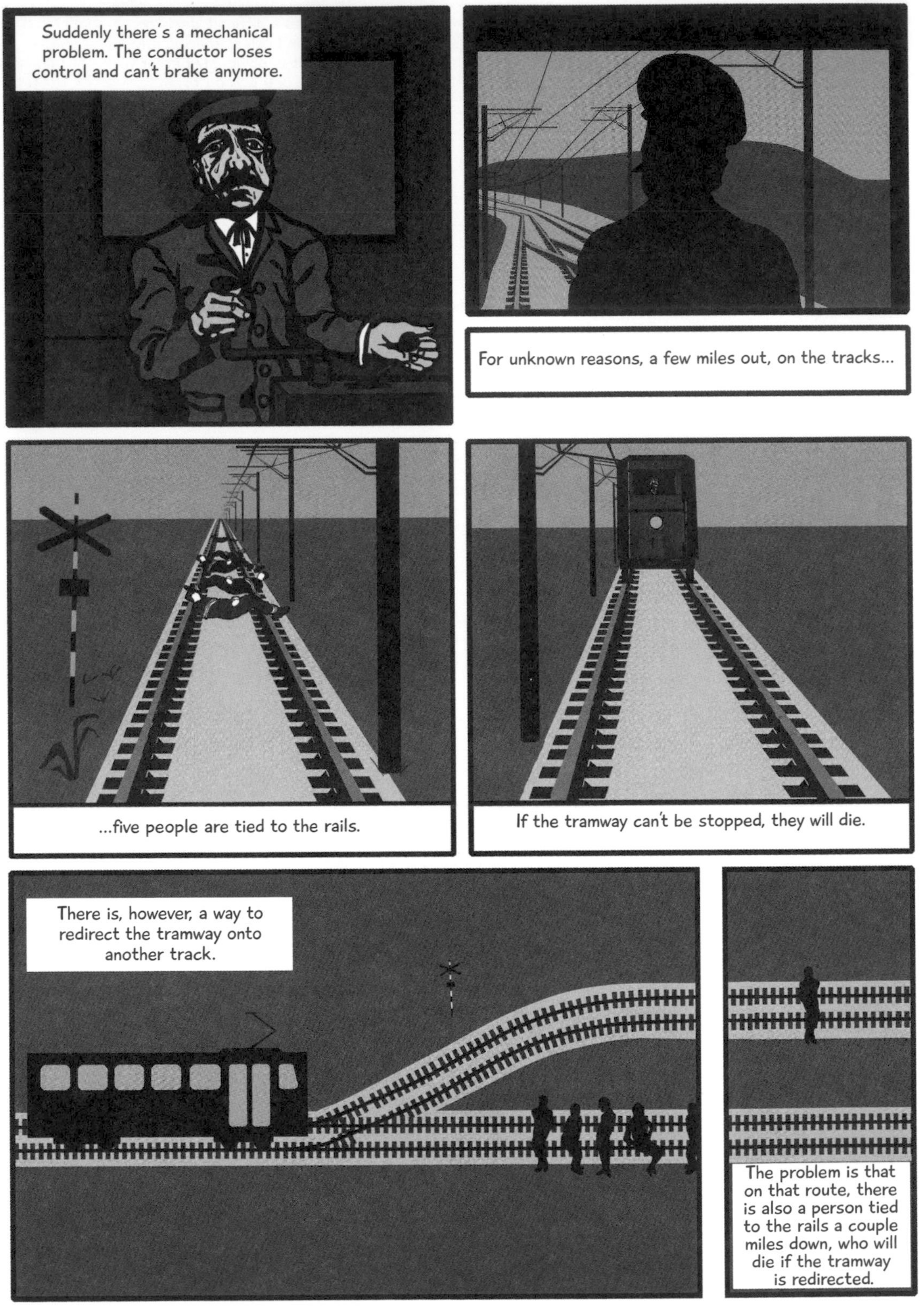
Suddenly there's a mechanical problem. The conductor loses control and can't brake anymore.
For unknown reasons, a few miles out, on the tracks...
...five people are tied to the rails.
If the tramway can't be stopped, they will die.
There is, however, a way to redirect the tramway onto another track.
The problem is that on that route, there is also a person tied to the rails a couple miles down, who will die if the tramway is redirected.

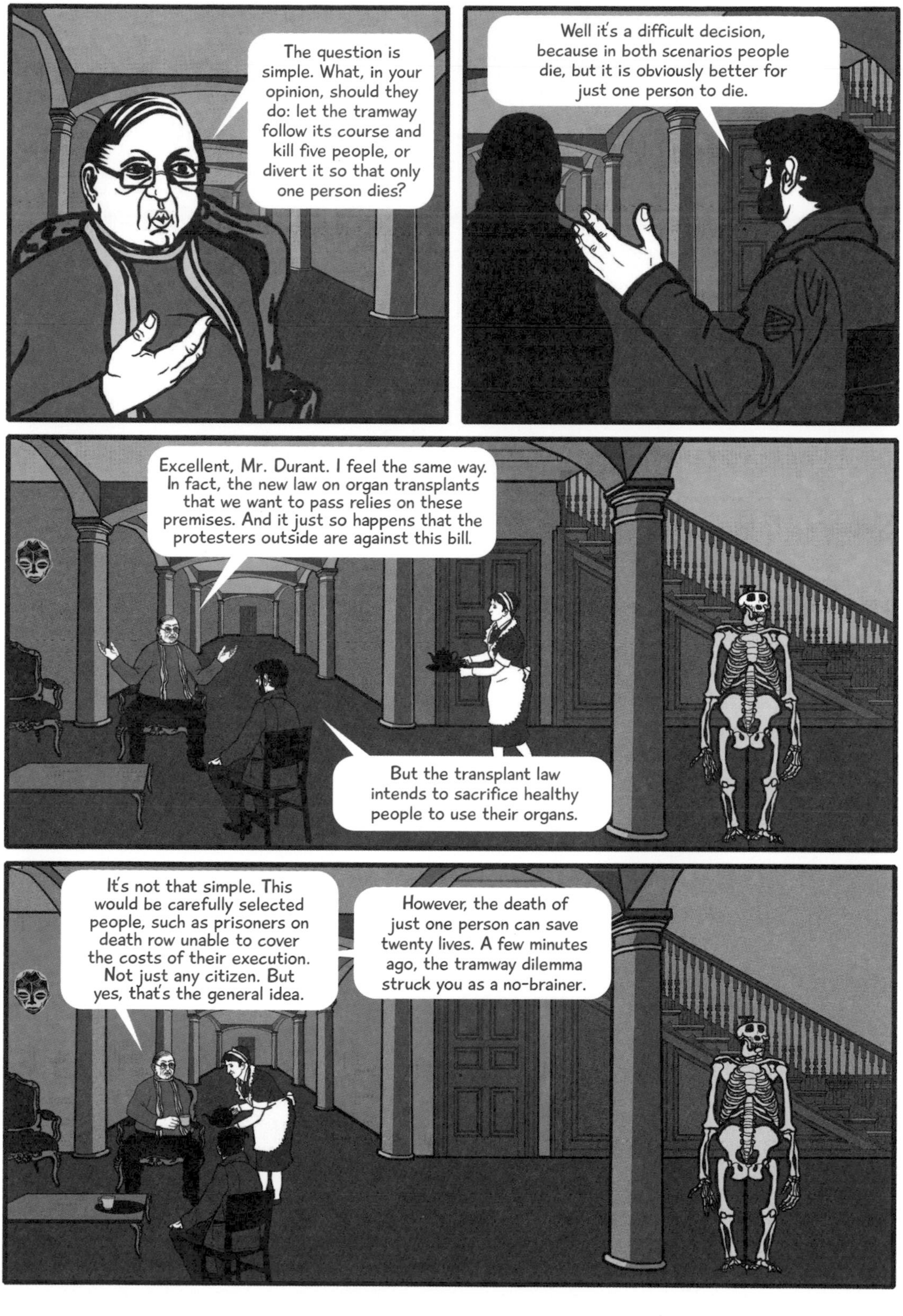
The question is simple. What, in your opinion, should they do: let the tramway follow its course and kill five people, or divert it so that only one person dies?
Well it's a difficult decision, because in both scenarios people die, but it is obviously better for just one person to die.
Excellent, Mr. Durant. I feel the same way. In fact, the new law on organ transplants that we want to pass relies on these premises. And it just so happens that the protesters outside are against this bill.
But the transplant law intends to sacrifice healthy people to use their organs.
It's not that simple. This would be carefully selected people, such as prisoners on death row unable to cover the costs of their execution. Not just any citizen. But yes, that's the general idea.
However, the death of just one person can save twenty lives. A few minutes ago, the tramway dilemma struck you as a no-brainer.

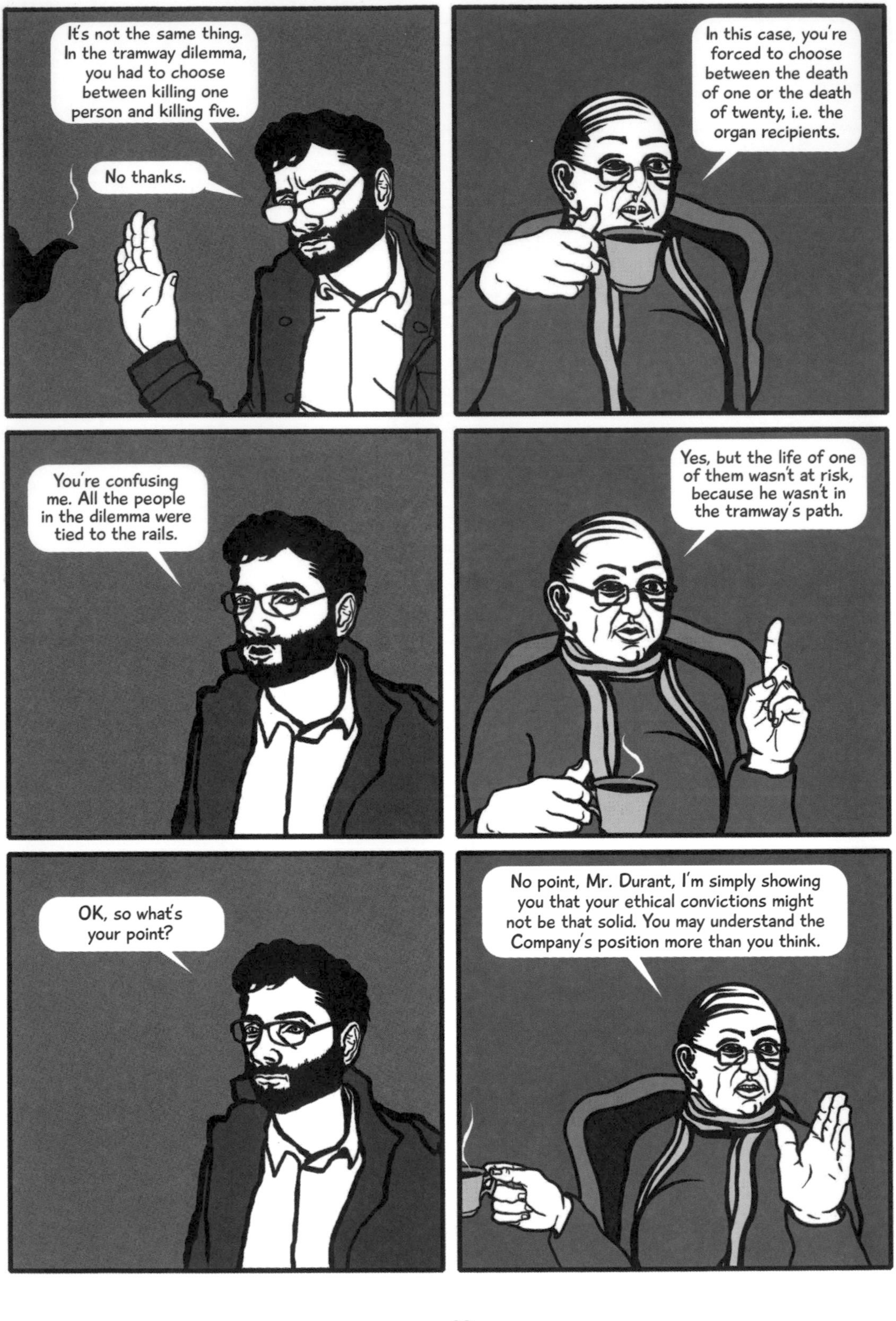
It's not the same thing. In the tramway dilemma, you had to choose between killing one person and killing five.
No thanks.
In this case, you're forced to choose between the death of one or the death of twenty, i.e. the organ recipients.
You're confusing me. All the people in the dilemma were tied to the rails.
Yes, but the life of one of them wasn't at risk, because he wasn't in the tramway's path.
OK, so what's your point?
No point, Mr. Durant, I'm simply showing you that your ethical convictions might not be that solid. You may understand the Company's position more than you think.

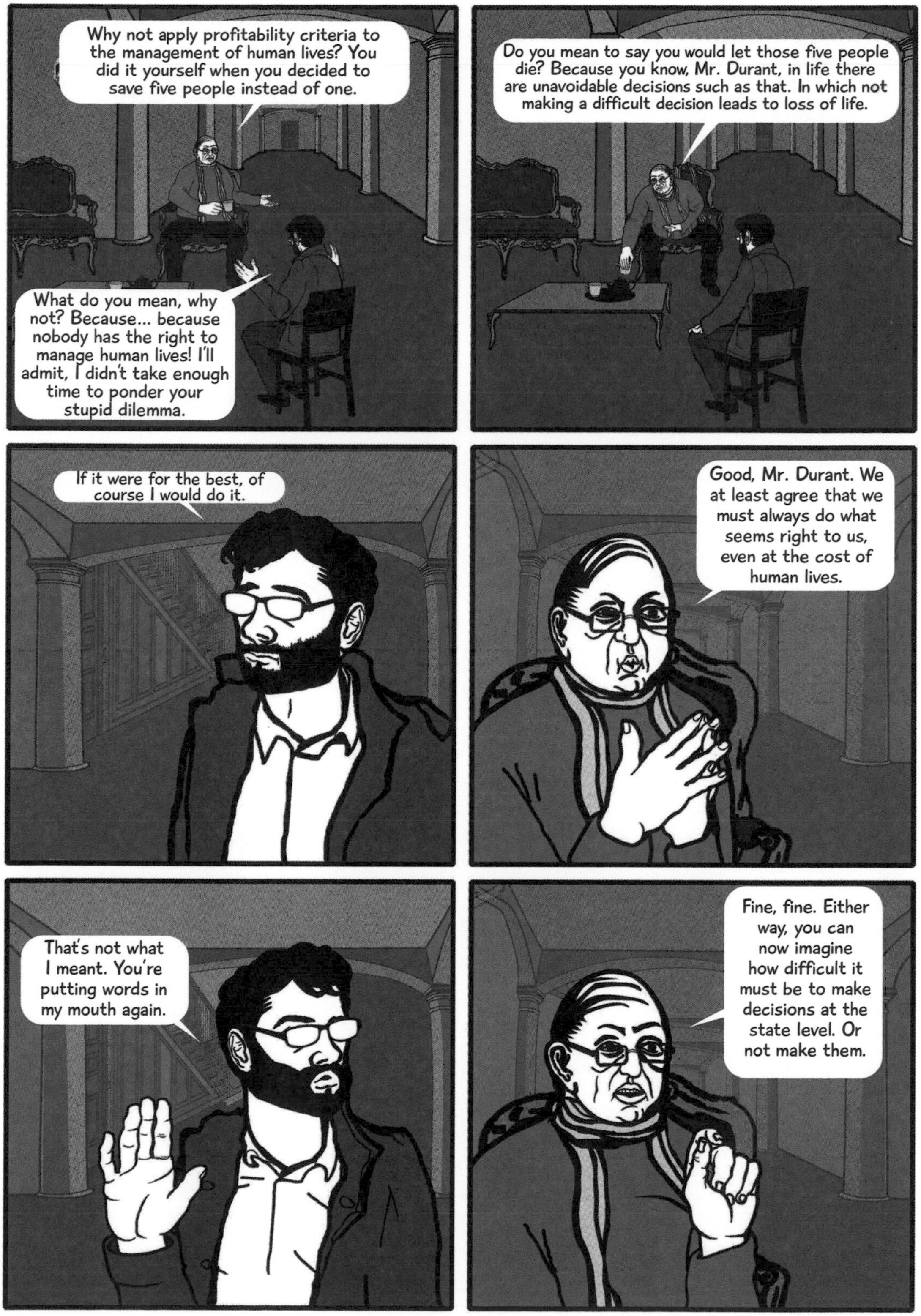

Why not apply profitability criteria to the management of human lives? You did it yourself when you decided to save five people instead of one.
What do you mean, why not? Because... because nobody has the right to manage human lives! I'll admit, I didn't take enough time to ponder your stupid dilemma.
Do you mean to say you would let those five people die? Because you know, Mr. Durant, in life there are unavoidable decisions such as that. In which not making a difficult decision leads to loss of life.
If it were for the best, of course I would do it.
Good, Mr. Durant. We at least agree that we must always do what seems right to us, even at the cost of human lives.
That's not what I meant. You're putting words in my mouth again.
Fine, fine. Either way, you can now imagine how difficult it must be to make decisions at the state level. Or not make them.

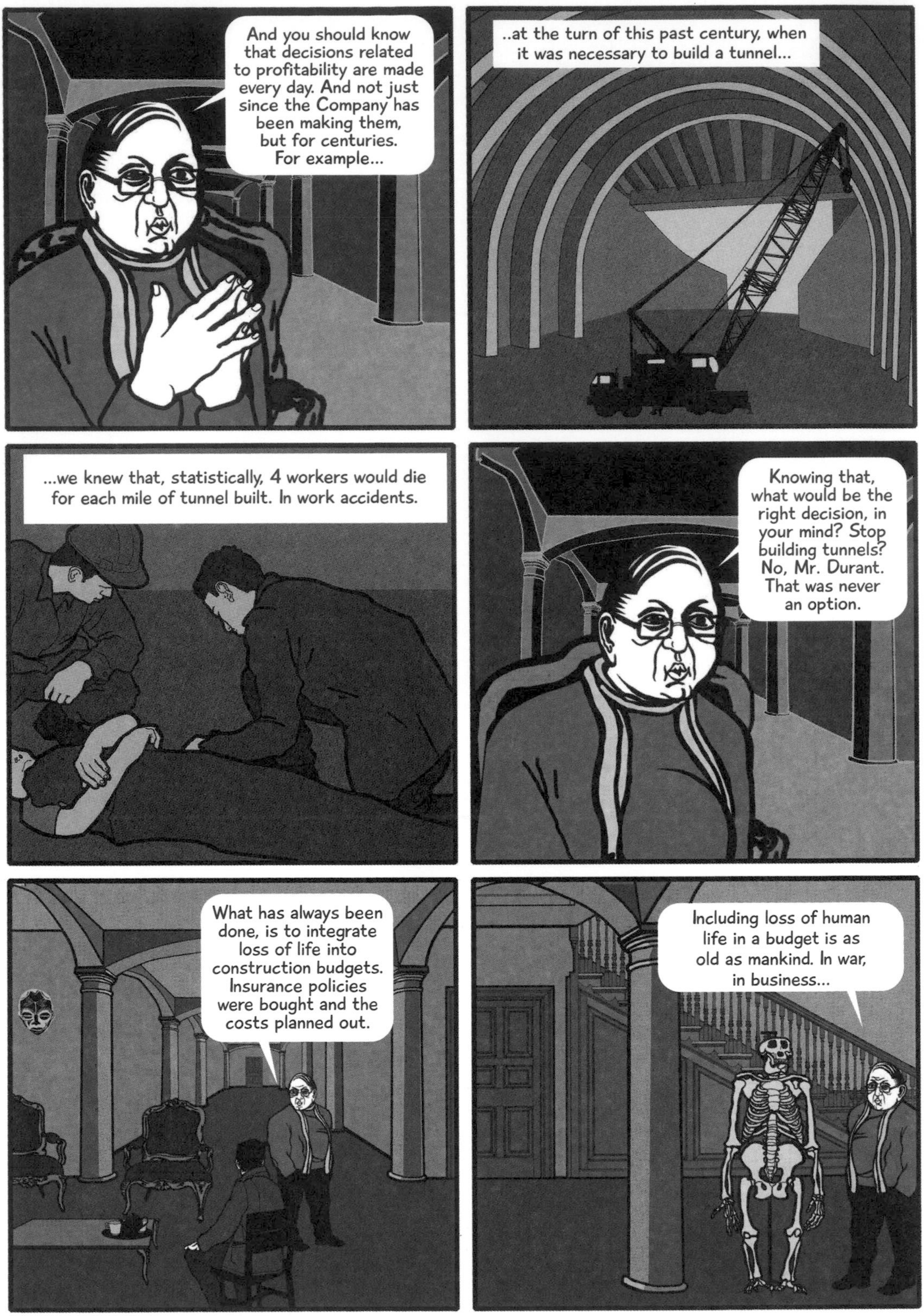

And you should know that decisions related to profitability are made every day. And not just since the Company has been making them, but for centuries. For example...
..at the turn of this past century, when it was necessary to build a tunnel...
...we knew that, statistically, 4 workers would die for each mile of tunnel built. In work accidents.
Knowing that, what would be the right decision, in your mind? Stop building tunnels? No, Mr. Durant. That was never an option.
What has always been done, is to integrate loss of life into construction budgets. Insurance policies were bought and the costs planned out.
Including loss of human life in a budget is as old as mankind. In war, in business...

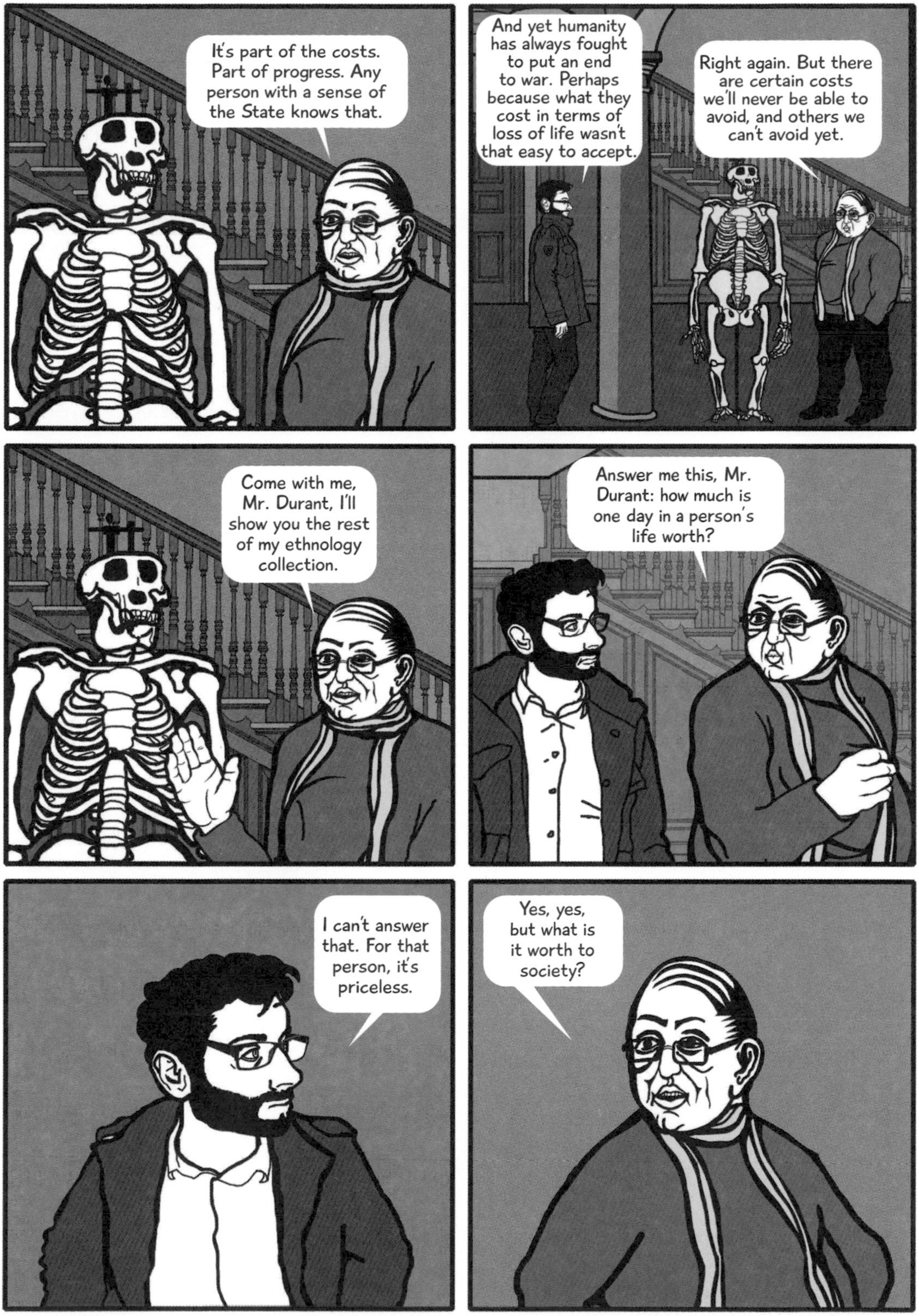
It's part of the costs. Part of progress. Any person with a sense of the State knows that.
And yet humanity has always fought to put an end to war. Perhaps because what they cost in terms of loss of life wasn't that easy to accept.
Right again. But there are certain costs we'll never be able to avoid, and others we can't avoid yet.
Come with me, Mr. Durant, I'll show you the rest of my ethnology collection.
Answer me this, Mr. Durant: how much is one day in a person's life worth?
I can't answer that. For that person, it's priceless.
Yes, yes, but what is it worth to society?

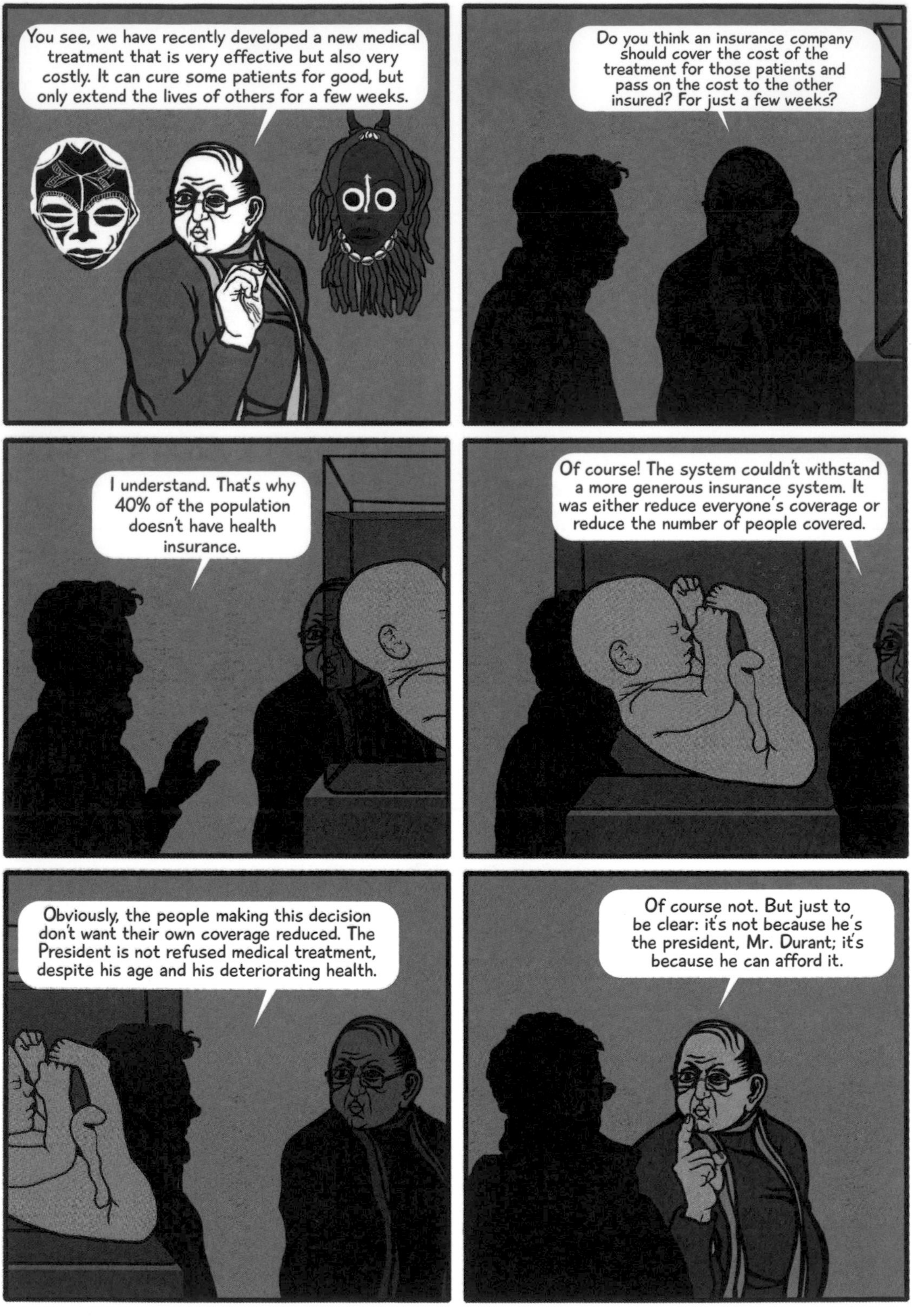
You see, we have recently developed a new medical treatment that is very effective but also very costly. It can cure some patients for good, but only extend the lives of others for a few weeks.
Do you think an insurance company should cover the cost of the treatment for those patients and pass on the cost to the other insured? For just a few weeks?
I understand. That's why 40% of the population doesn't have health insurance.
Of course! The system couldn't withstand a more generous insurance system. It was either reduce everyone's coverage or reduce the number of people covered.
Obviously, the people making this decision don't want their own coverage reduced. The President is not refused medical treatment, despite his age and his deteriorating health.
Of course not. But just to be clear: it's not because he's the president, Mr. Durant; it's because he can afford it.

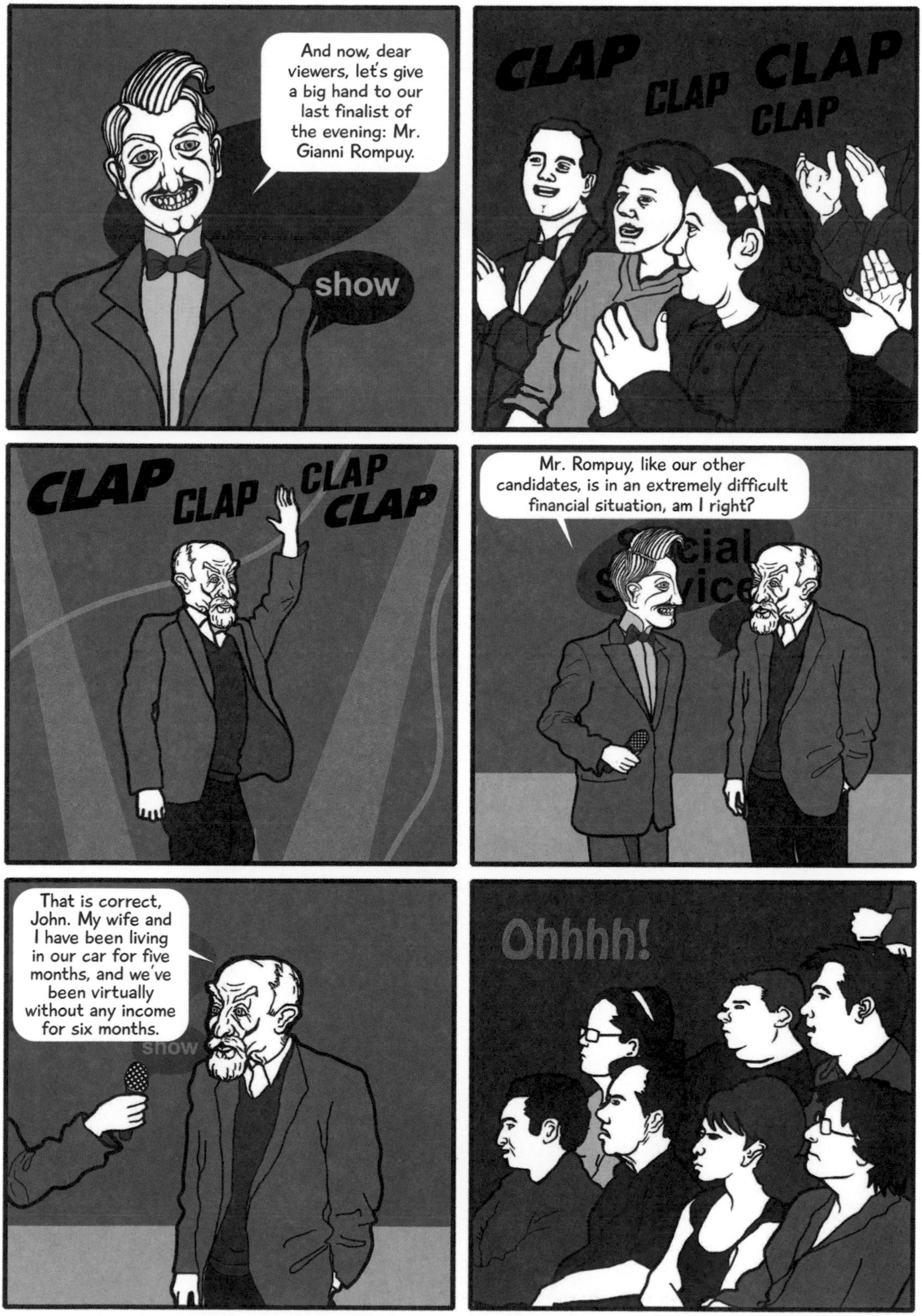
And now, dear viewers, let's give a big hand to our last finalist of the evening: Mr. Gianni Rompuy.
show
CLAP CLAP CLAP CLAP
CLAP CLAP CLAP CLAP
Mr. Rompuy, like our other candidates, is in an extremely difficult financial situation, am I right?
That is correct, John. My wife and I have been living in our car for five months, and we've been virtually without any income for six months.
Ohhhh!

Admittedly not an ideal situation, Mr. Rompuy. But that's why the Social Services program is here: to give people like you...

The possibility of becoming productive members of society!

Exactly!

OK, Mr. Rompuy, as you can see, we want to help you and you've come to the right place. Let's see what the wheel of fortune can do for you. Among the categories it lands on, you must choose the one that can best help get you out of your situation.

Thank you, John.

Here's your first option! Compete for one year of unemployment benefits, like in the past...

...for an amount that will be determined by the results of your question round.

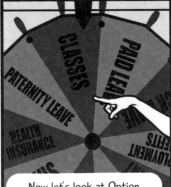

Now let's look at Option 2: free accounting classes! Careful though, for this class, it's all or nothing depending on your question round.

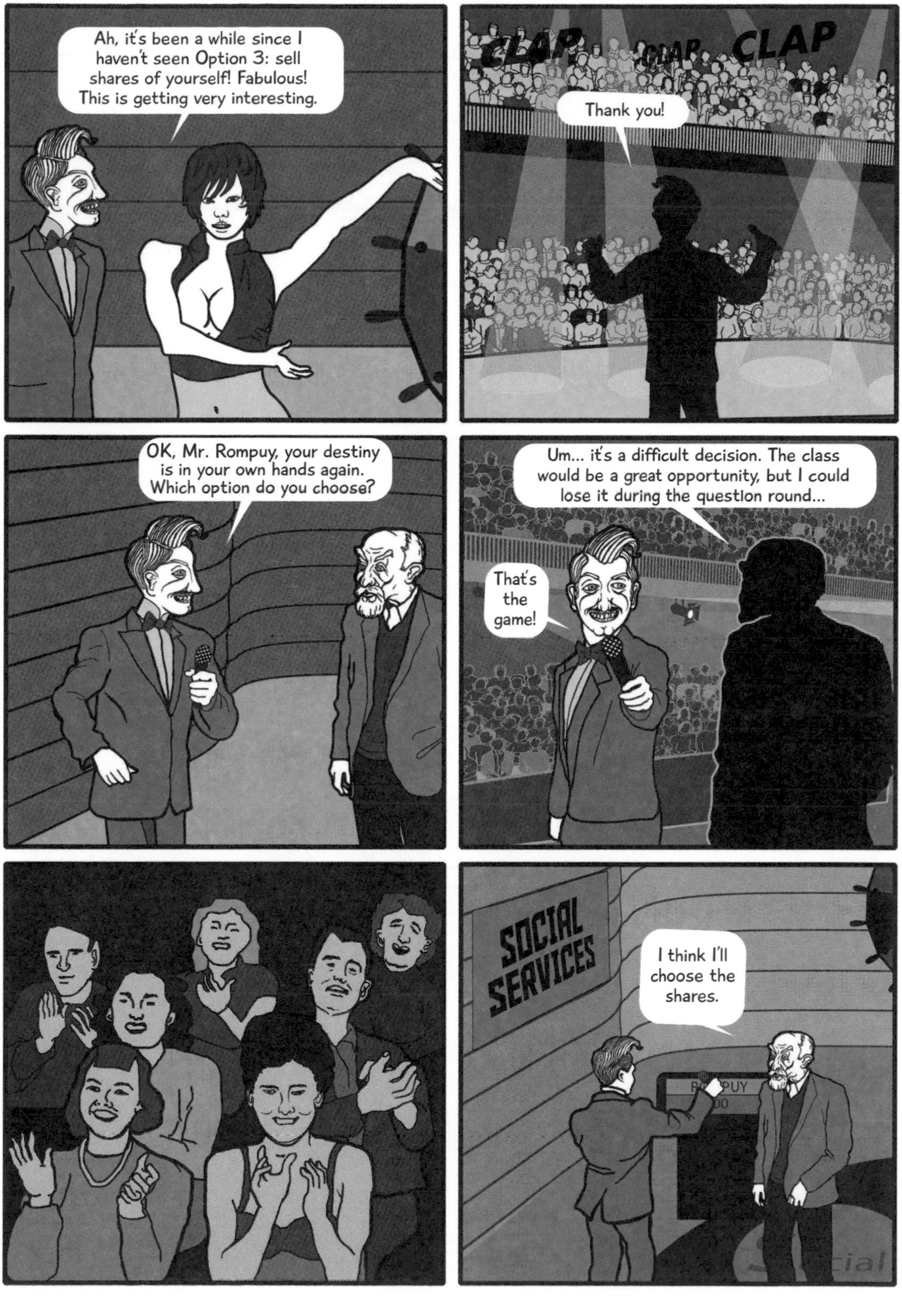
Ah, it's been a while since I haven't seen Option 3: sell shares of yourself! Fabulous! This is getting very interesting.
CLAP CLAP CLAP
Thank you!
OK, Mr. Rompuy, your destiny is in your own hands again. Which option do you choose?
Um... it's a difficult decision. The class would be a great opportunity, but I could lose it during the question round...
That's the game!
SOCIAL SERVICES
I think I'll choose the shares.

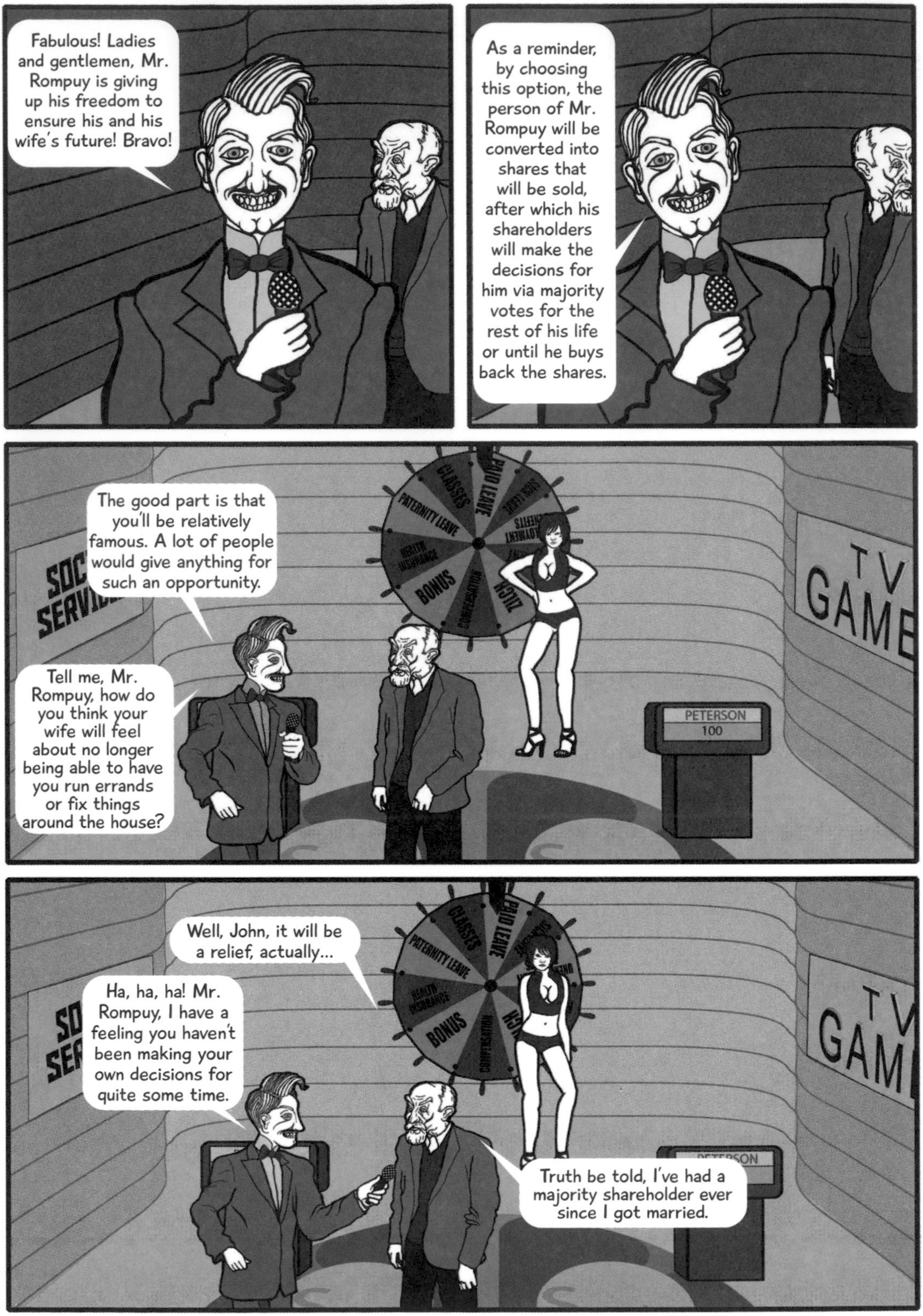
Fabulous! Ladies and gentlemen, Mr. Rompuy is giving up his freedom to ensure his and his wife's future! Bravo!
As a reminder, by choosing this option, the person of Mr. Rompuy will be converted into shares that will be sold, after which his shareholders will make the decisions for him via majority votes for the rest of his life or until he buys back the shares.
The good part is that you'll be relatively famous. A lot of people would give anything for such an opportunity.
Tell me, Mr. Rompuy, how do you think your wife will feel about no longer being able to have you run errands or fix things around the house?
CLASSES
PAID LEAVE
PATERNITY LEAVE
BONUS
ZILCH
PETERSON
100
Well, John, it will be a relief, actually...
Ha, ha, ha! Mr. Rompuy, I have a feeling you haven't been making your own decisions for quite some time.
Truth be told, I've had a majority shareholder ever since I got married.

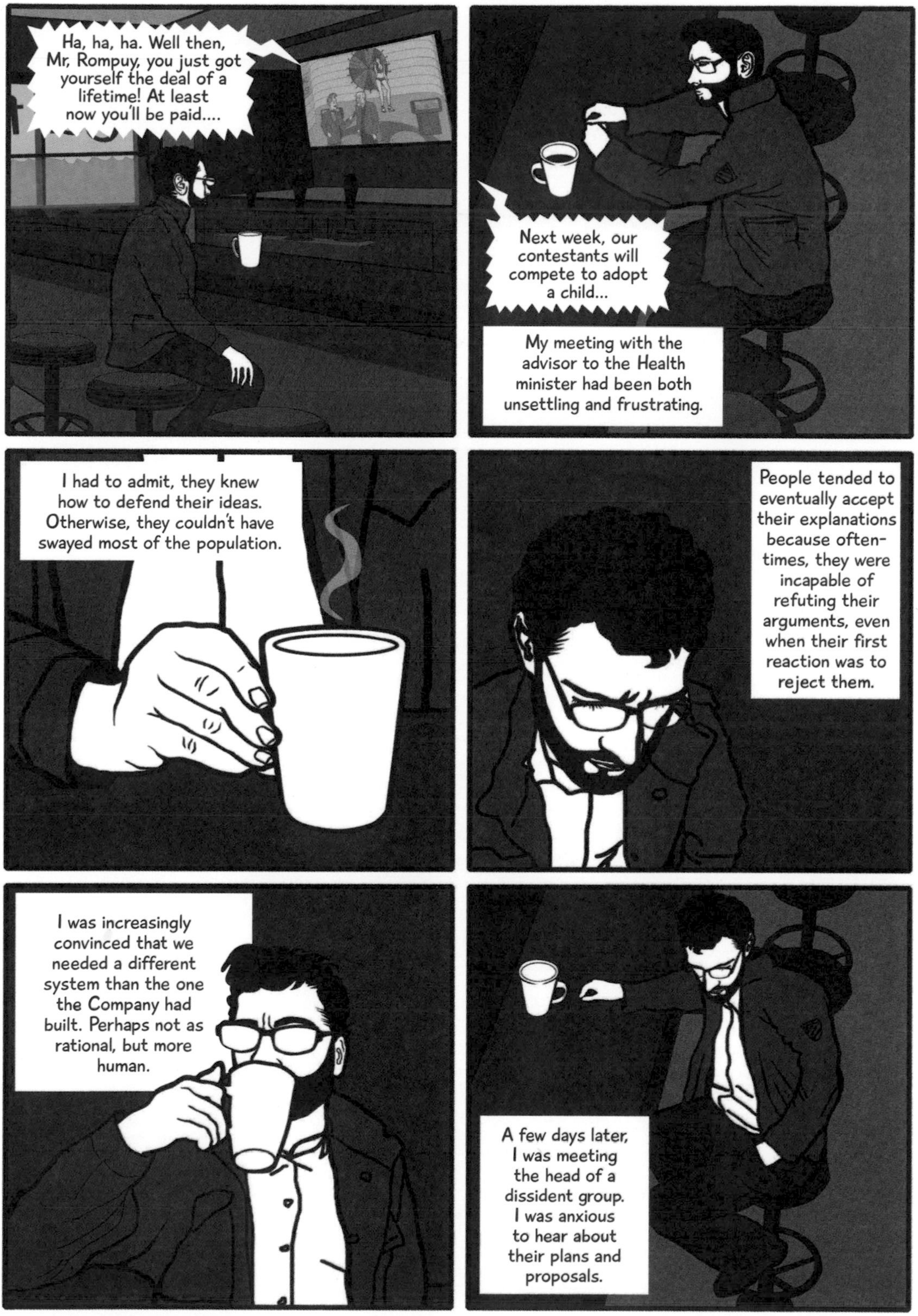
Ha, ha, ha. Well then, Mr, Rompuy, you just got yourself the deal of a lifetime! At least now you'll be paid....
Next week, our contestants will compete to adopt a child...
My meeting with the advisor to the Health minister had been both unsettling and frustrating.
I had to admit, they knew how to defend their ideas. Otherwise, they couldn't have swayed most of the population.
People tended to eventually accept their explanations because often-times, they were incapable of refuting their arguments, even when their first reaction was to reject them.
I was increasingly convinced that we needed a different system than the one the Company had built. Perhaps not as rational, but more human.
A few days later, I was meeting the head of a dissident group. I was anxious to hear about their plans and proposals.

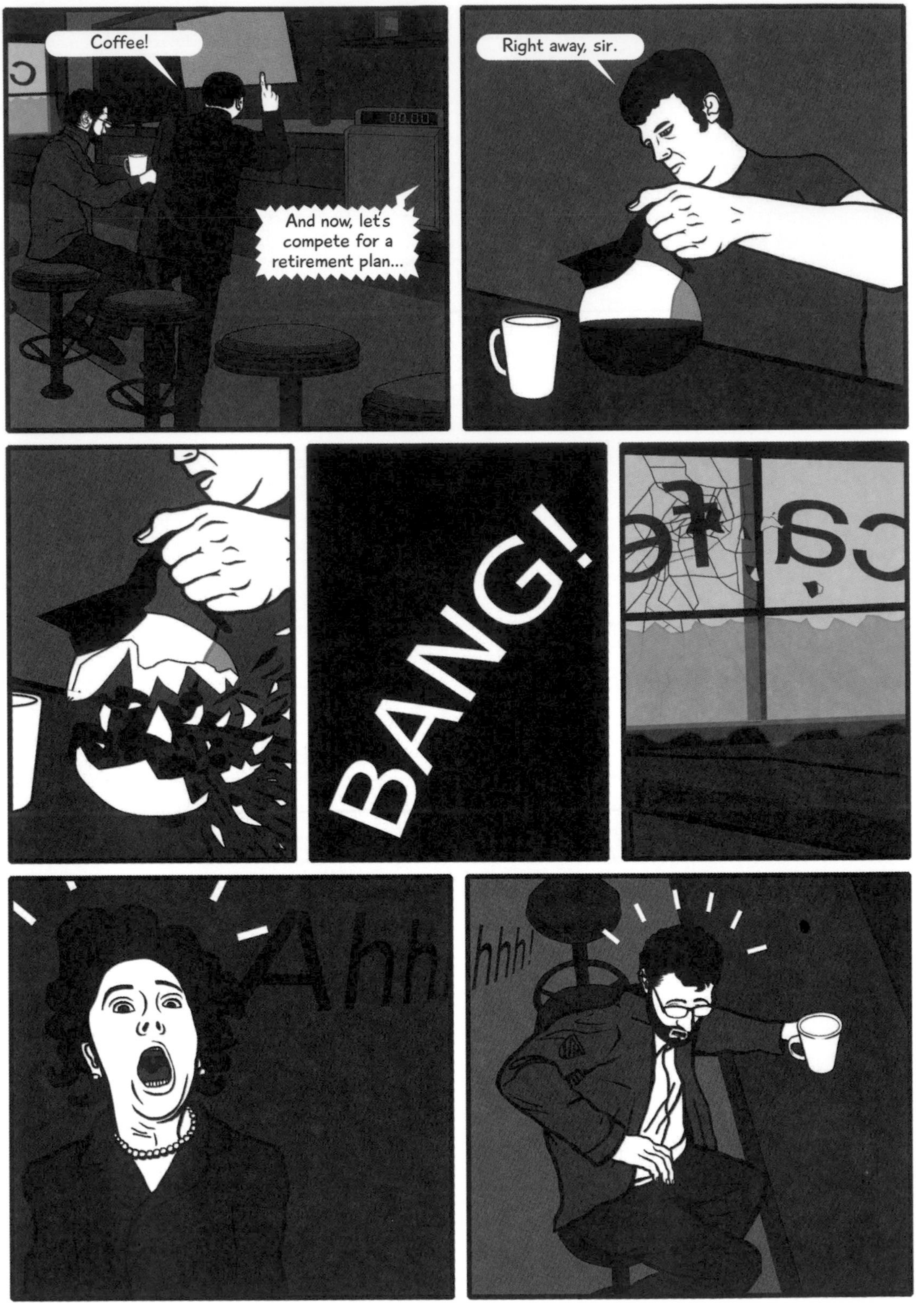
Coffee!
And now, let's compete for a retirement plan...
Right away, sir.
BANG!
Ahh
hhh!

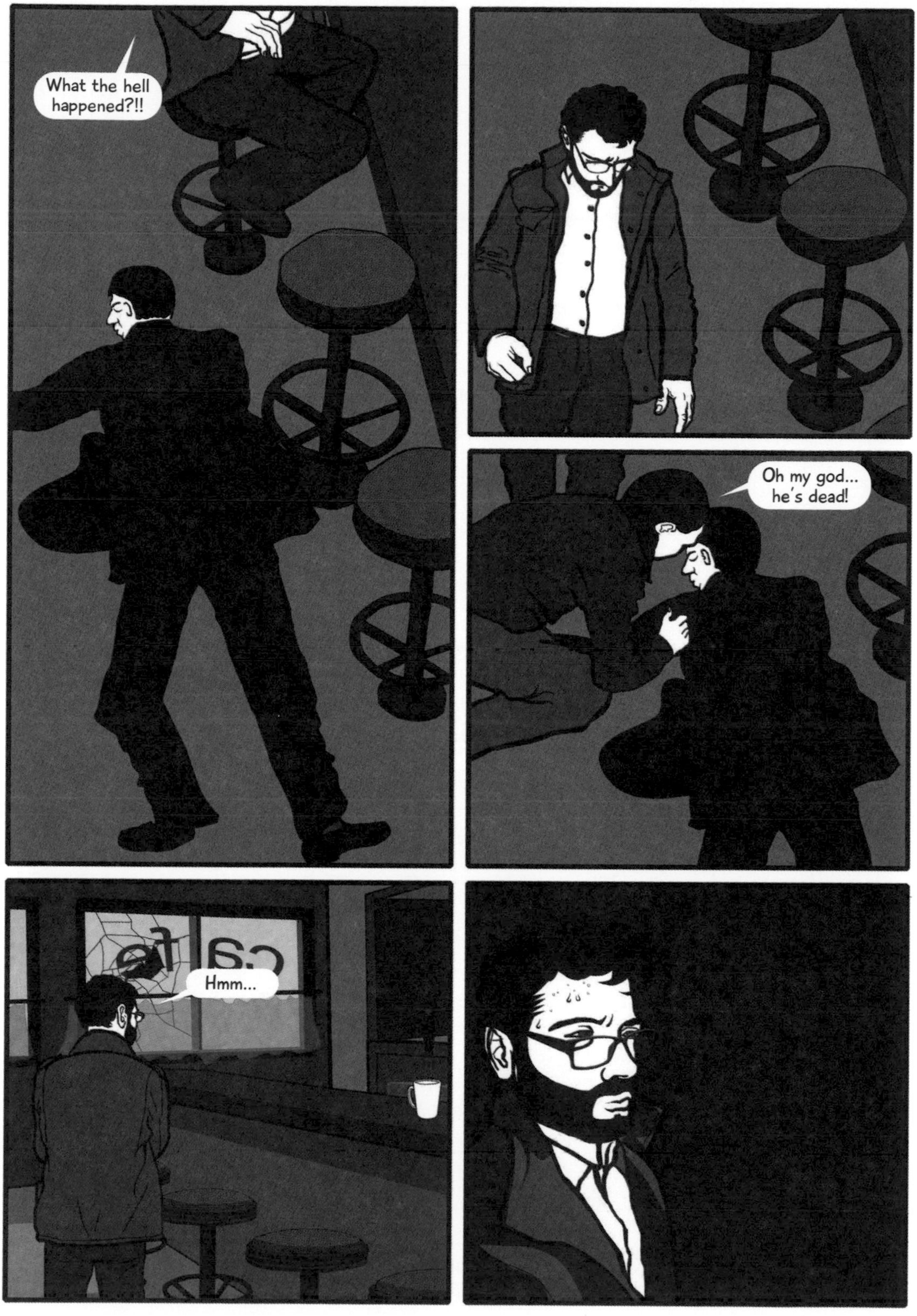
What the hell happened?!!
Oh my god... he's dead!
Hmm...

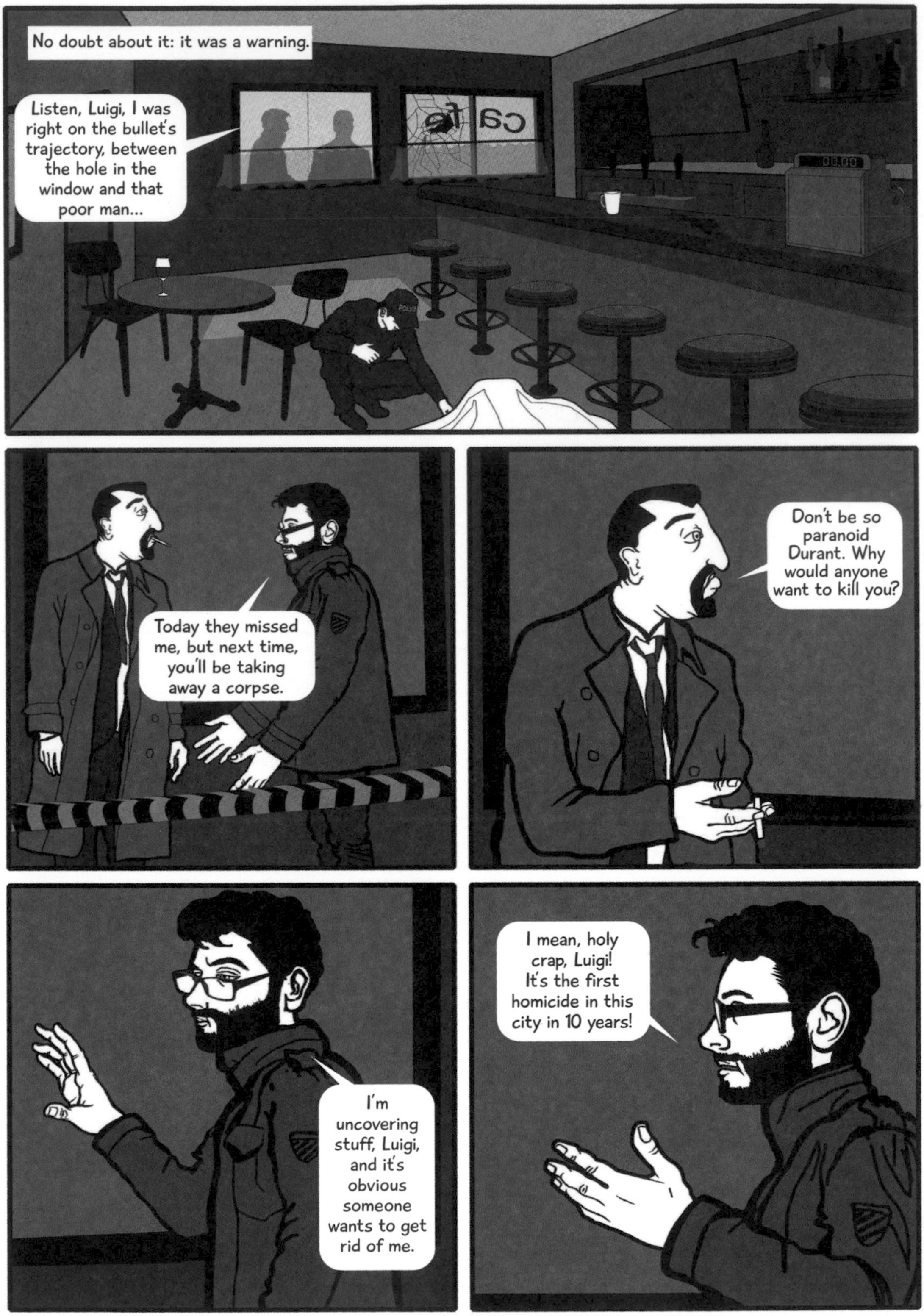
No doubt about it: it was a warning.
Listen, Luigi, I was right on the bullet's trajectory, between the hole in the window and that poor man...
Today they missed me, but next time, you'll be taking away a corpse.
Don't be so paranoid Durant. Why would anyone want to kill you?
I'm uncovering stuff, Luigi, and it's obvious someone wants to get rid of me.
I mean, holy crap, Luigi! It's the first homicide in this city in 10 years!

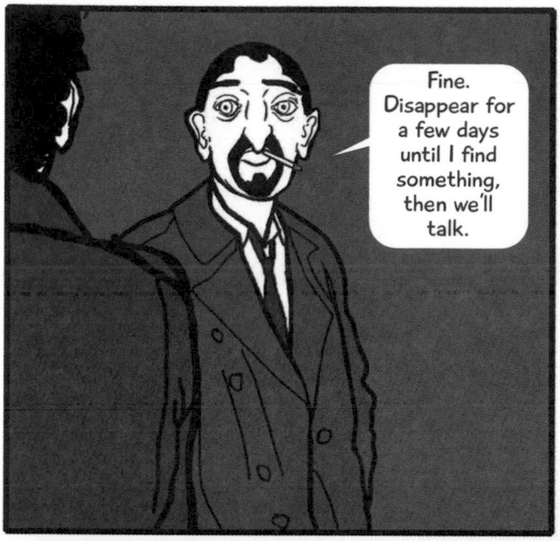
Fine. Disappear for a few days until I find something, then we'll talk.

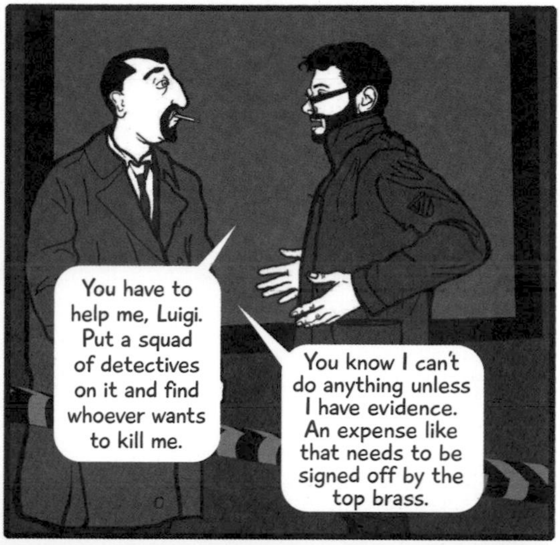
You have to help me, Luigi. Put a squad of detectives on it and find whoever wants to kill me.
You know I can't do anything unless I have evidence. An expense like that needs to be signed off by the top brass.

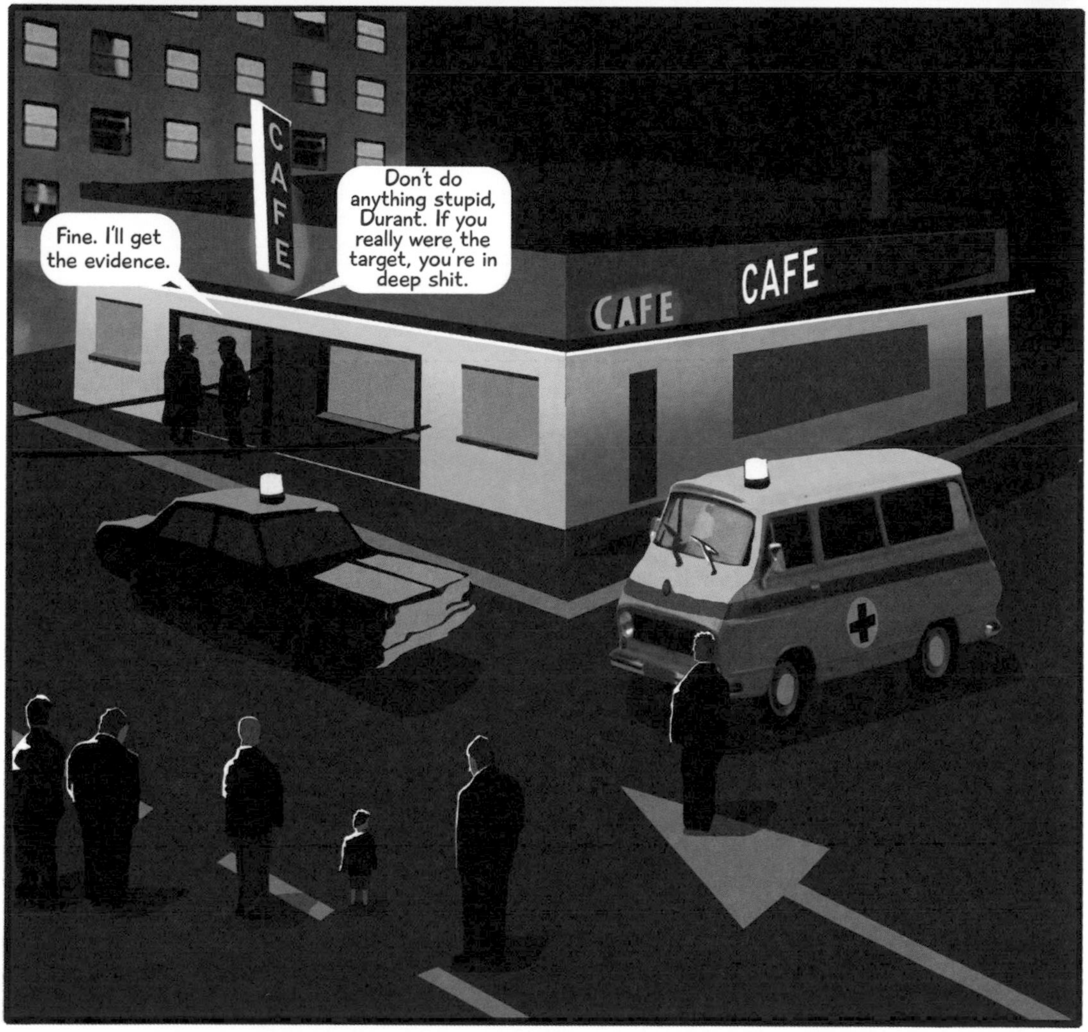
CAFE
Fine. I'll get the evidence.
Don't do anything stupid, Durant. If you really were the target, you're in deep shit.
CAFE
CAFE

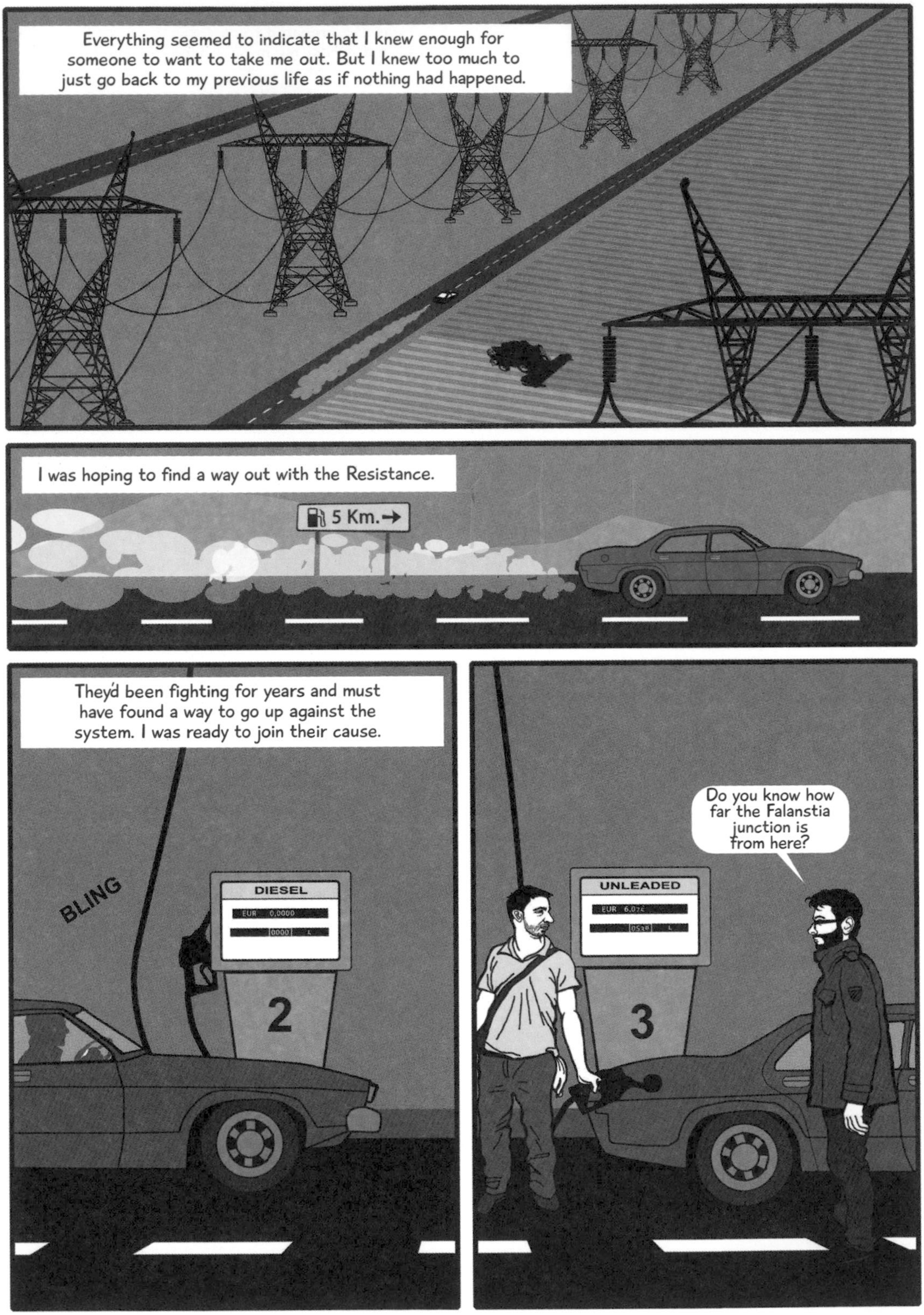
Everything seemed to indicate that I knew enough for someone to want to take me out. But I knew too much to just go back to my previous life as if nothing had happened.
I was hoping to find a way out with the Resistance.
5 Km.→
They'd been fighting for years and must have found a way to go up against the system. I was ready to join their cause.
BLING
DIESEL
2
UNLEADED
3
Do you know how far the Falanstia junction is from here?

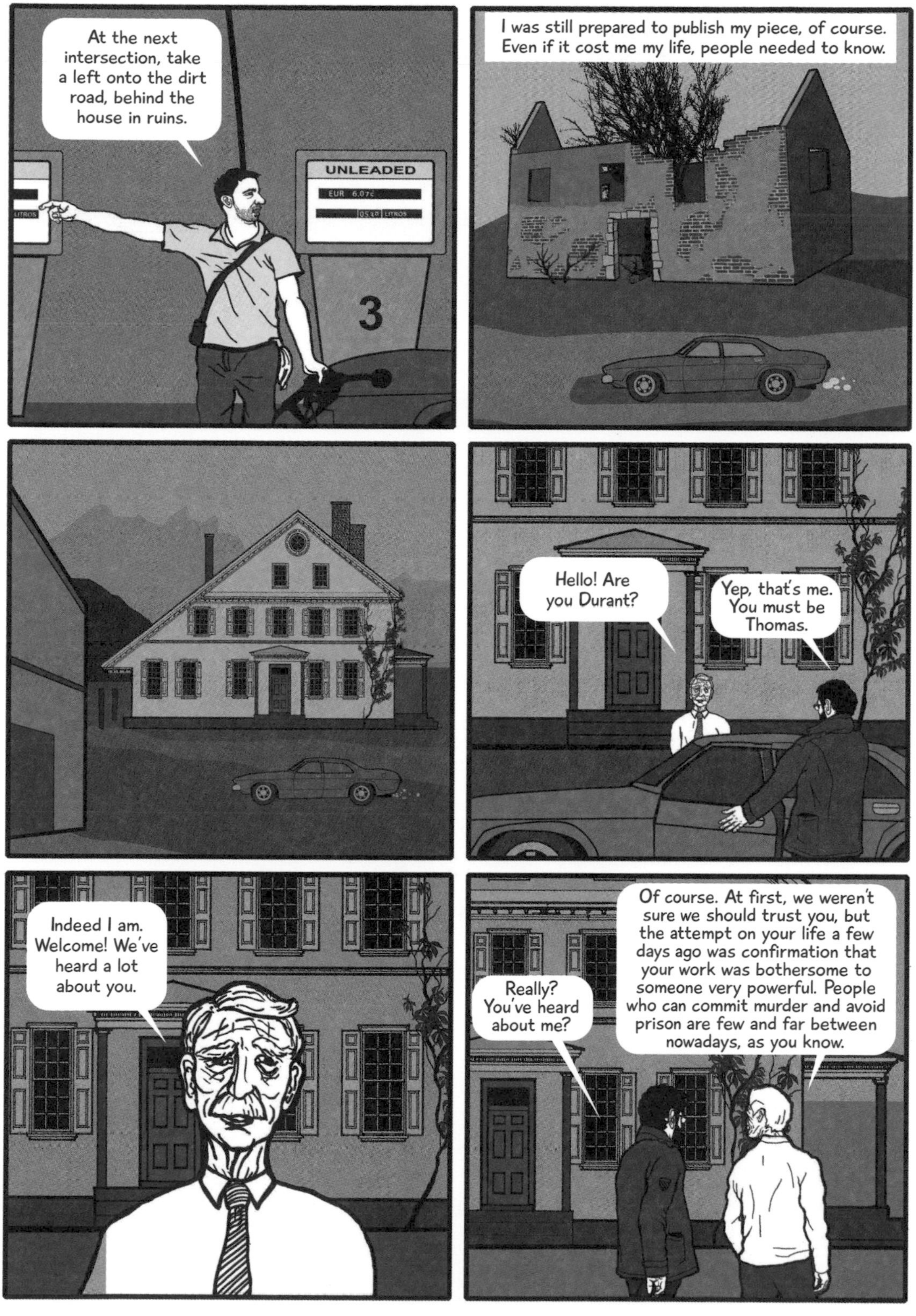
At the next intersection, take a left onto the dirt road, behind the house in ruins.
UNLEADED
3
I was still prepared to publish my piece, of course. Even if it cost me my life, people needed to know.
Hello! Are you Durant?
Yep, that's me. You must be Thomas.
Indeed I am. Welcome! We've heard a lot about you.
Really? You've heard about me?
Of course. At first, we weren't sure we should trust you, but the attempt on your life a few days ago was confirmation that your work was bothersome to someone very powerful. People who can commit murder and avoid prison are few and far between nowadays, as you know.

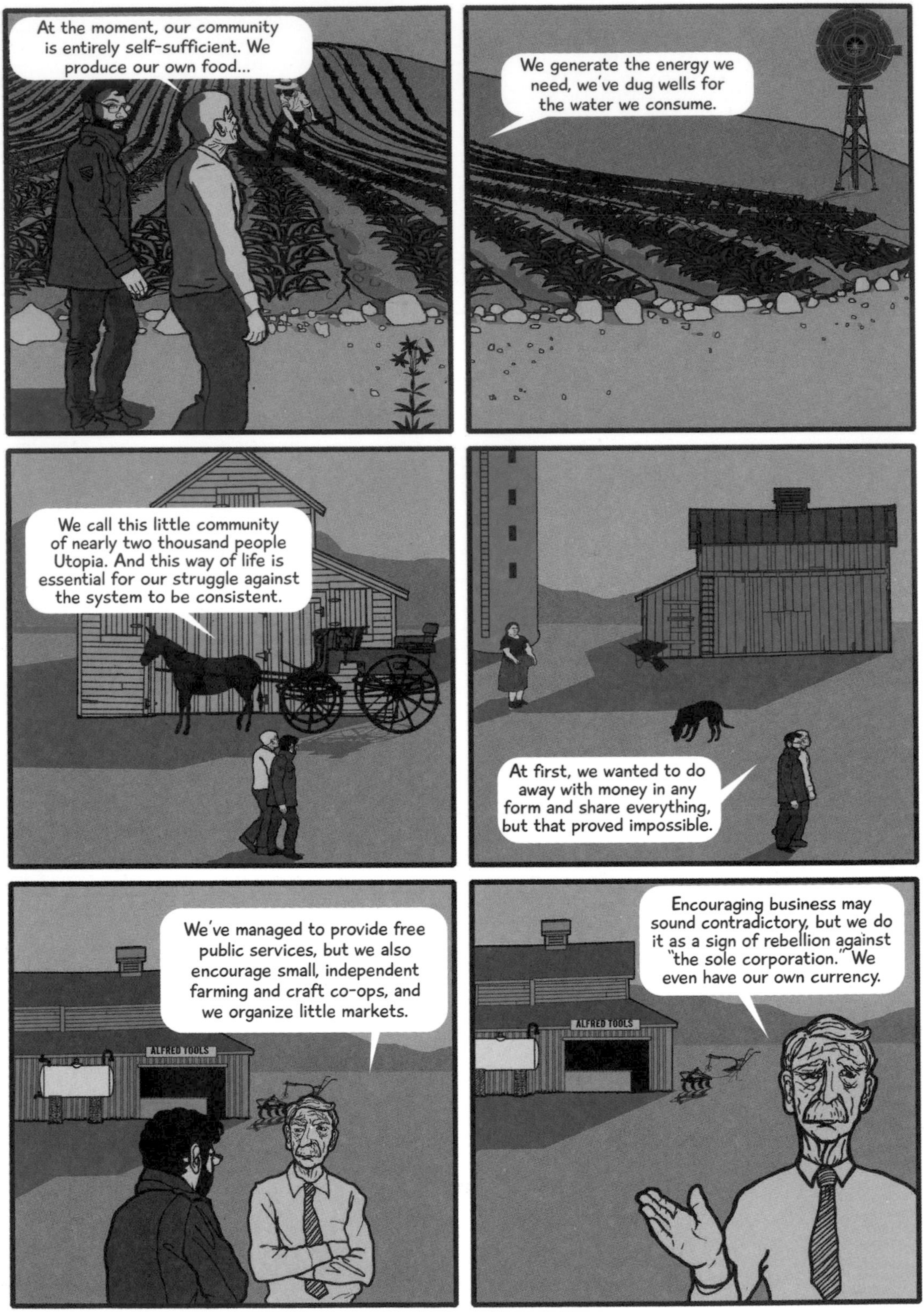
At the moment, our community is entirely self-sufficient. We produce our own food...
We generate the energy we need, we've dug wells for the water we consume.
We call this little community of nearly two thousand people Utopia. And this way of life is essential for our struggle against the system to be consistent.
At first, we wanted to do away with money in any form and share everything, but that proved impossible.
We've managed to provide free public services, but we also encourage small, independent farming and craft co-ops, and we organize little markets.
ALFRED TOOLS
ALFRED TOOLS
Encouraging business may sound contradictory, but we do it as a sign of rebellion against "the sole corporation." We even have our own currency.

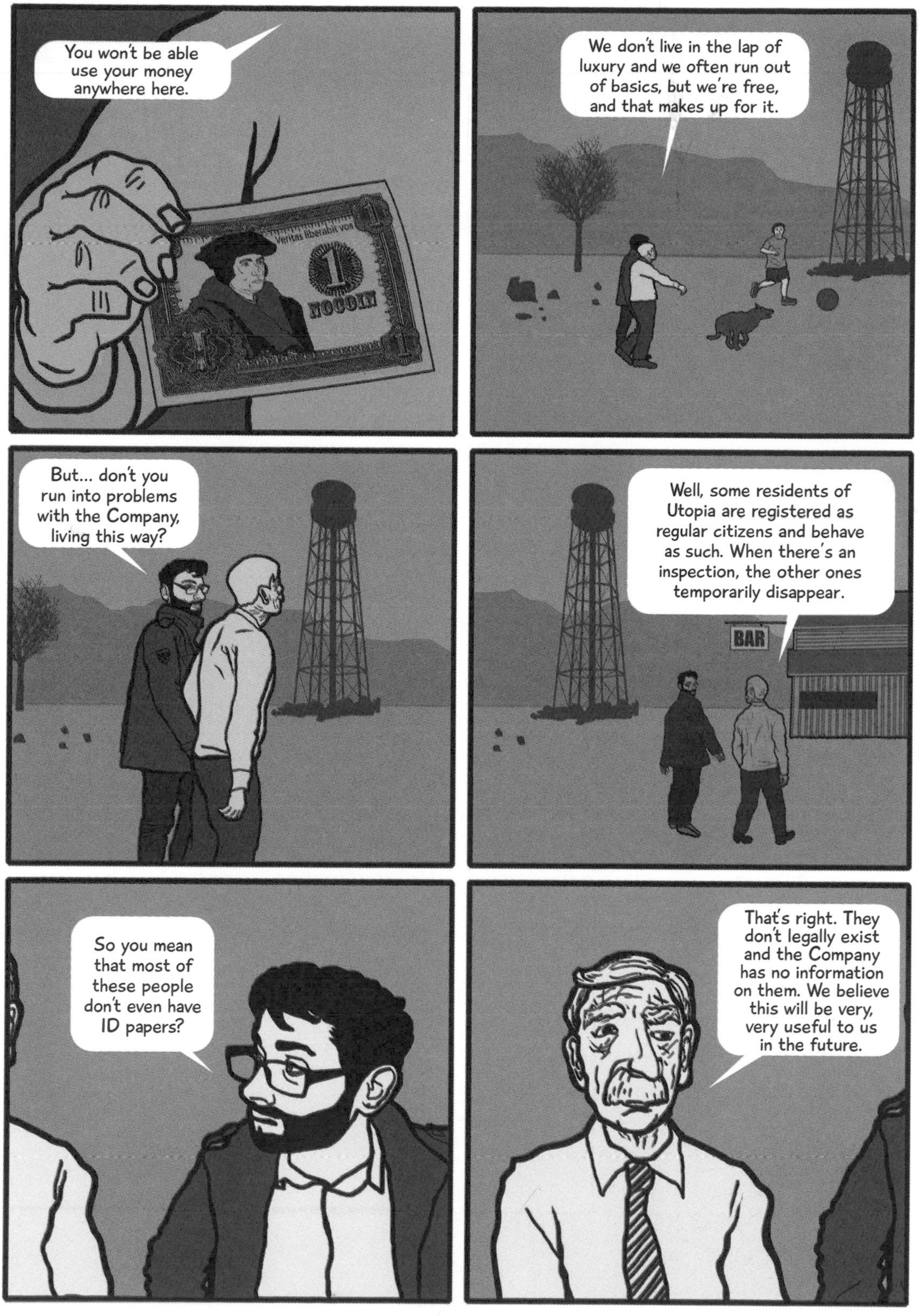
You won't be able use your money anywhere here.
Veritas liberabit vos
1
NOCOIN
We don't live in the lap of luxury and we often run out of basics, but we're free, and that makes up for it.
But... don't you run into problems with the Company, living this way?
Well, some residents of Utopia are registered as regular citizens and behave as such. When there's an inspection, the other ones temporarily disappear.
BAR
So you mean that most of these people don't even have ID papers?
That's right. They don't legally exist and the Company has no information on them. We believe this will be very, very useful to us in the future.

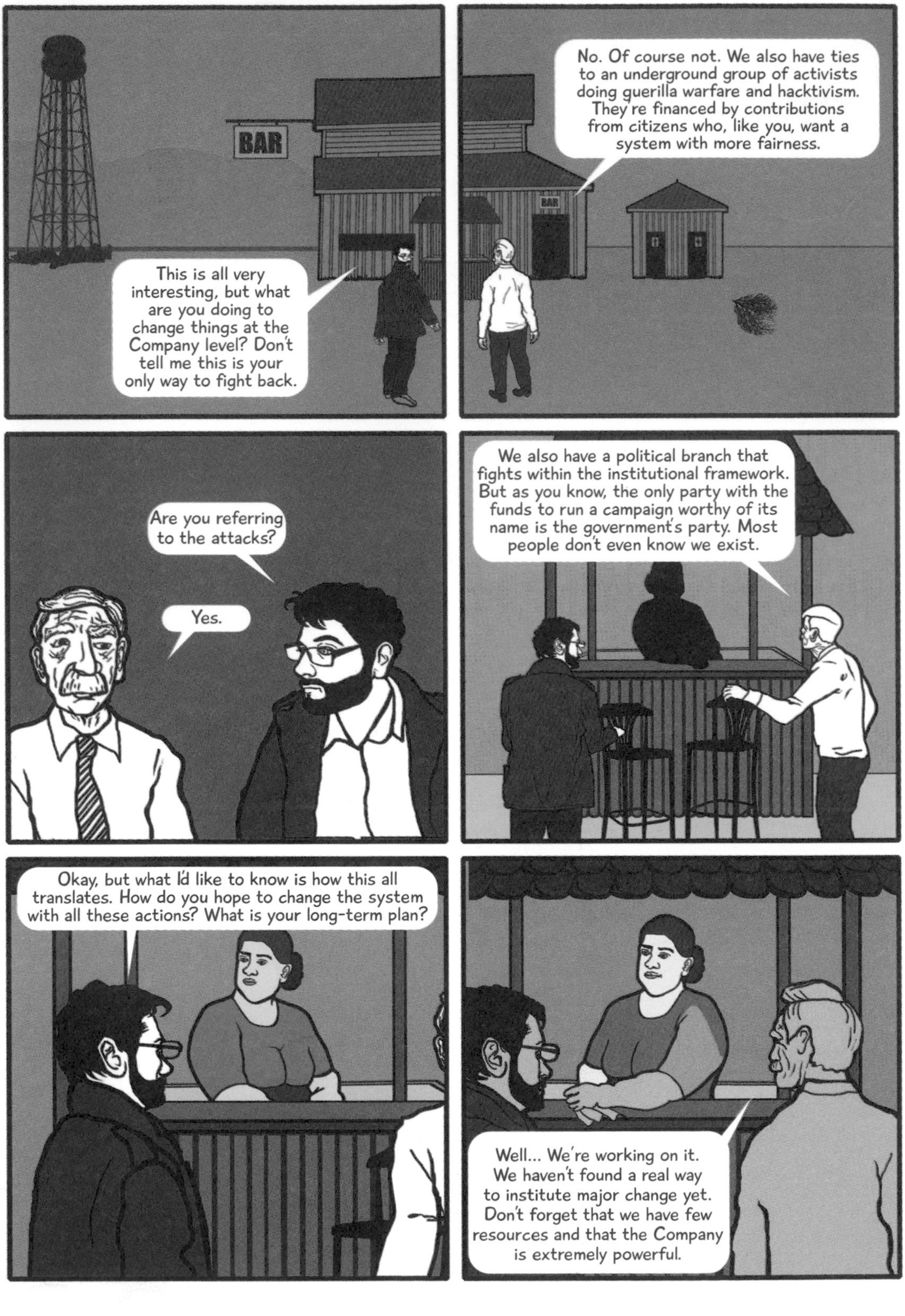
BAR
This is all very interesting, but what are you doing to change things at the Company level? Don't tell me this is your only way to fight back.
No. Of course not. We also have ties to an underground group of activists doing guerilla warfare and hacktivism. They're financed by contributions from citizens who, like you, want a system with more fairness.
BAR
Are you referring to the attacks?
Yes.
We also have a political branch that fights within the institutional framework. But as you know, the only party with the funds to run a campaign worthy of its name is the government's party. Most people don't even know we exist.
Okay, but what I'd like to know is how this all translates. How do you hope to change the system with all these actions? What is your long-term plan?
Well... We're working on it. We haven't found a real way to institute major change yet. Don't forget that we have few resources and that the Company is extremely powerful.

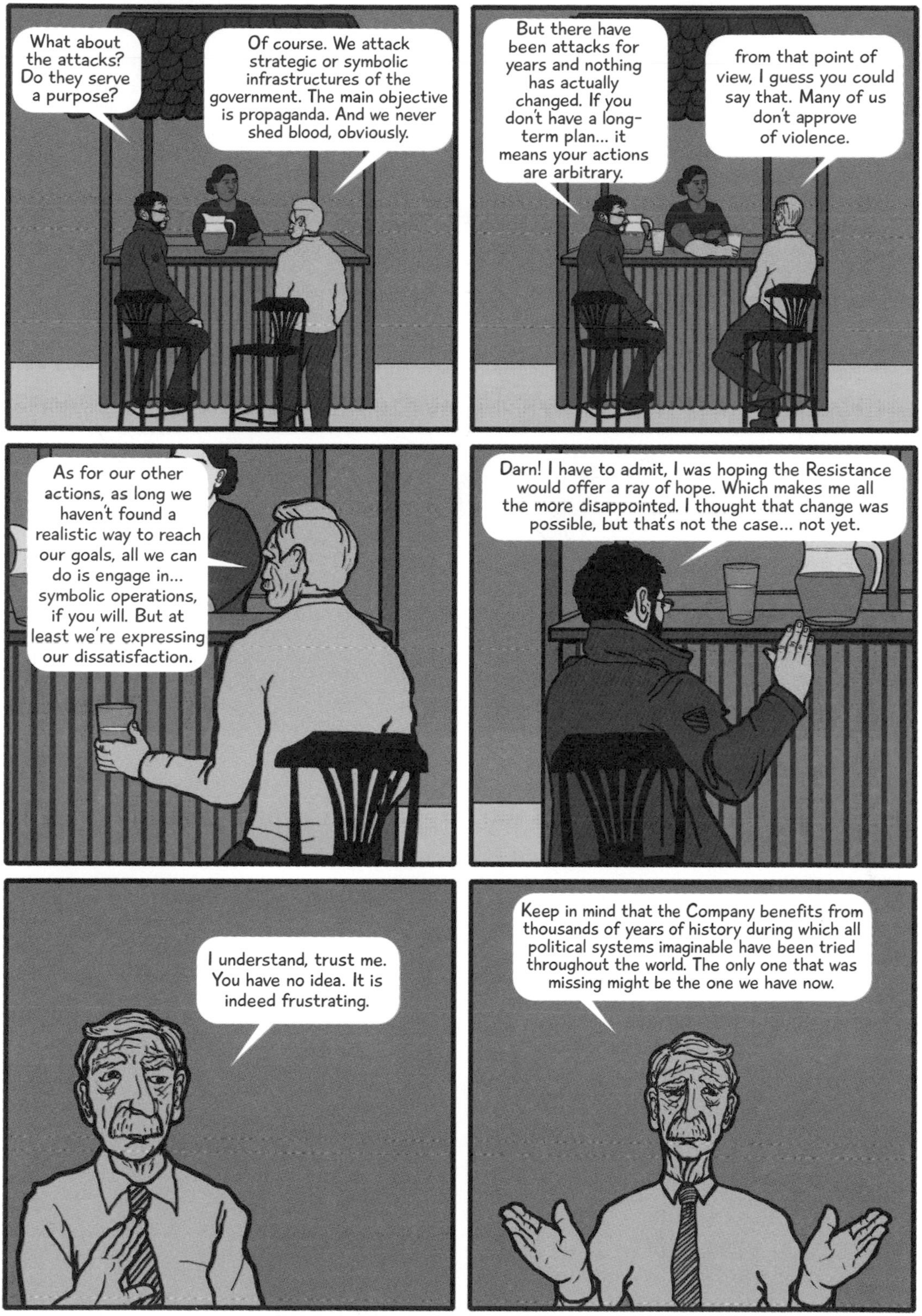
What about the attacks? Do they serve a purpose?
Of course. We attack strategic or symbolic infrastructures of the government. The main objective is propaganda. And we never shed blood, obviously.
But there have been attacks for years and nothing has actually changed. If you don't have a long-term plan... it means your actions are arbitrary.
from that point of view, I guess you could say that. Many of us don't approve of violence.
As for our other actions, as long we haven't found a realistic way to reach our goals, all we can do is engage in... symbolic operations, if you will. But at least we're expressing our dissatisfaction.
Darn! I have to admit, I was hoping the Resistance would offer a ray of hope. Which makes me all the more disappointed. I thought that change was possible, but that's not the case... not yet.
I understand, trust me. You have no idea. It is indeed frustrating.
Keep in mind that the Company benefits from thousands of years of history during which all political systems imaginable have been tried throughout the world. The only one that was missing might be the one we have now.

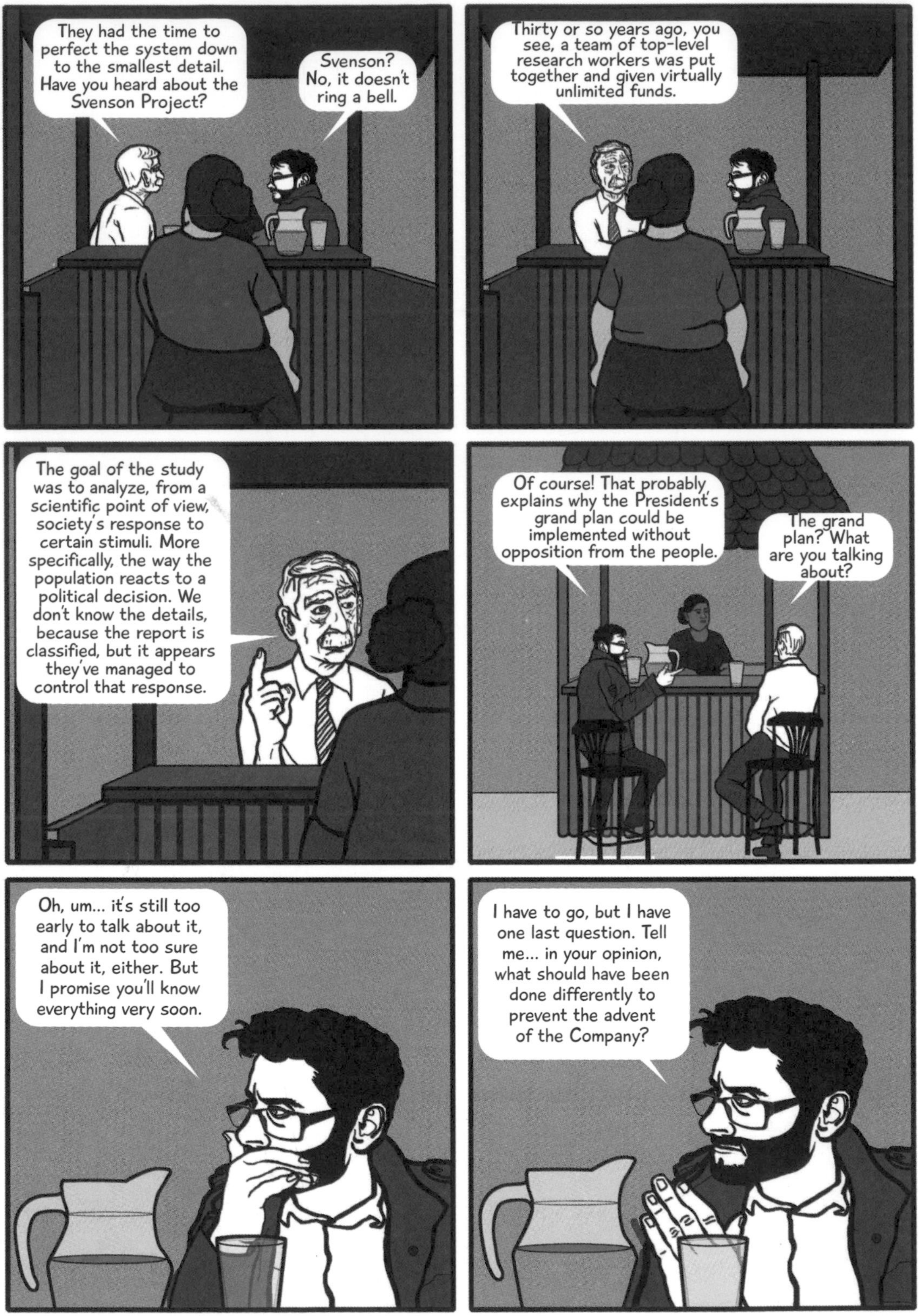
They had the time to perfect the system down to the smallest detail. Have you heard about the Svenson Project?
Svenson? No, it doesn't ring a bell.
Thirty or so years ago, you see, a team of top-level research workers was put together and given virtually unlimited funds.
The goal of the study was to analyze, from a scientific point of view, society's response to certain stimuli. More specifically, the way the population reacts to a political decision. We don't know the details, because the report is classified, but it appears they've managed to control that response.
Of course! That probably explains why the President's grand plan could be implemented without opposition from the people.
The grand plan? What are you talking about?
Oh, um... it's still too early to talk about it, and I'm not too sure about it, either. But I promise you'll know everything very soon.
I have to go, but I have one last question. Tell me... in your opinion, what should have been done differently to prevent the advent of the Company?

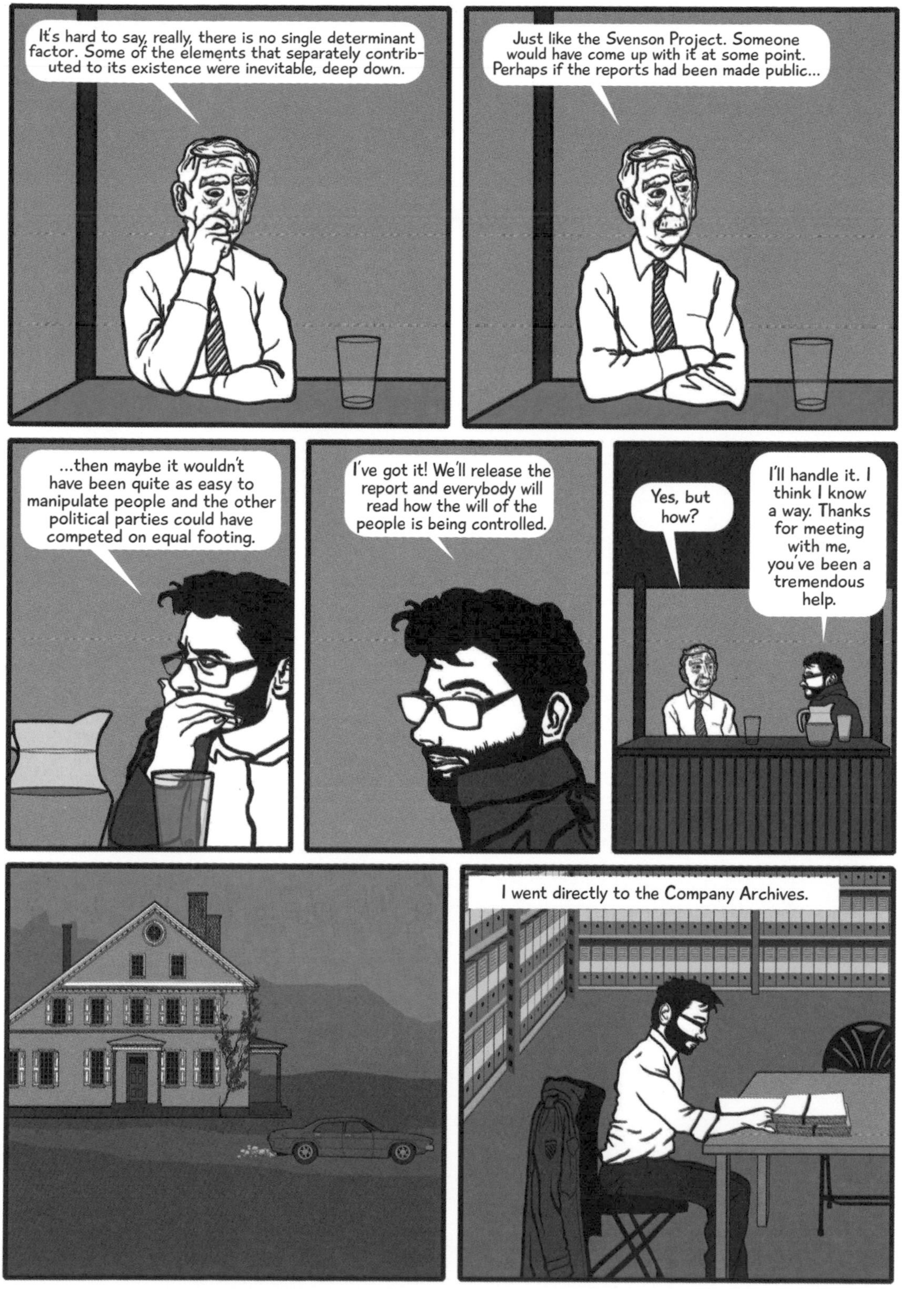
It's hard to say, really, there is no single determinant factor. Some of the elements that separately contributed to its existence were inevitable, deep down.
Just like the Svenson Project. Someone would have come up with it at some point. Perhaps if the reports had been made public...
...then maybe it wouldn't have been quite as easy to manipulate people and the other political parties could have competed on equal footing.
I've got it! We'll release the report and everybody will read how the will of the people is being controlled.
Yes, but how?
I'll handle it. I think I know a way. Thanks for meeting with me, you've been a tremendous help.
I went directly to the Company Archives.

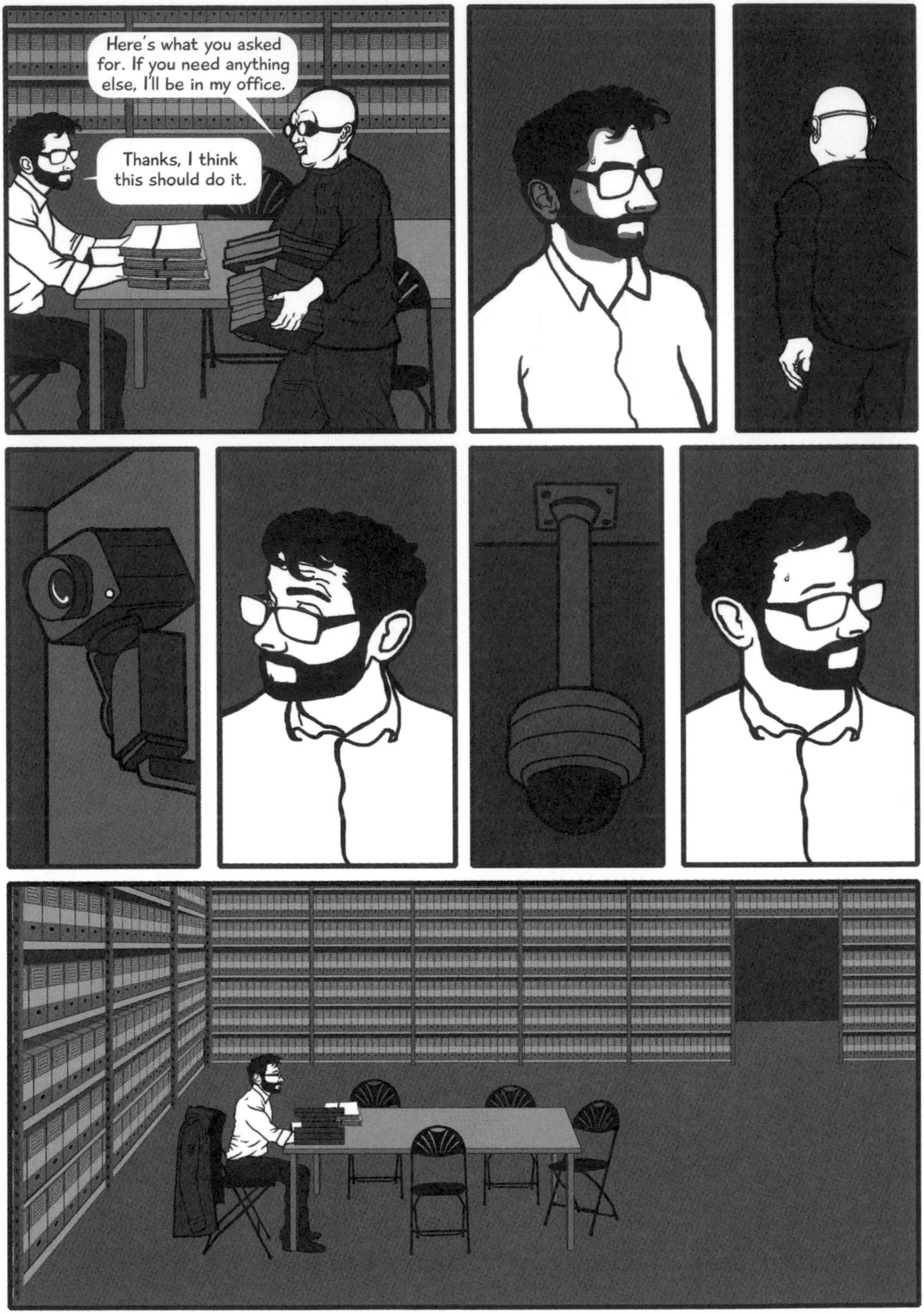
Here's what you asked for. If you need anything else, I'll be in my office.
Thanks, I think this should do it.

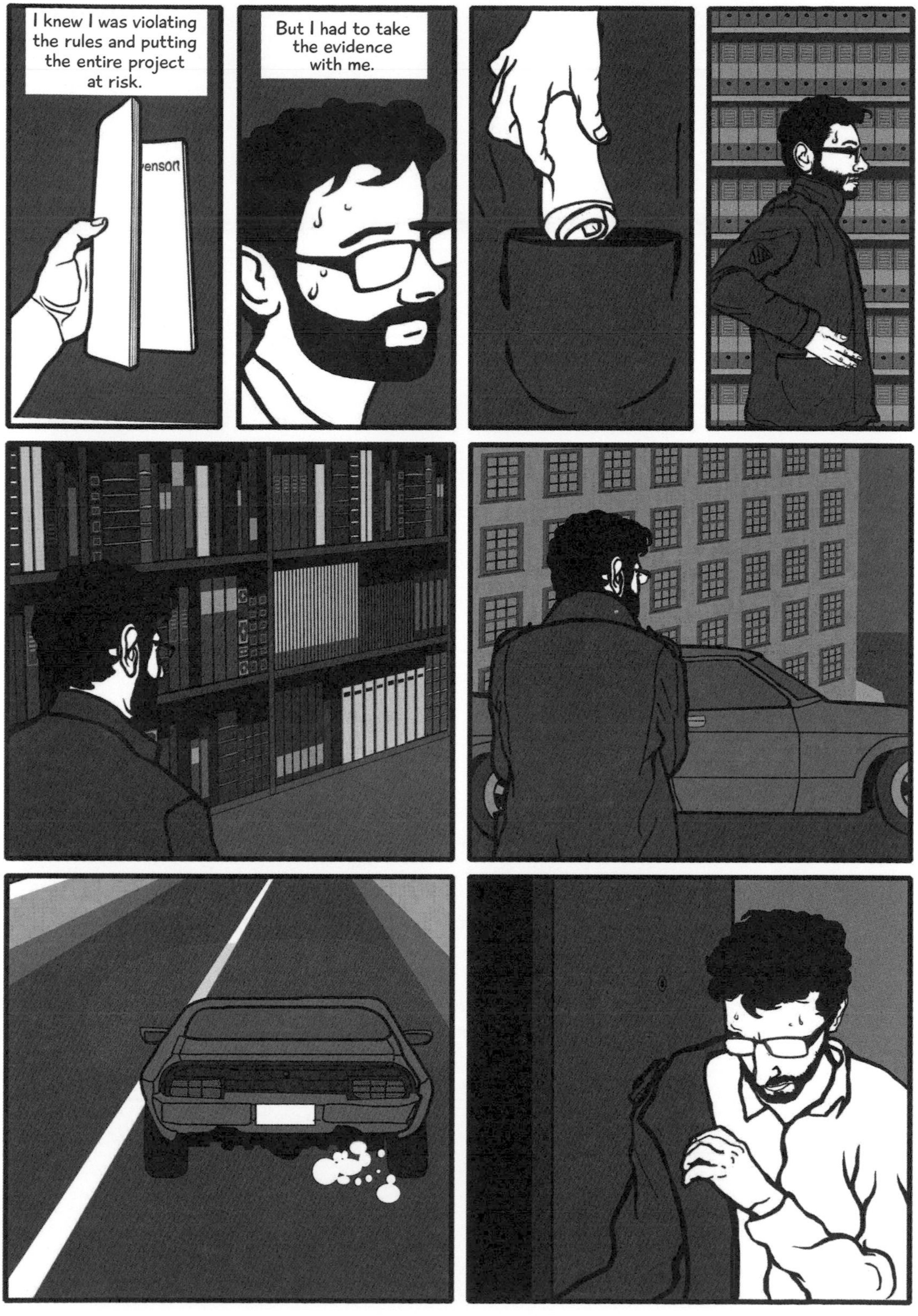
I knew I was violating the rules and putting the entire project at risk.
But I had to take the evidence with me.
ensoп

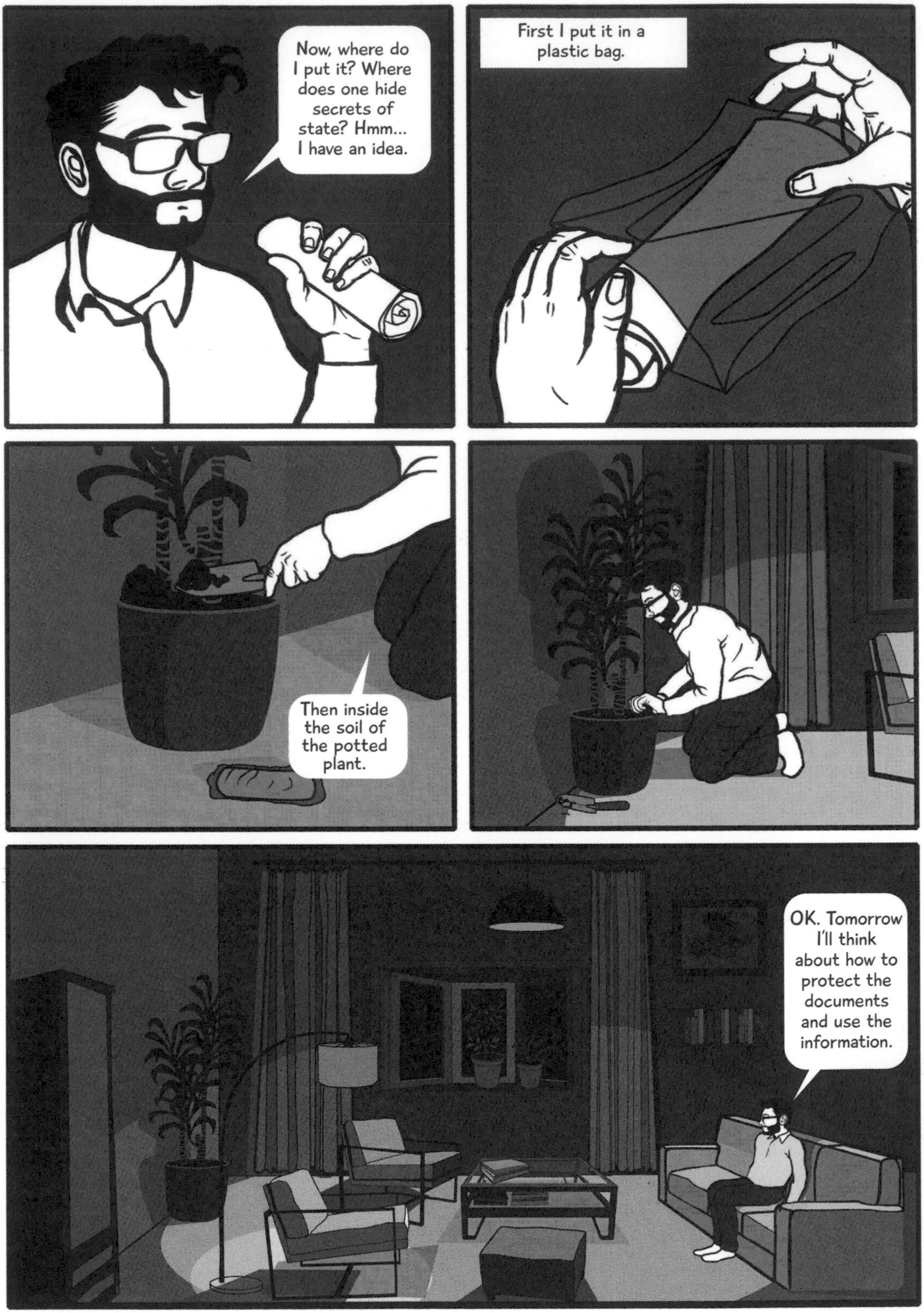
Now, where do I put it? Where does one hide secrets of state? Hmm... I have an idea.
First I put it in a plastic bag.
Then inside the soil of the potted plant.
OK. Tomorrow I'll think about how to protect the documents and use the information.

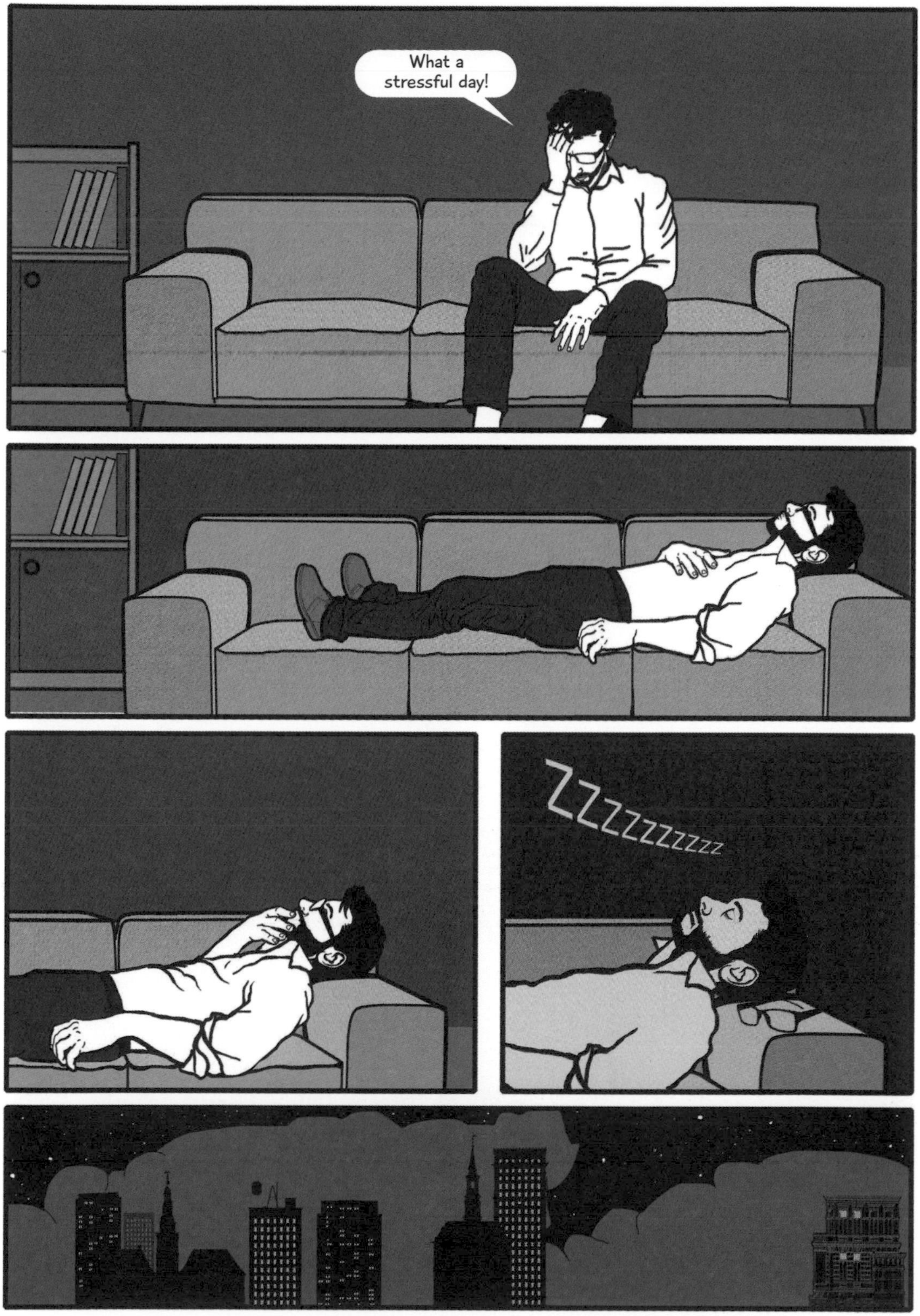
What a stressful day!
ZZZZZZZZZZZ

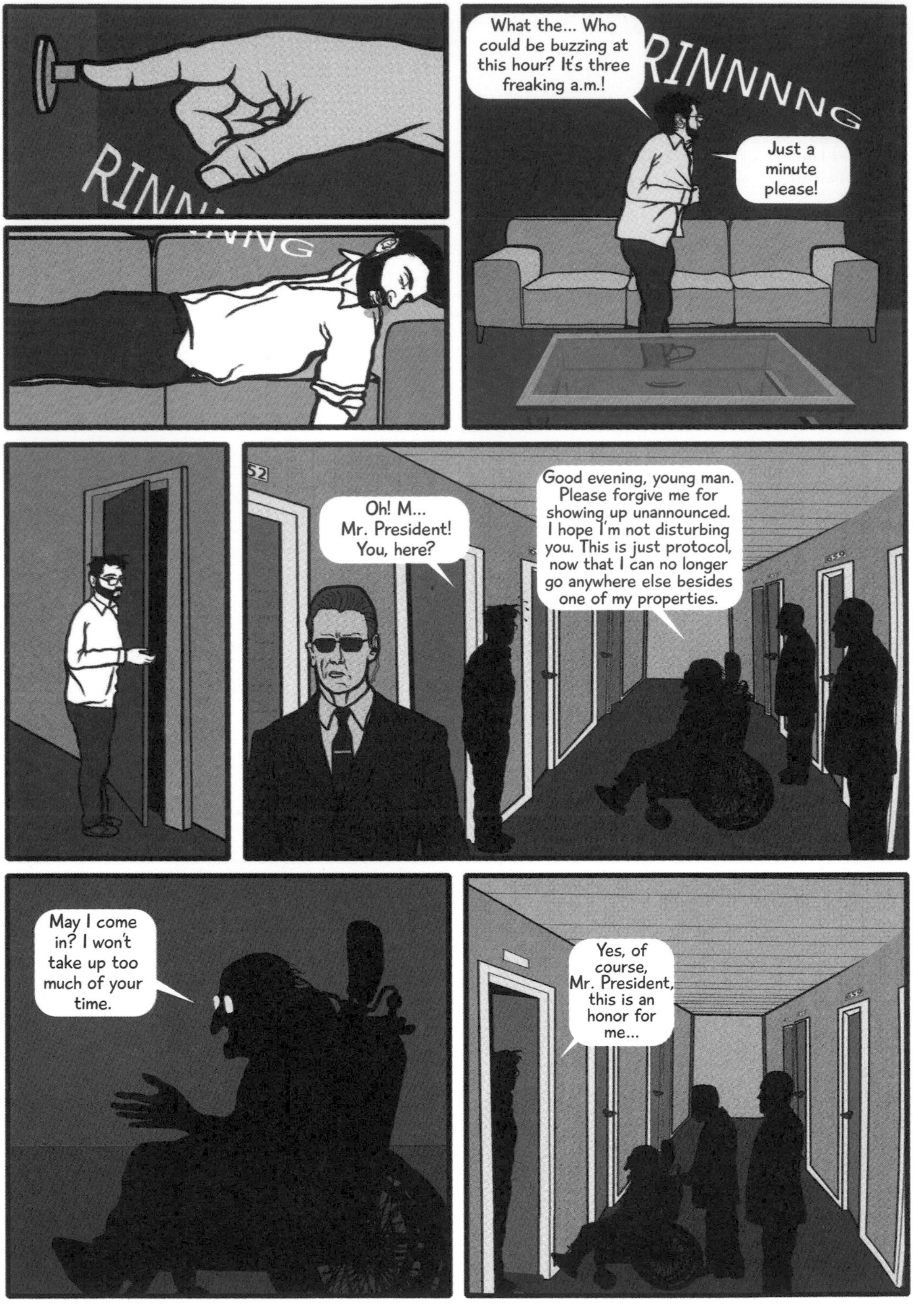
RINNNNNG
What the... Who could be buzzing at this hour? It's three freaking a.m.!
RINNNNNG
Just a minute please!
Oh! M... Mr. President! You, here?
Good evening, young man. Please forgive me for showing up unannounced. I hope I'm not disturbing you. This is just protocol, now that I can no longer go anywhere else besides one of my properties.
May I come in? I won't take up too much of your time.
Yes, of course, Mr. President, this is an honor for me...

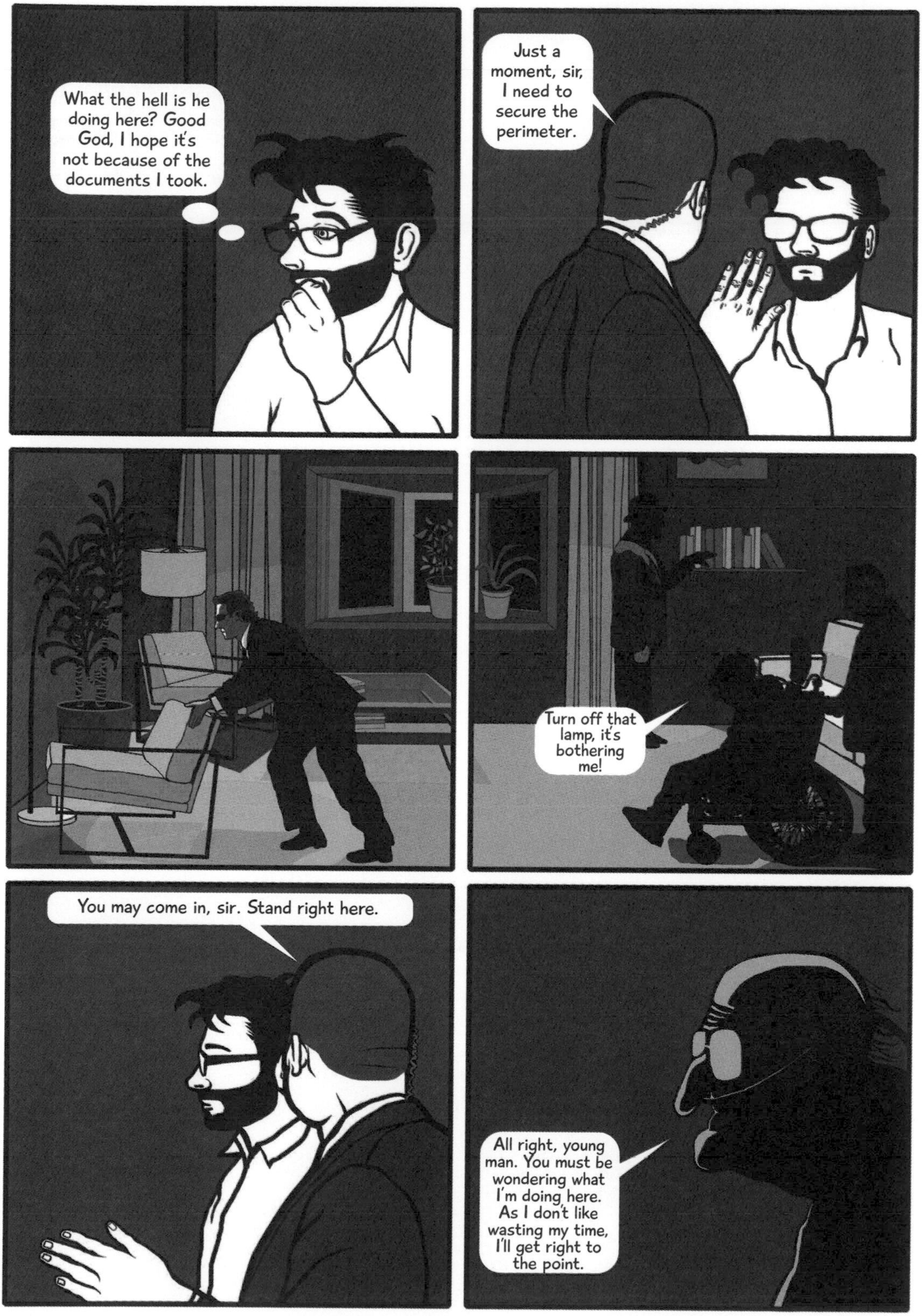
What the hell is he doing here? Good God, I hope it's not because of the documents I took.
Just a moment, sir, I need to secure the perimeter.
Turn off that lamp, it's bothering me!
You may come in, sir. Stand right here.
All right, young man. You must be wondering what I'm doing here. As I don't like wasting my time, I'll get right to the point.

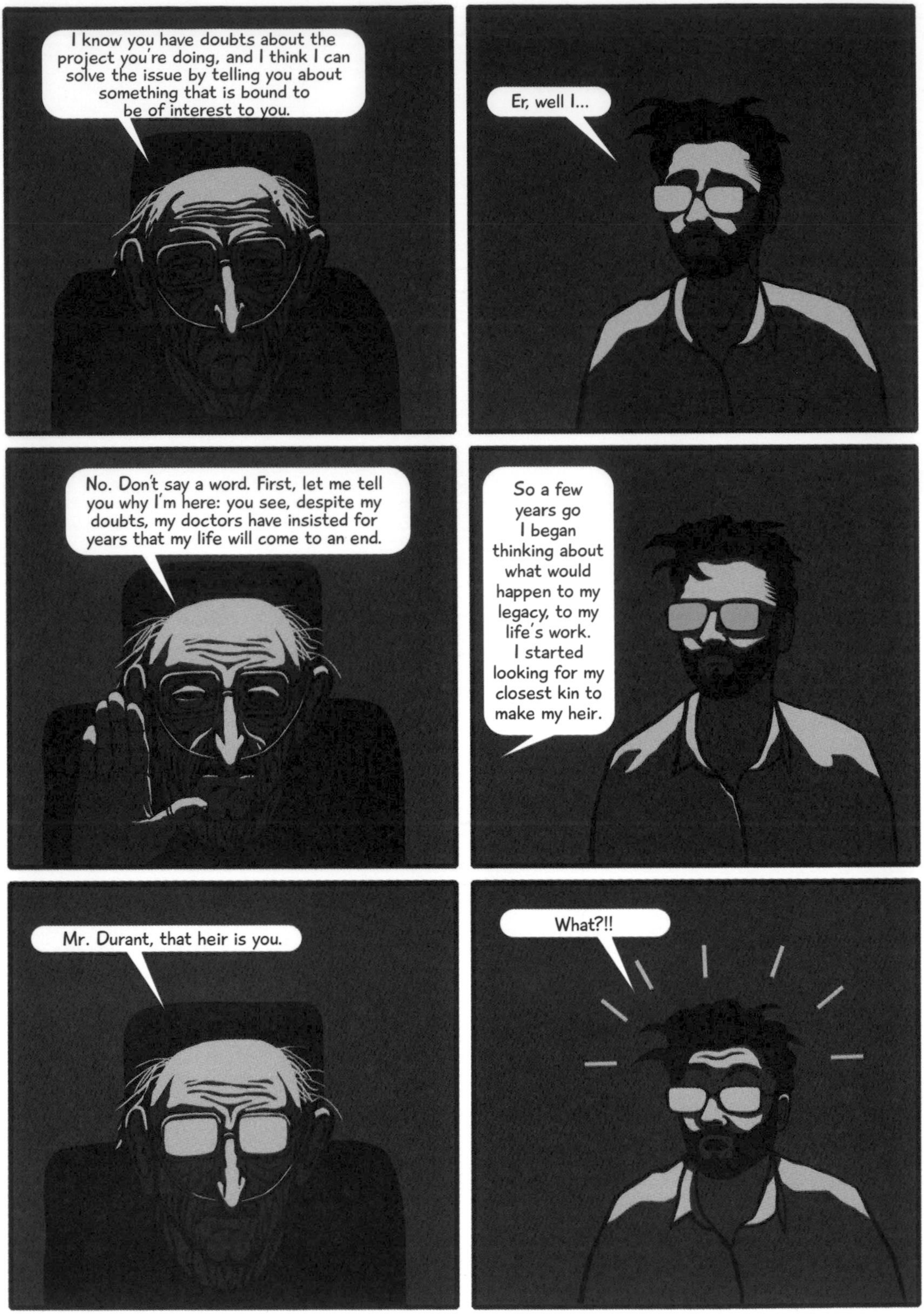
I know you have doubts about the project you're doing, and I think I can solve the issue by telling you about something that is bound to be of interest to you.
Er, well I...
No. Don't say a word. First, let me tell you why I'm here: you see, despite my doubts, my doctors have insisted for years that my life will come to an end.
So a few years go I began thinking about what would happen to my legacy, to my life's work. I started looking for my closest kin to make my heir.
Mr. Durant, that heir is you.
What?!!

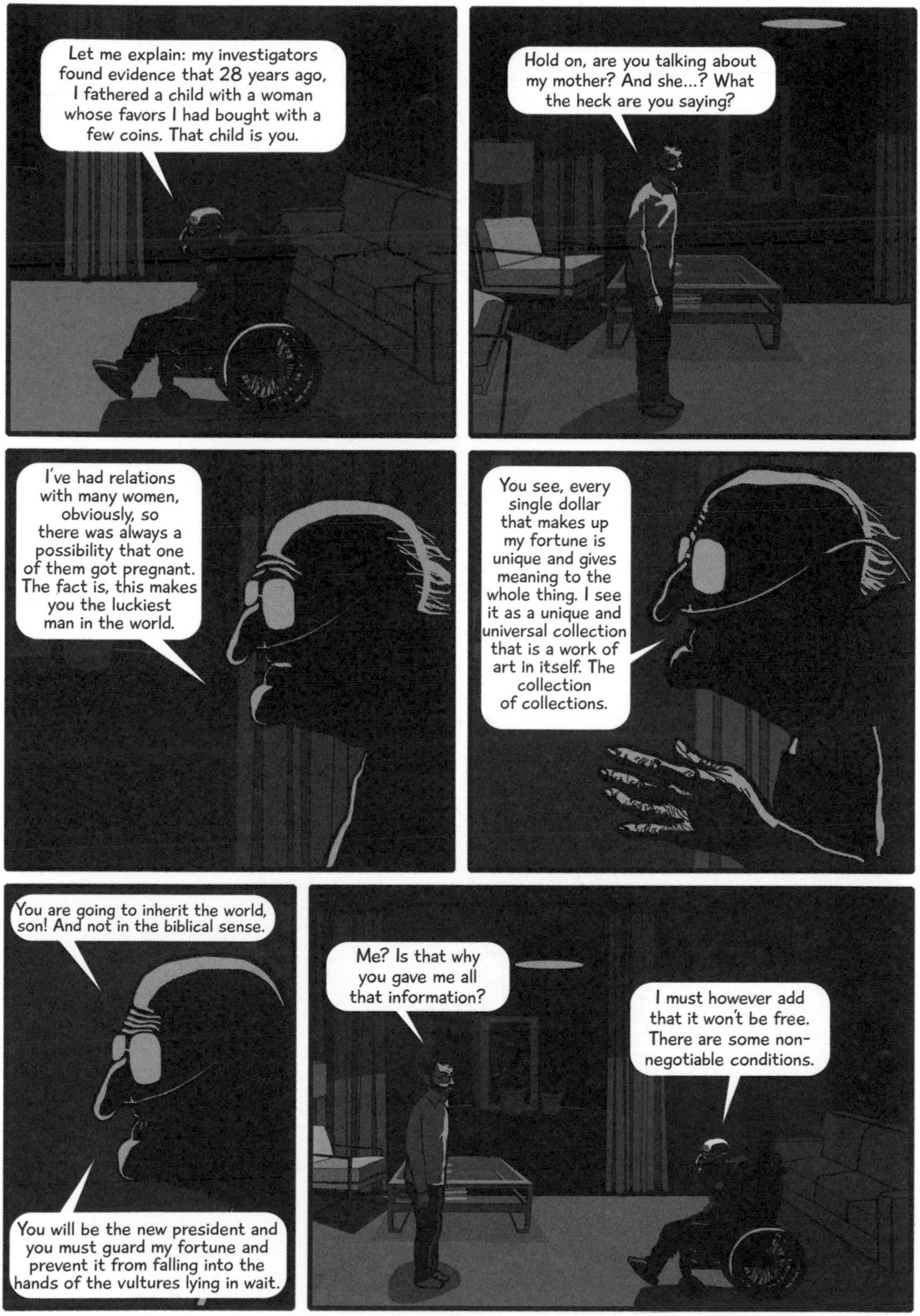
Let me explain: my investigators found evidence that 28 years ago, I fathered a child with a woman whose favors I had bought with a few coins. That child is you.
Hold on, are you talking about my mother? And she...? What the heck are you saying?
I've had relations with many women, obviously, so there was always a possibility that one of them got pregnant. The fact is, this makes you the luckiest man in the world.
You see, every single dollar that makes up my fortune is unique and gives meaning to the whole thing. I see it as a unique and universal collection that is a work of art in itself. The collection of collections.
You are going to inherit the world, son! And not in the biblical sense.
You will be the new president and you must guard my fortune and prevent it from falling into the hands of the vultures lying in wait.
Me? Is that why you gave me all that information?
I must however add that it won't be free. There are some non-negotiable conditions.

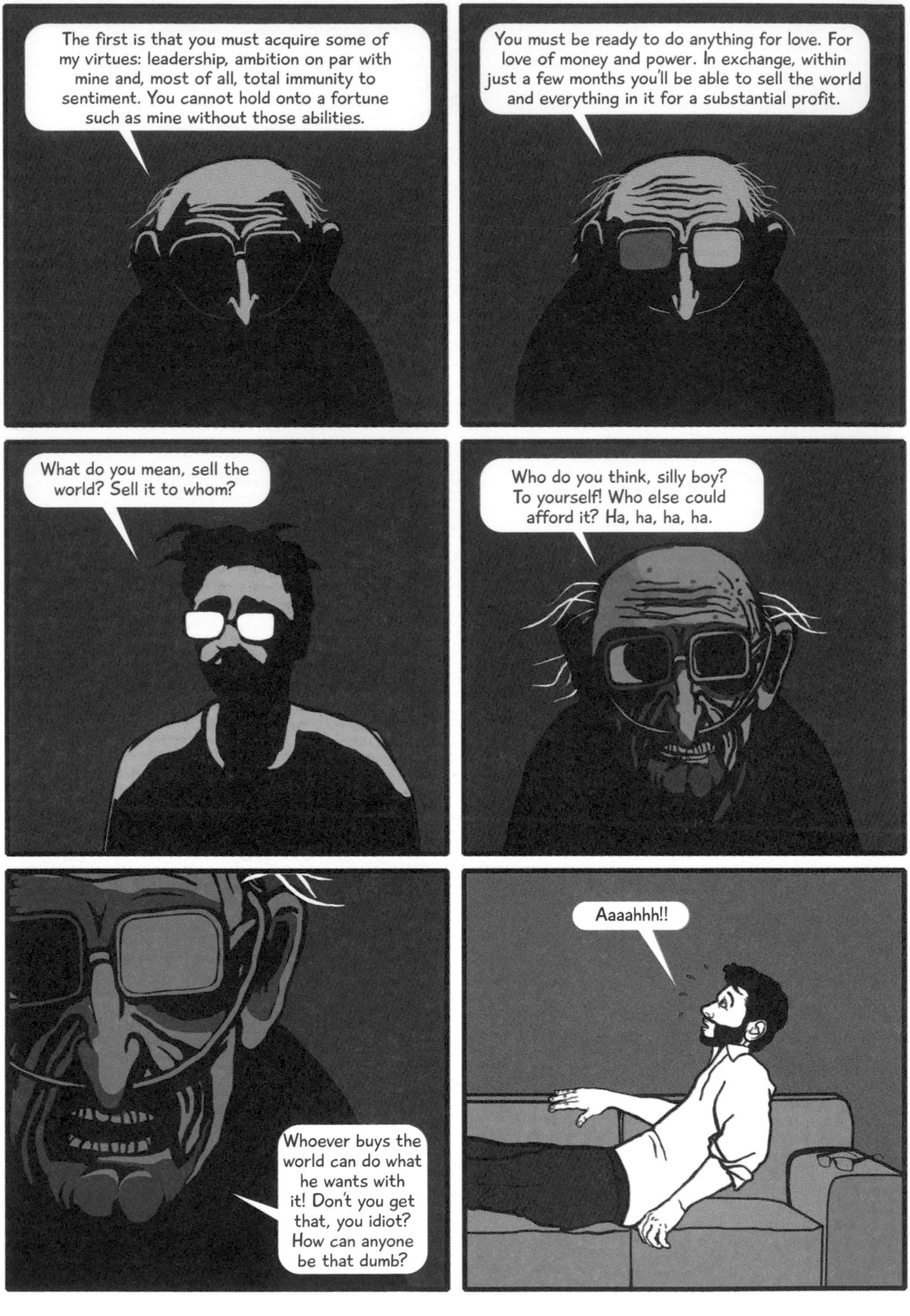
The first is that you must acquire some of my virtues: leadership, ambition on par with mine and, most of all, total immunity to sentiment. You cannot hold onto a fortune such as mine without those abilities.
You must be ready to do anything for love. For love of money and power. In exchange, within just a few months you'll be able to sell the world and everything in it for a substantial profit.
What do you mean, sell the world? Sell it to whom?
Who do you think, silly boy? To yourself! Who else could afford it? Ha, ha, ha, ha.
Whoever buys the world can do what he wants with it! Don't you get that, you idiot? How can anyone be that dumb?
Aaaahhh!!

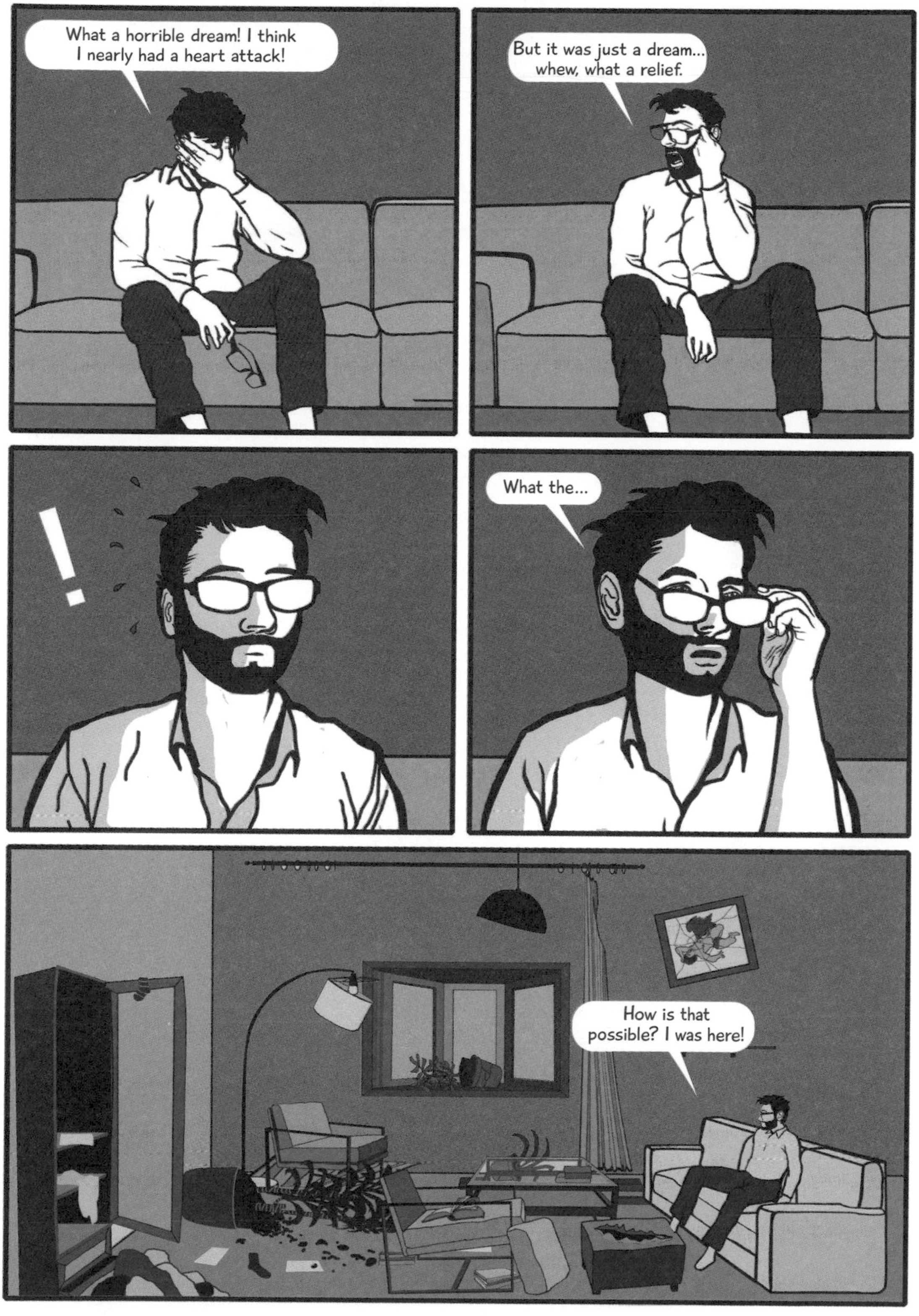
What a horrible dream! I think I nearly had a heart attack!
But it was just a dream... whew, what a relief.
!
What the...
How is that possible? I was here!

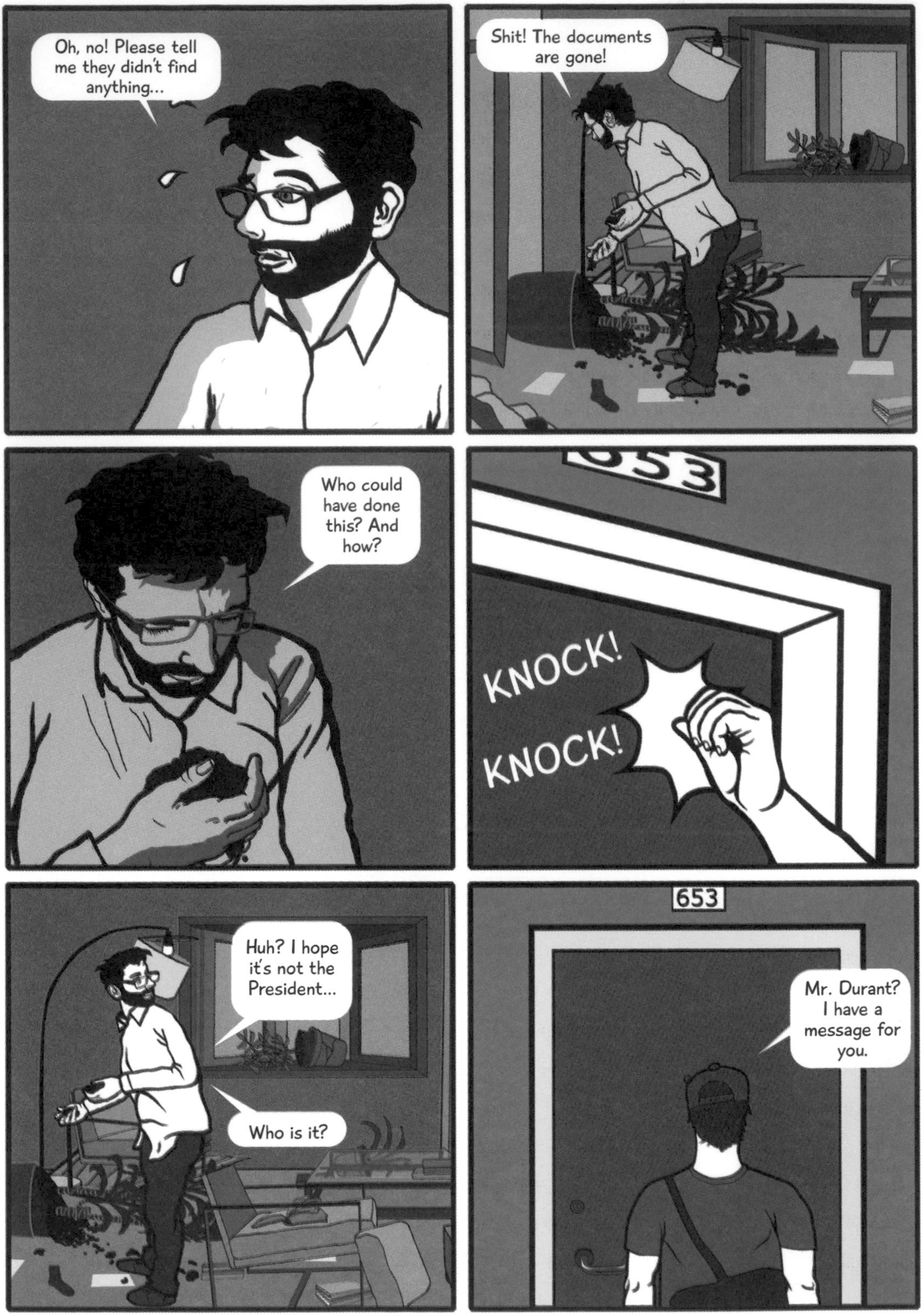
Oh, no! Please tell me they didn't find anything...
Shit! The documents are gone!
Who could have done this? And how?
653
KNOCK!
KNOCK!
Huh? I hope it's not the President...
Who is it?
653
Mr. Durant? I have a message for you.

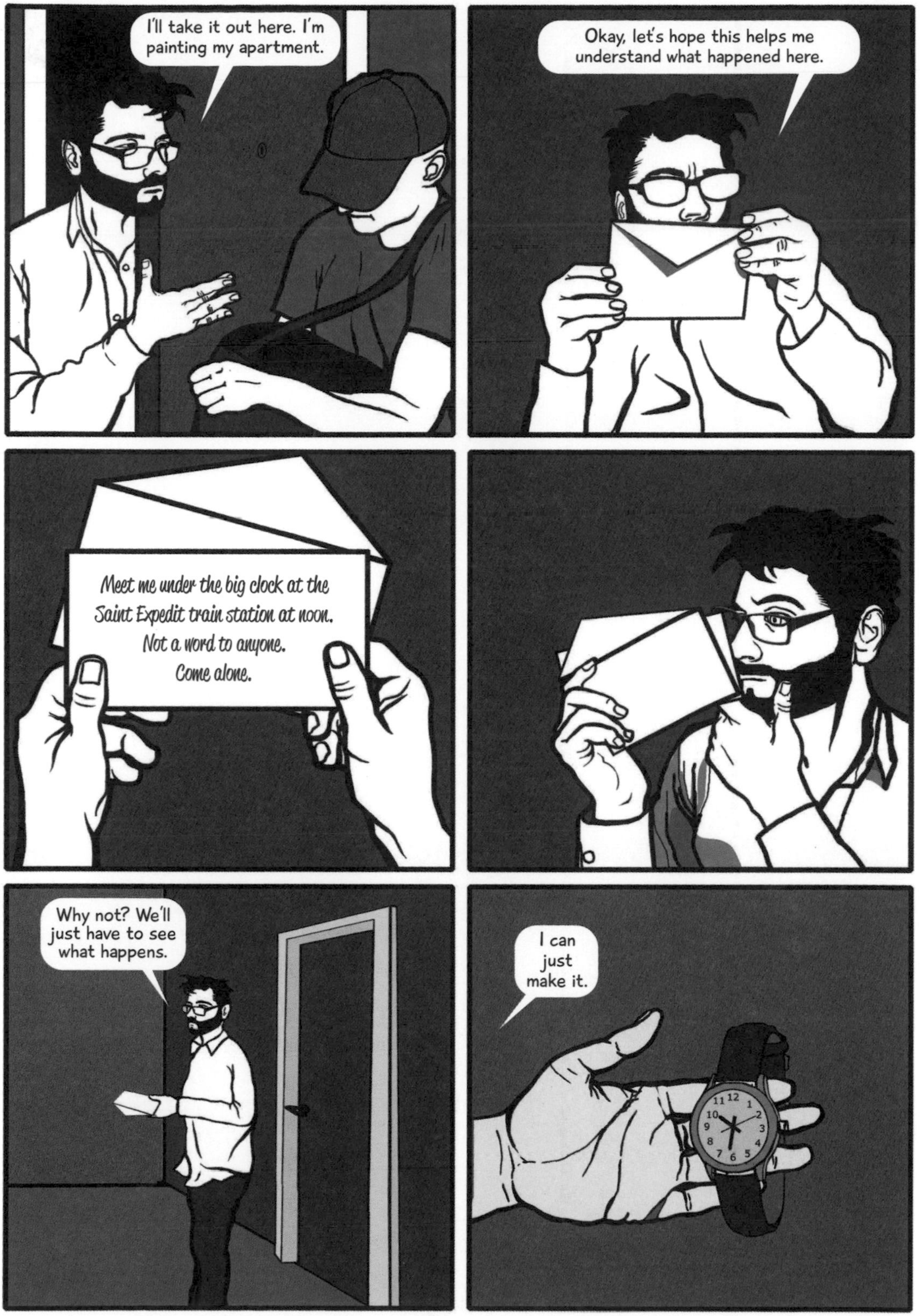
I'll take it out here. I'm painting my apartment.
Okay, let's hope this helps me understand what happened here.
Meet me under the big clock at the Saint Expedit train station at noon. Not a word to anyone. Come alone.
Why not? We'll just have to see what happens.
I can just make it.

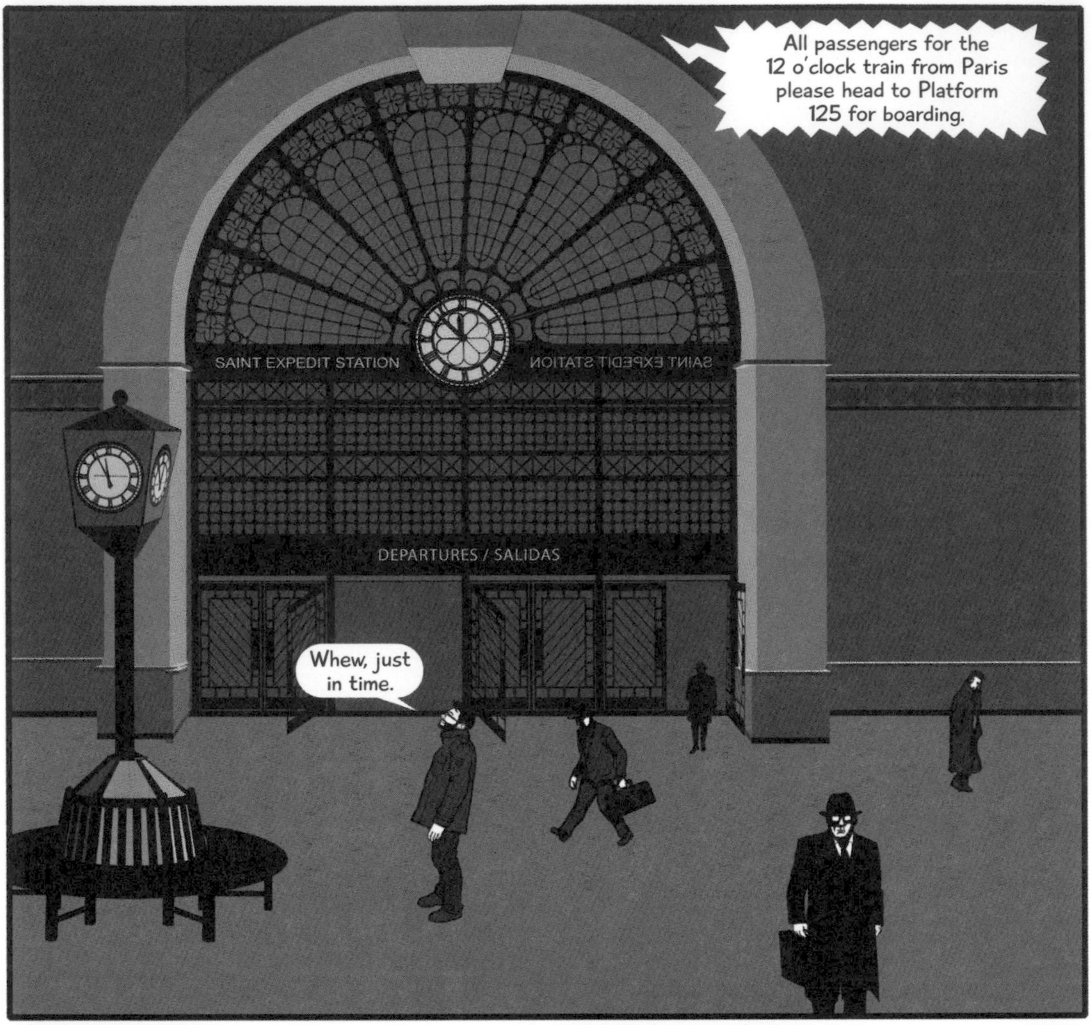
All passengers for the 12 o'clock train from Paris please head to Platform 125 for boarding.
SAINT EXPEDIT STATION
DEPARTURES / SALIDAS
Whew, just in time.

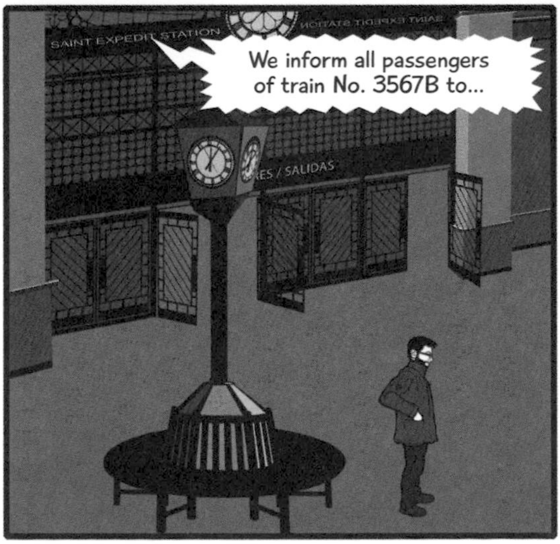
We inform all passengers of train No. 3567B to...

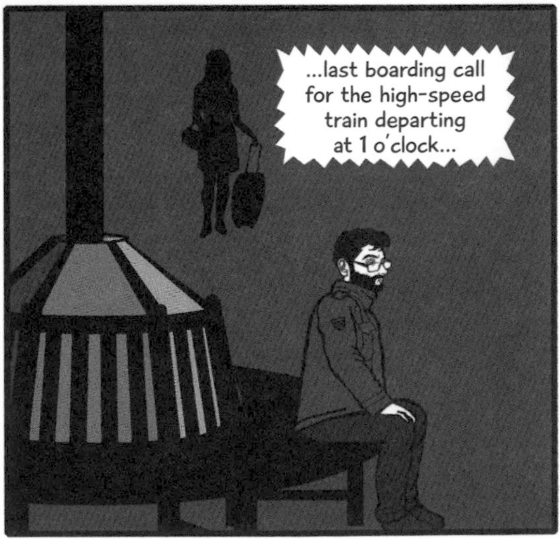
...last boarding call for the high-speed train departing at 1 o'clock...

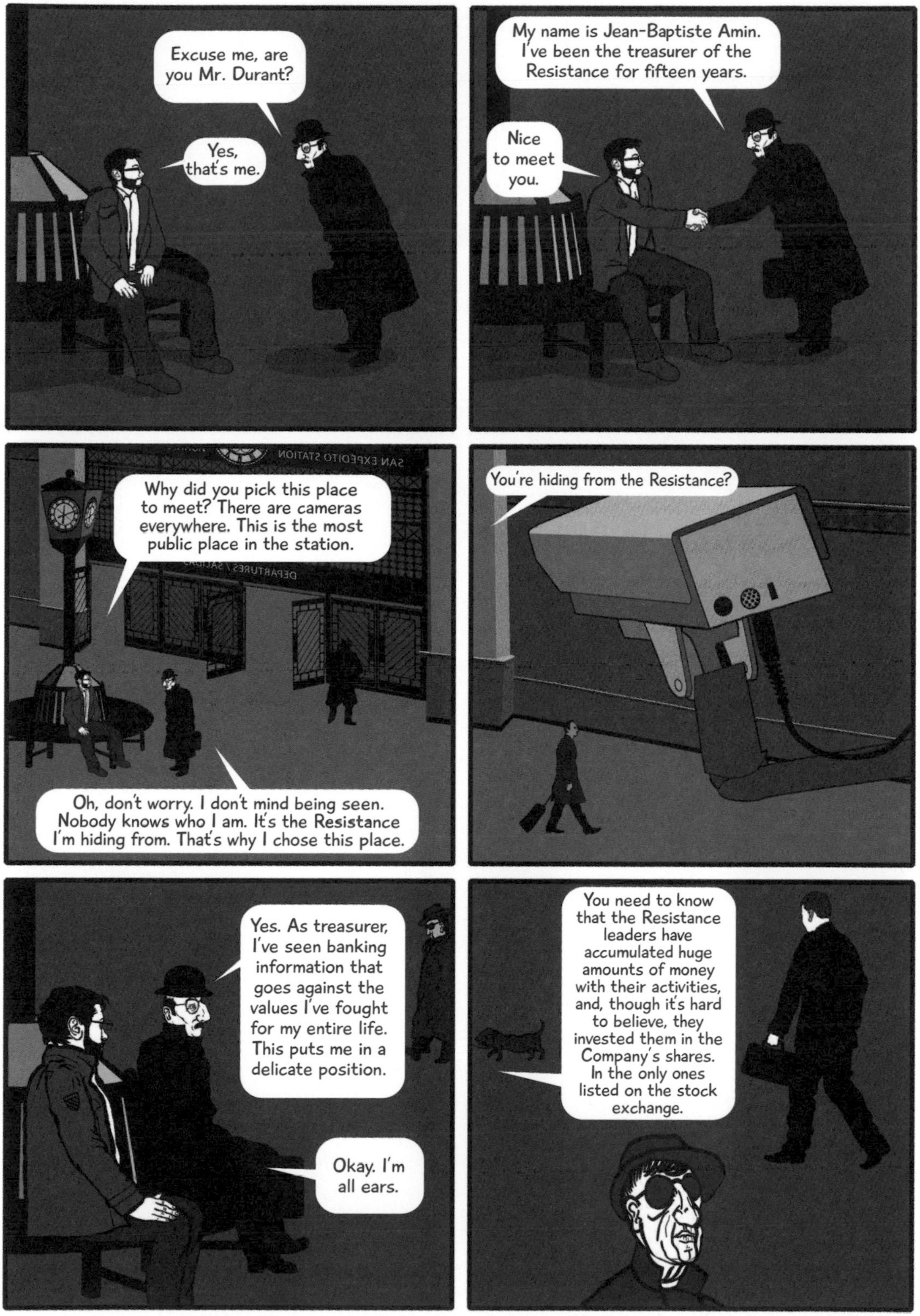

Excuse me, are you Mr. Durant?
Yes, that's me.
My name is Jean-Baptiste Amin. I've been the treasurer of the Resistance for fifteen years.
Nice to meet you.
Why did you pick this place to meet? There are cameras everywhere. This is the most public place in the station.
Oh, don't worry. I don't mind being seen. Nobody knows who I am. It's the Resistance I'm hiding from. That's why I chose this place.
You're hiding from the Resistance?
Yes. As treasurer, I've seen banking information that goes against the values I've fought for my entire life. This puts me in a delicate position.
Okay. I'm all ears.
You need to know that the Resistance leaders have accumulated huge amounts of money with their activities, and, though it's hard to believe, they invested them in the Company's shares. In the only ones listed on the stock exchange.

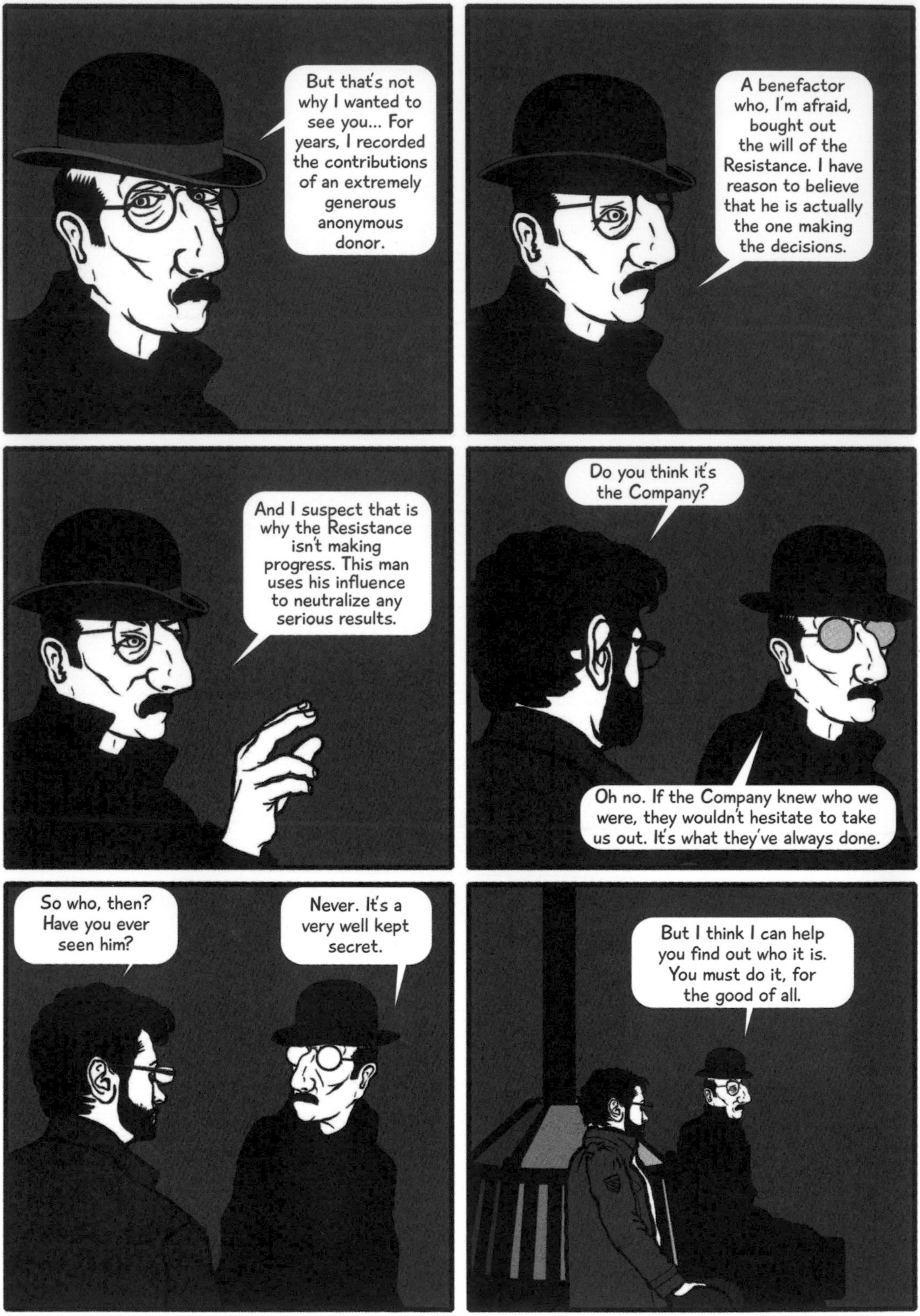
But that's not why I wanted to see you... For years, I recorded the contributions of an extremely generous anonymous donor.
A benefactor who, I'm afraid, bought out the will of the Resistance. I have reason to believe that he is actually the one making the decisions.
And I suspect that is why the Resistance isn't making progress. This man uses his influence to neutralize any serious results.
Do you think it's the Company?
Oh no. If the Company knew who we were, they wouldn't hesitate to take us out. It's what they've always done.
So who, then? Have you ever seen him?
Never. It's a very well kept secret.
But I think I can help you find out who it is. You must do it, for the good of all.

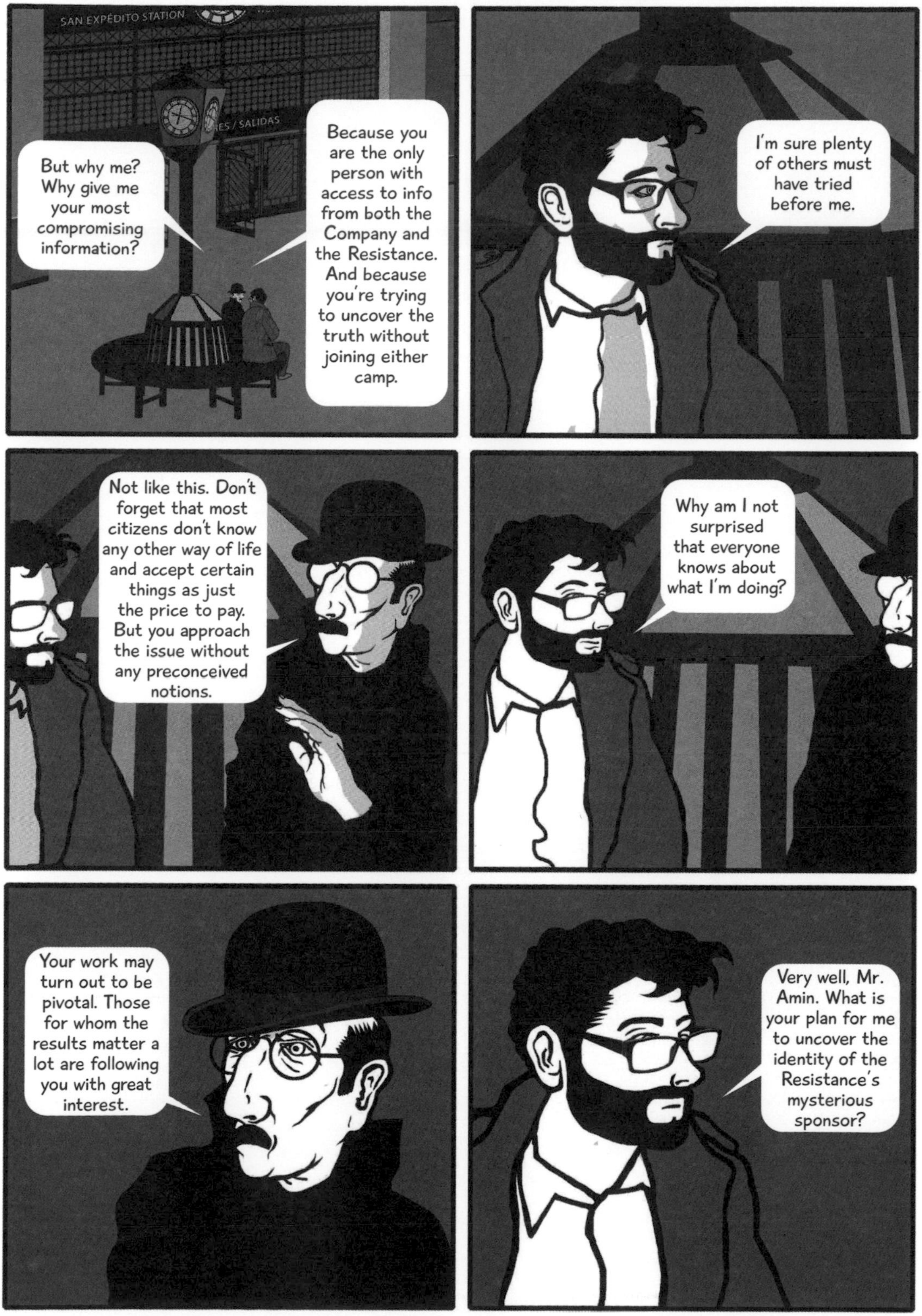
SAN EXPEDITO STATION
SALIDAS
But why me? Why give me your most compromising information?
Because you are the only person with access to info from both the Company and the Resistance. And because you're trying to uncover the truth without joining either camp.
I'm sure plenty of others must have tried before me.
Not like this. Don't forget that most citizens don't know any other way of life and accept certain things as just the price to pay. But you approach the issue without any preconceived notions.
Why am I not surprised that everyone knows about what I'm doing?
Your work may turn out to be pivotal. Those for whom the results matter a lot are following you with great interest.
Very well, Mr. Amin. What is your plan for me to uncover the identity of the Resistance's mysterious sponsor?

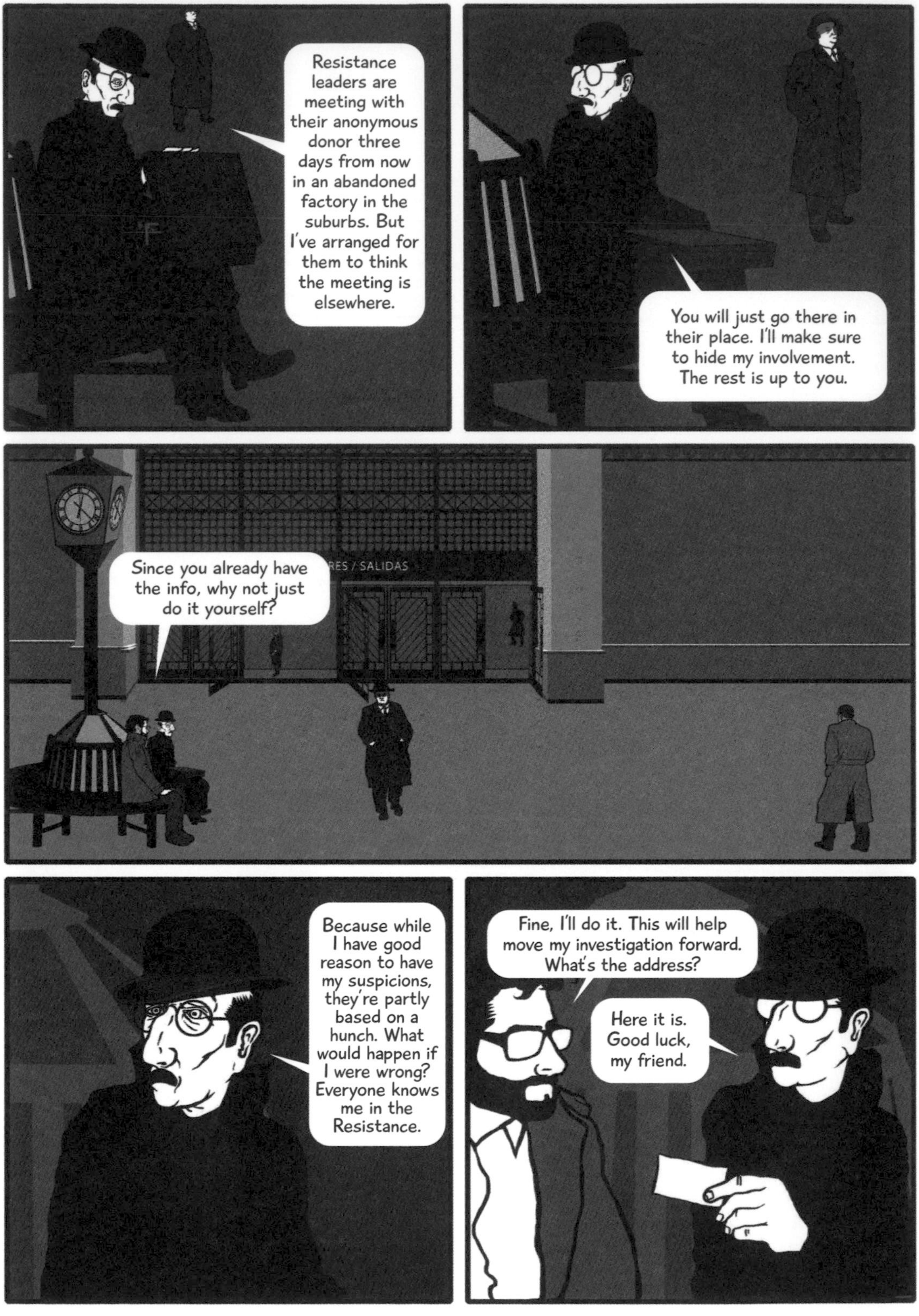
Resistance leaders are meeting with their anonymous donor three days from now in an abandoned factory in the suburbs. But I've arranged for them to think the meeting is elsewhere.
You will just go there in their place. I'll make sure to hide my involvement. The rest is up to you.
Since you already have the info, why not just do it yourself?
RES / SALIDAS
Because while I have good reason to have my suspicions, they're partly based on a hunch. What would happen if I were wrong? Everyone knows me in the Resistance.
Fine, I'll do it. This will help move my investigation forward. What's the address?
Here it is. Good luck, my friend.

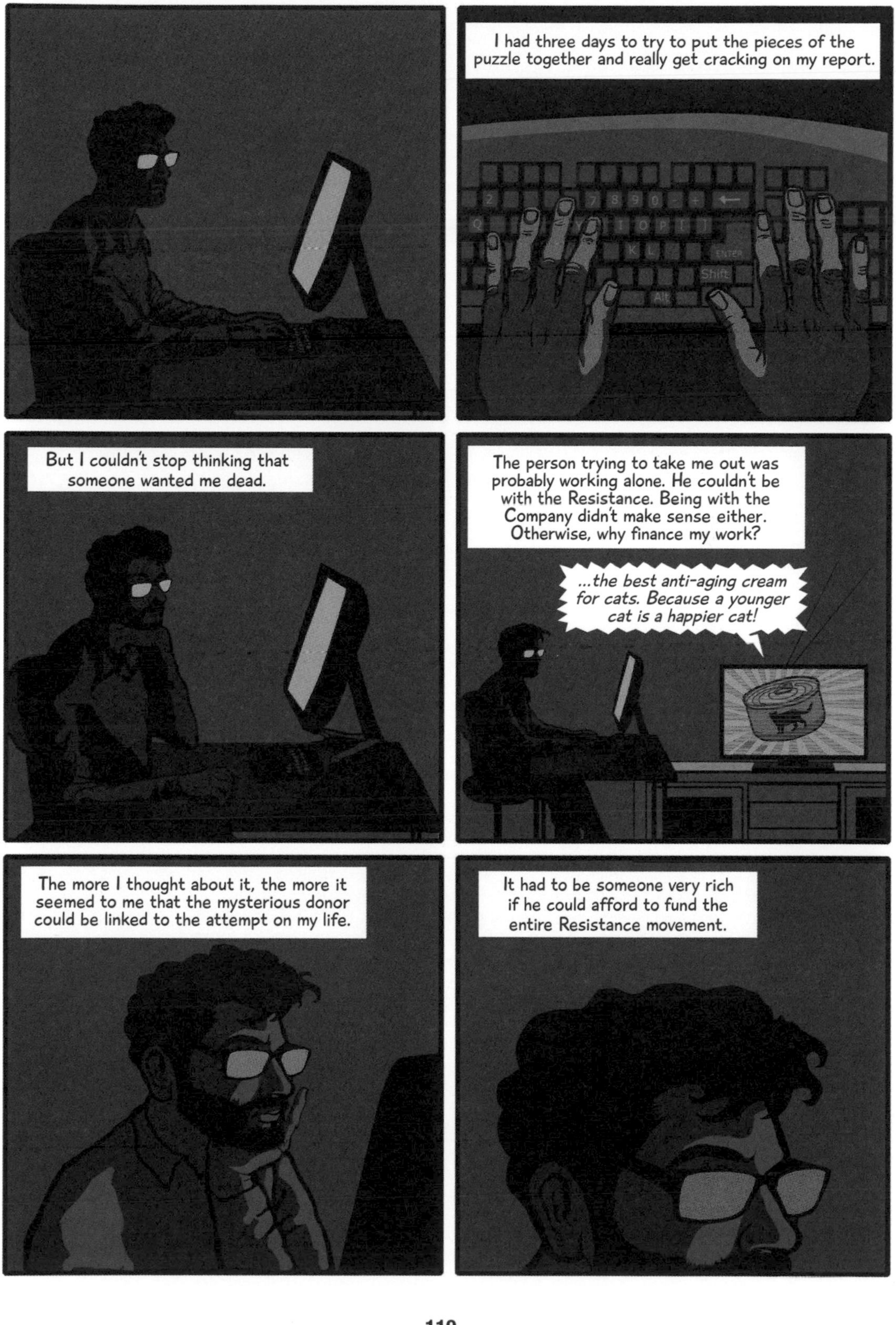
I had three days to try to put the pieces of the puzzle together and really get cracking on my report.
But I couldn't stop thinking that someone wanted me dead.
The person trying to take me out was probably working alone. He couldn't be with the Resistance. Being with the Company didn't make sense either. Otherwise, why finance my work?
...the best anti-aging cream for cats. Because a younger cat is a happier cat!
The more I thought about it, the more it seemed to me that the mysterious donor could be linked to the attempt on my life.
It had to be someone very rich if he could afford to fund the entire Resistance movement.

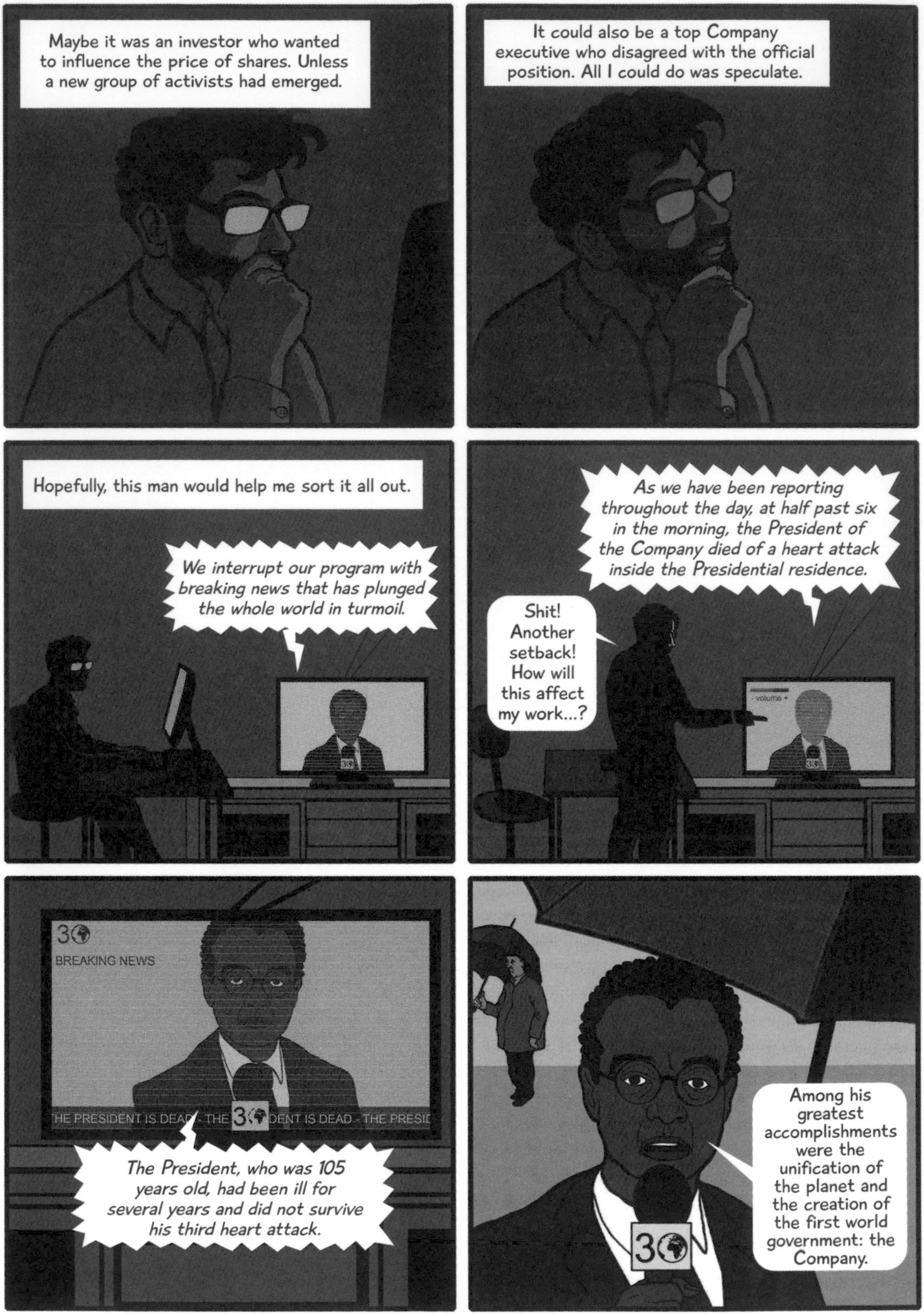
Maybe it was an investor who wanted to influence the price of shares. Unless a new group of activists had emerged.
It could also be a top Company executive who disagreed with the official position. All I could do was speculate.
Hopefully, this man would help me sort it all out.
We interrupt our program with breaking news that has plunged the whole world in turmoil.
As we have been reporting throughout the day, at half past six in the morning, the President of the Company died of a heart attack inside the Presidential residence.
Shit! Another setback! How will this affect my work...?
- volume +
BREAKING NEWS
HE PRESIDENT IS DEAD - THE 3 DENT IS DEAD - THE PRESID
The President, who was 105 years old, had been ill for several years and did not survive his third heart attack.
Among his greatest accomplishments were the unification of the planet and the creation of the first world government: the Company.

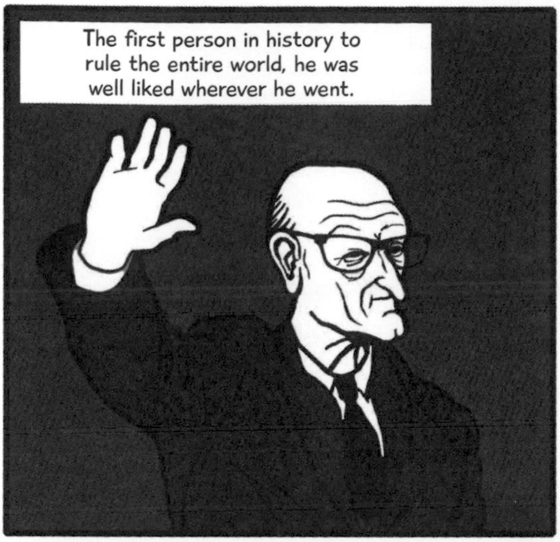
The first person in history to rule the entire world, he was well liked wherever he went.

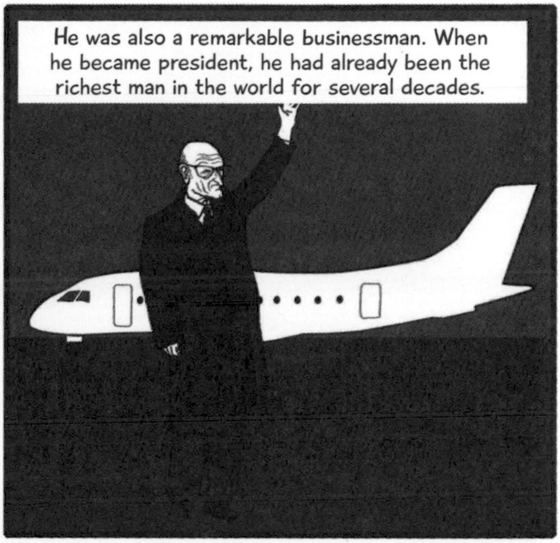
He was also a remarkable businessman. When he became president, he had already been the richest man in the world for several decades.

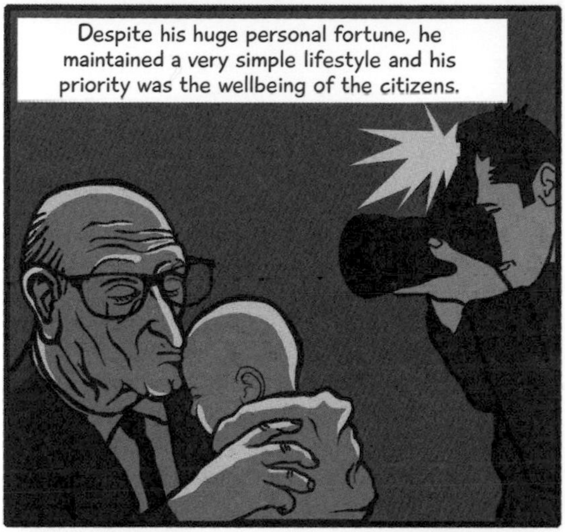
Despite his huge personal fortune, he maintained a very simple lifestyle and his priority was the wellbeing of the citizens.

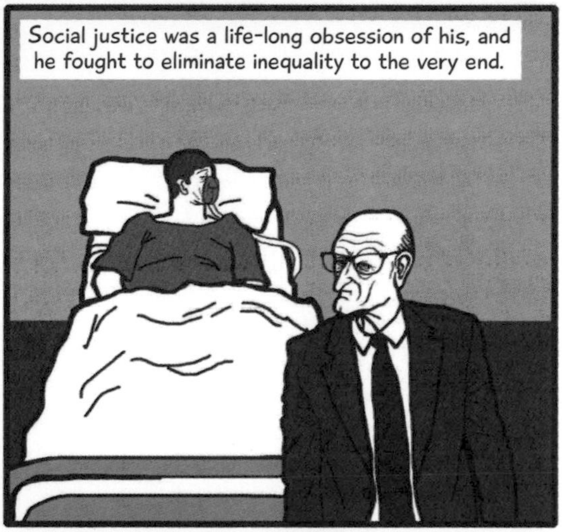
Social justice was a life-long obsession of his, and he fought to eliminate inequality to the very end.

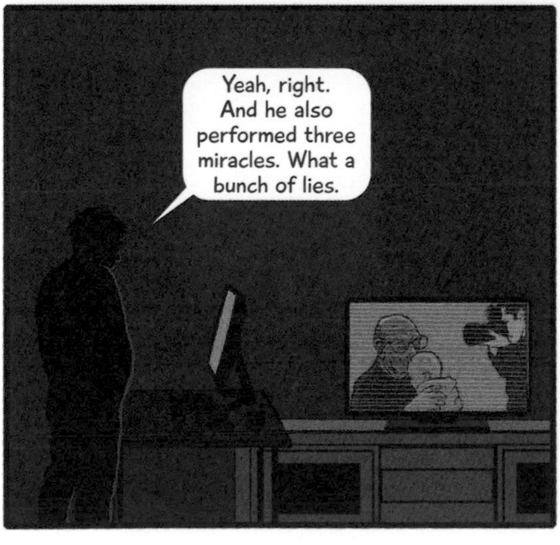
Yeah, right. And he also performed three miracles. What a bunch of lies.

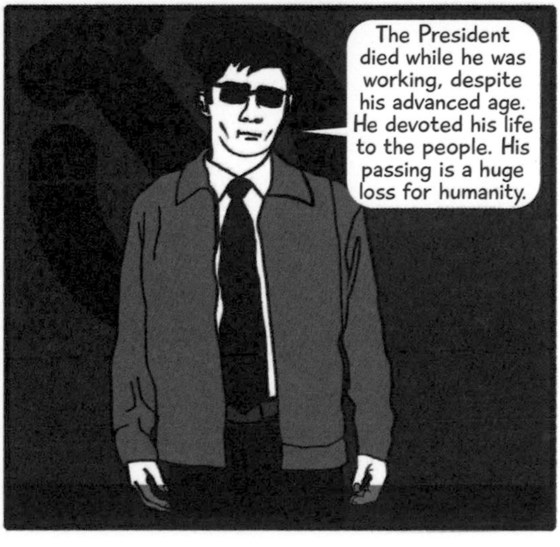
The President died while he was working, despite his advanced age. He devoted his life to the people. His passing is a huge loss for humanity.

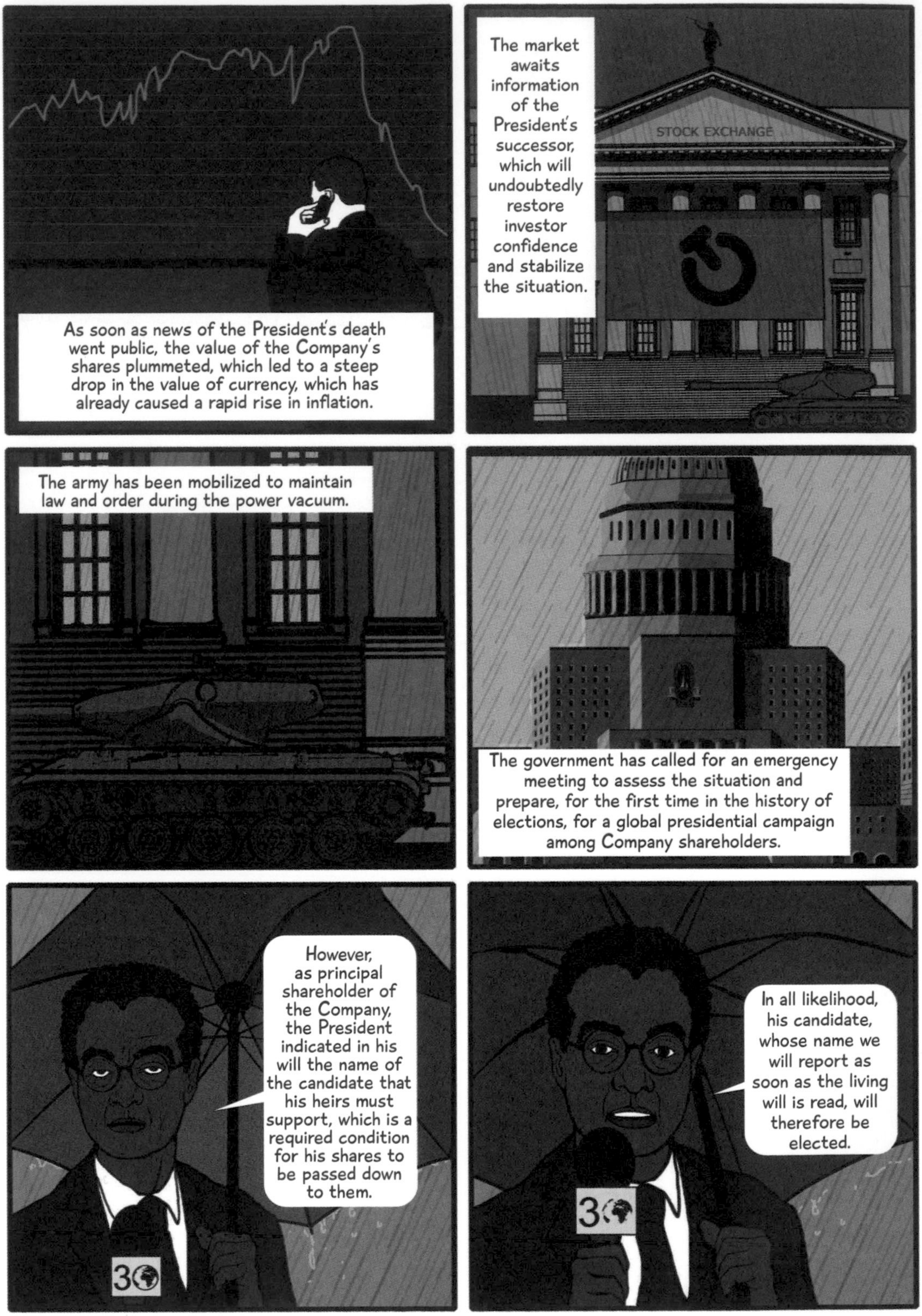
As soon as news of the President's death went public, the value of the Company's shares plummeted, which led to a steep drop in the value of currency, which has already caused a rapid rise in inflation.
The market awaits information of the President's successor, which will undoubtedly restore investor confidence and stabilize the situation.
STOCK EXCHANGE
The army has been mobilized to maintain law and order during the power vacuum.
The government has called for an emergency meeting to assess the situation and prepare, for the first time in the history of elections, for a global presidential campaign among Company shareholders.
However, as principal shareholder of the Company, the President indicated in his will the name of the candidate that his heirs must support, which is a required condition for his shares to be passed down to them.
In all likelihood, his candidate, whose name we will report as soon as the living will is read, will therefore be elected.

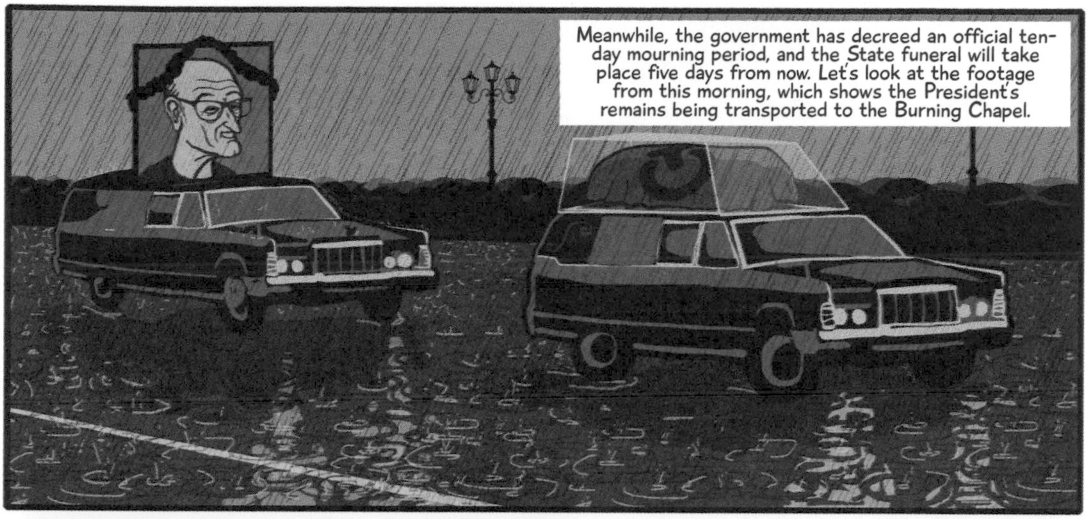
Meanwhile, the government has decreed an official ten-day mourning period, and the State funeral will take place five days from now. Let's look at the footage from this morning, which shows the President's remains being transported to the Burning Chapel.

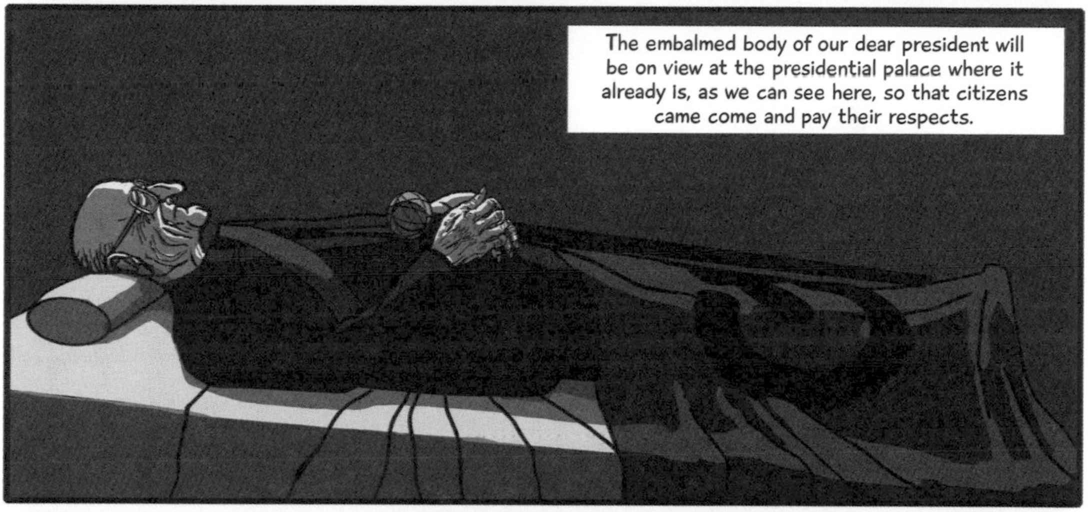
The embalmed body of our dear president will be on view at the presidential palace where it already is, as we can see here, so that citizens came come and pay their respects.

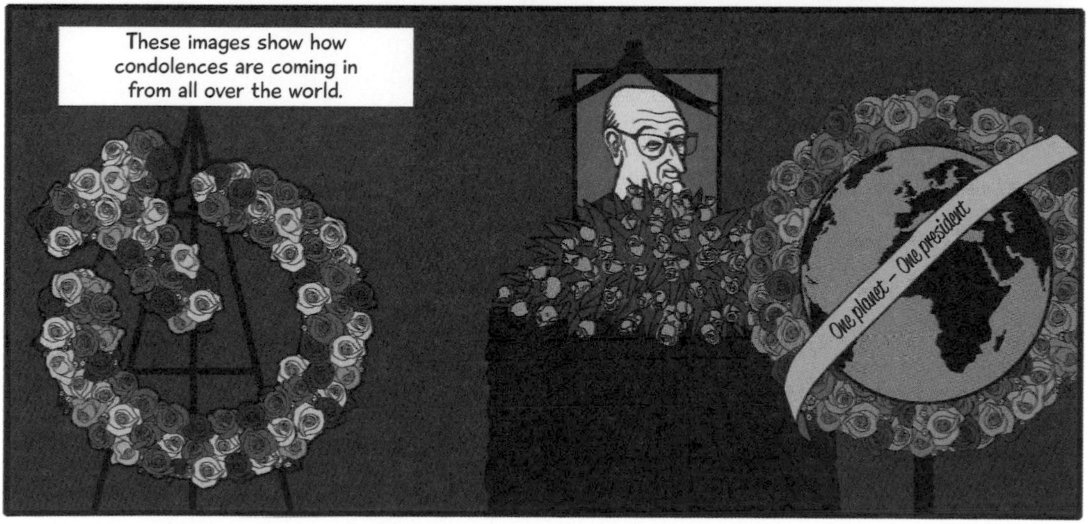
These images show how condolences are coming in from all over the world.
One planet – One president

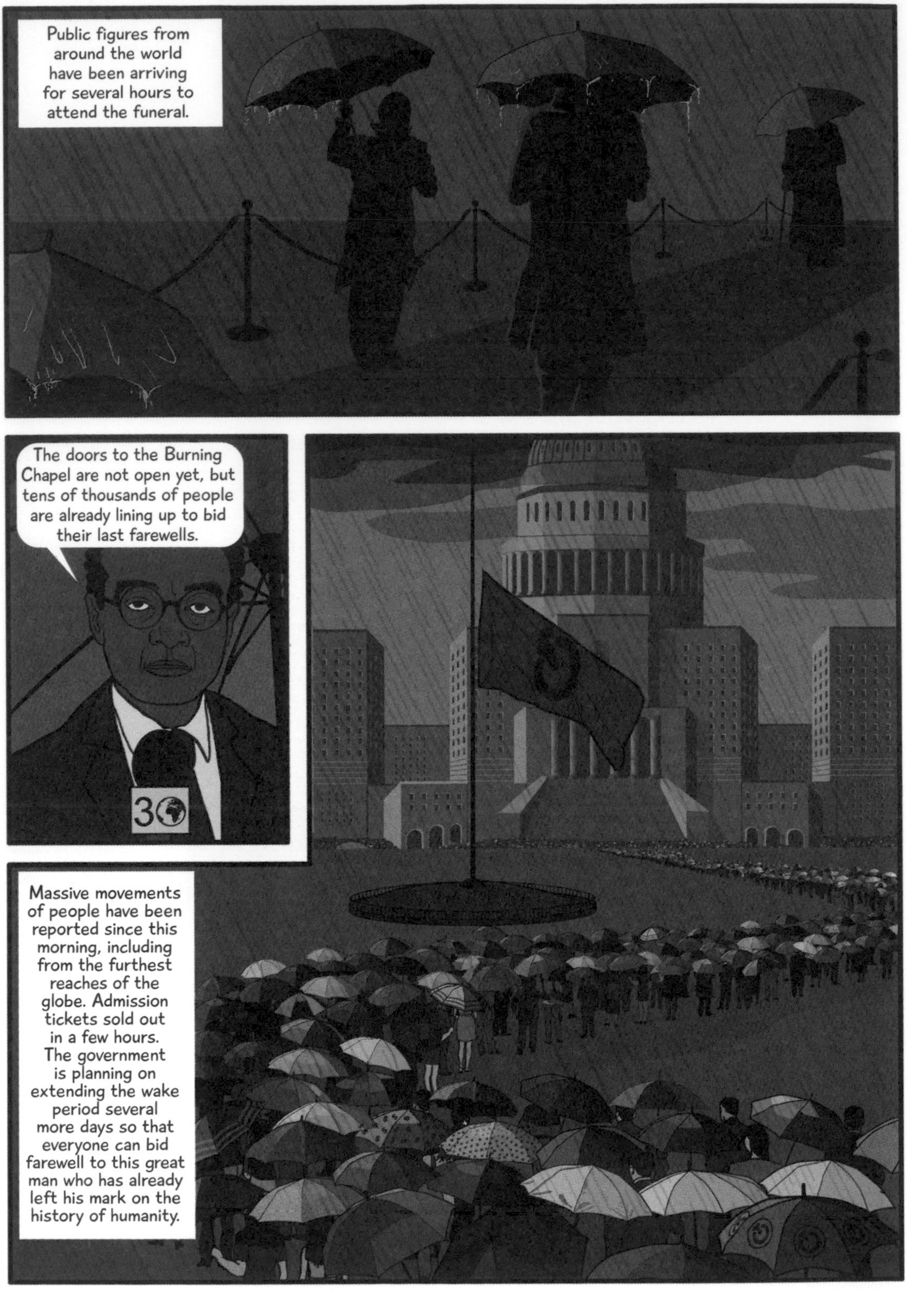

Public figures from around the world have been arriving for several hours to attend the funeral.
The doors to the Burning Chapel are not open yet, but tens of thousands of people are already lining up to bid their last farewells.
30
Massive movements of people have been reported since this morning, including from the furthest reaches of the globe. Admission tickets sold out in a few hours. The government is planning on extending the wake period several more days so that everyone can bid farewell to this great man who has already left his mark on the history of humanity.

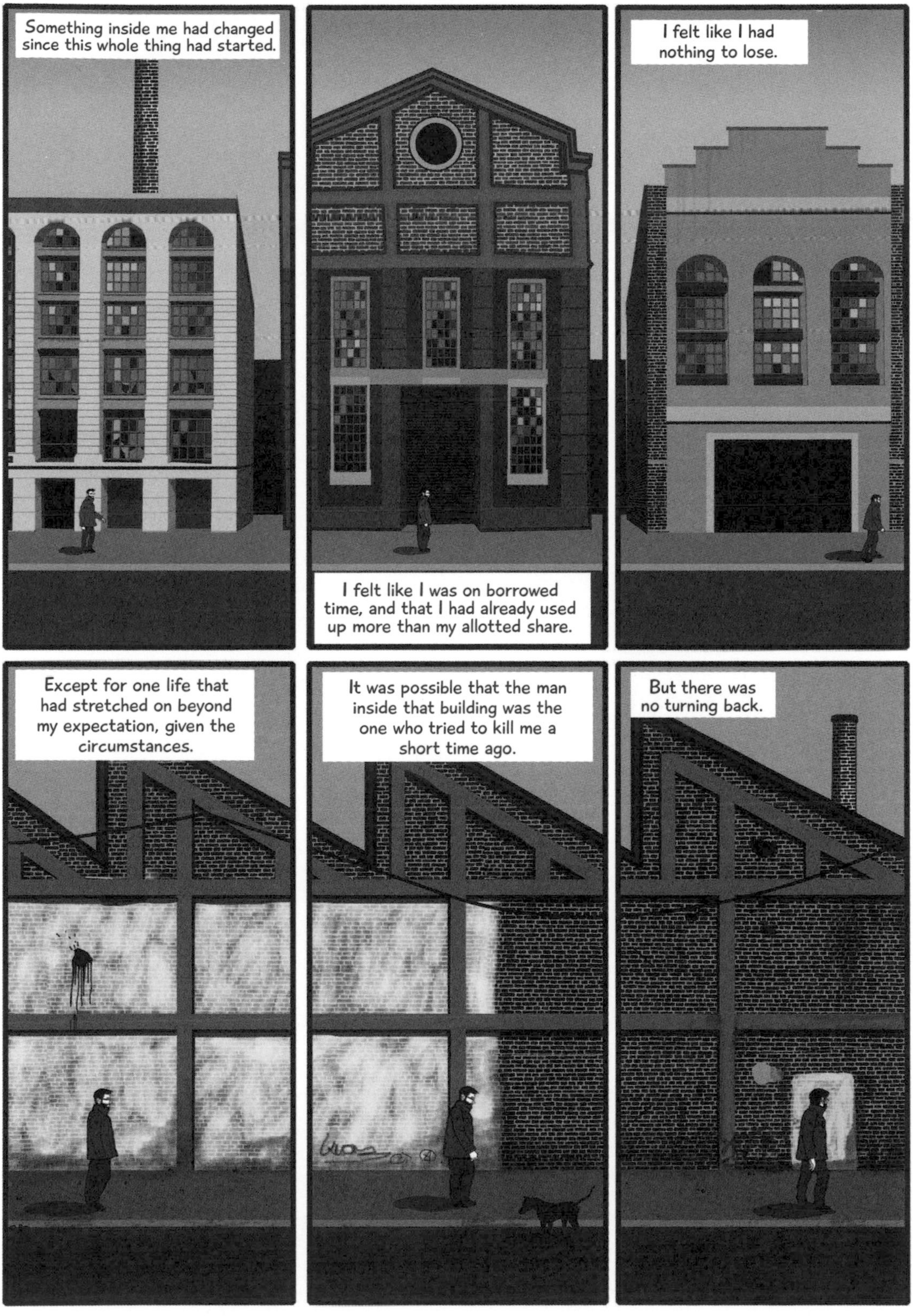
Something inside me had changed since this whole thing had started.
I felt like I was on borrowed time, and that I had already used up more than my allotted share.
I felt like I had nothing to lose.
Except for one life that had stretched on beyond my expectation, given the circumstances.
It was possible that the man inside that building was the one who tried to kill me a short time ago.
But there was no turning back.

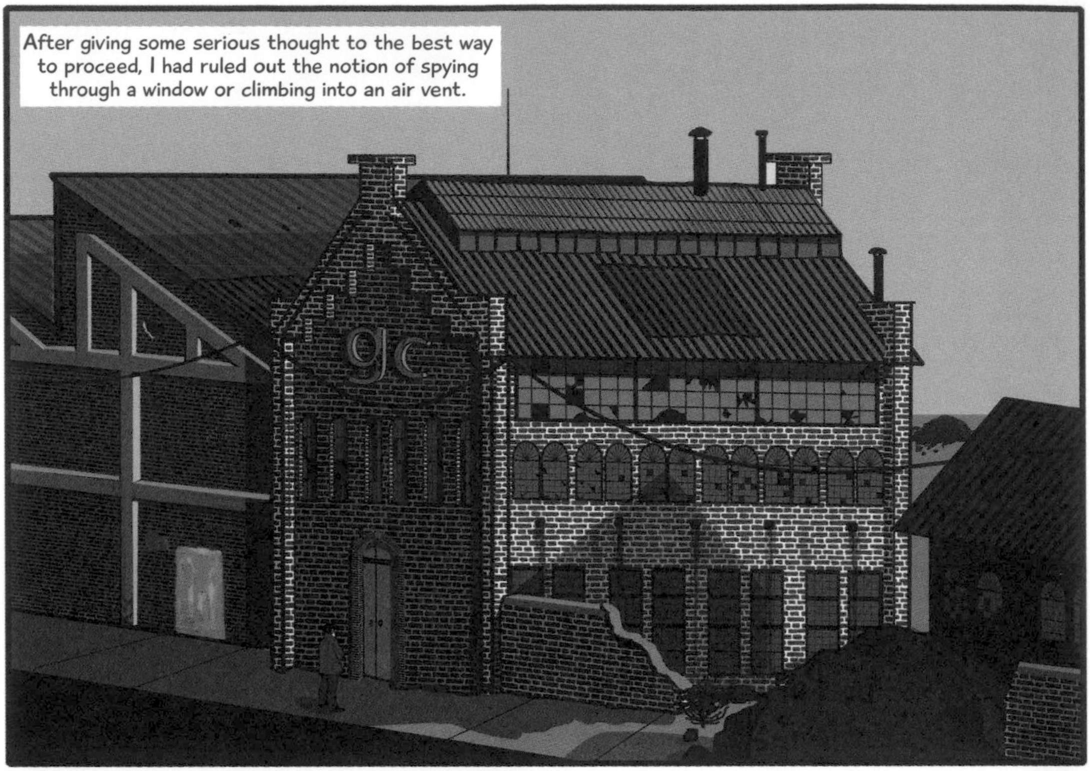
After giving some serious thought to the best way to proceed, I had ruled out the notion of spying through a window or climbing into an air vent.

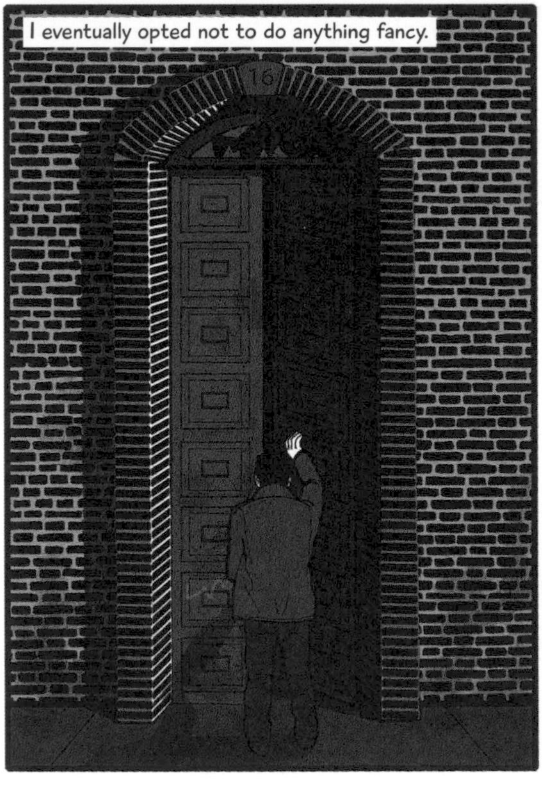
I eventually opted not to do anything fancy.
16

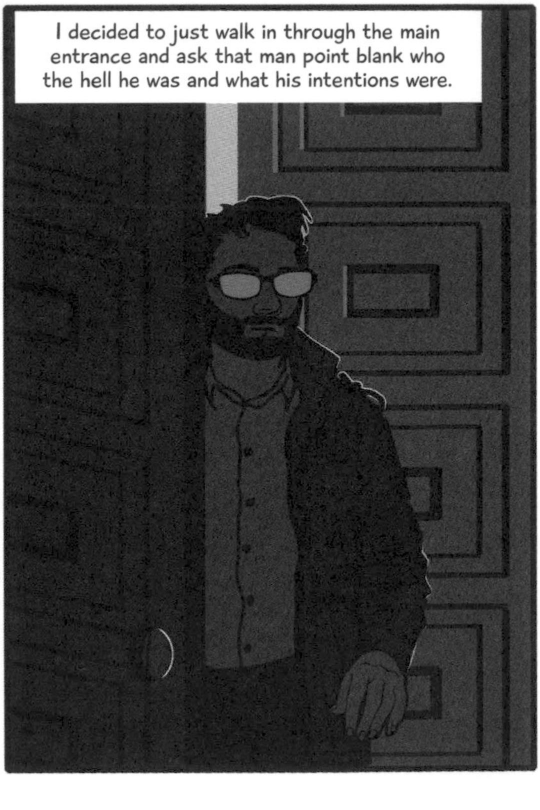
I decided to just walk in through the main entrance and ask that man point blank who the hell he was and what his intentions were.

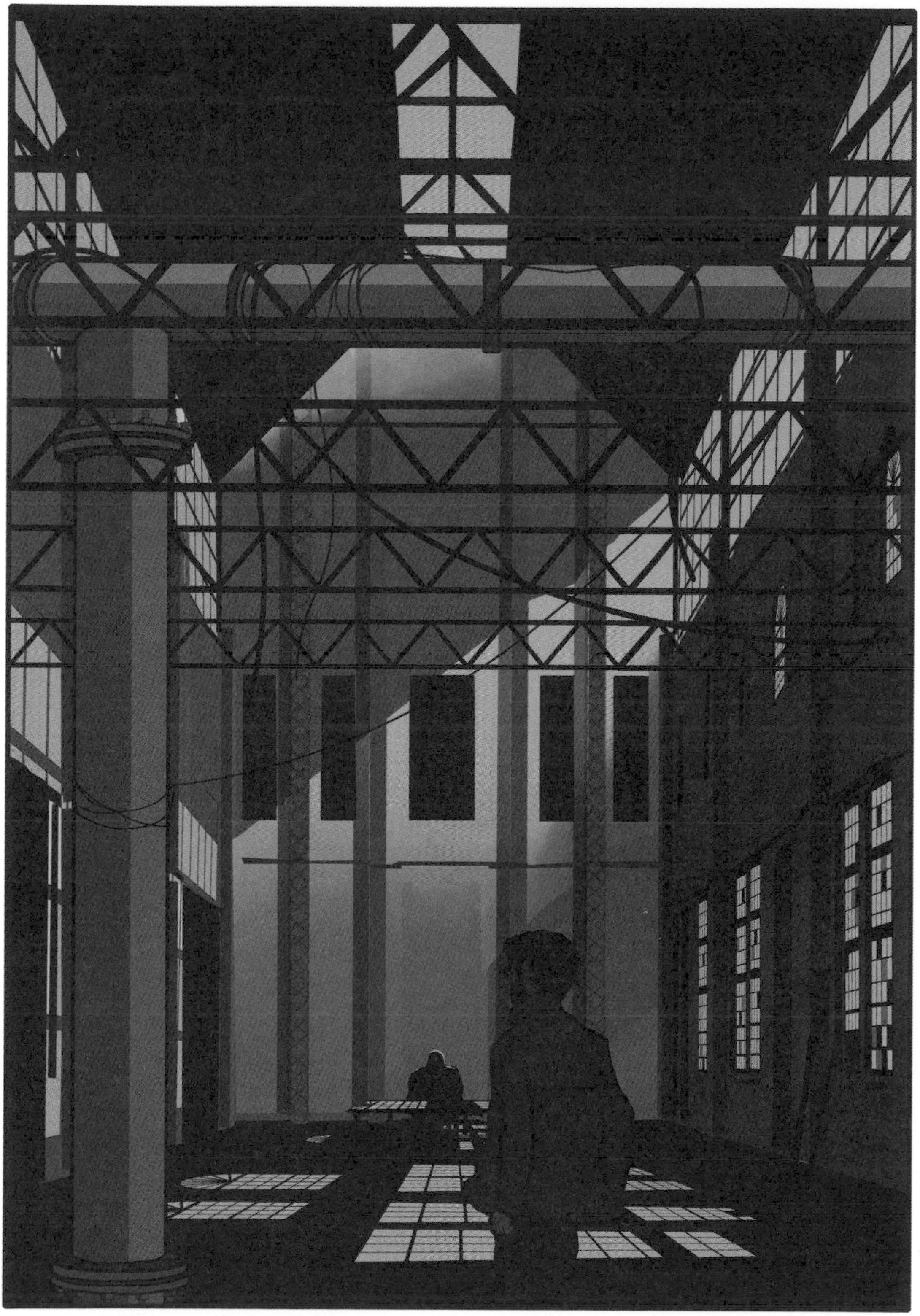

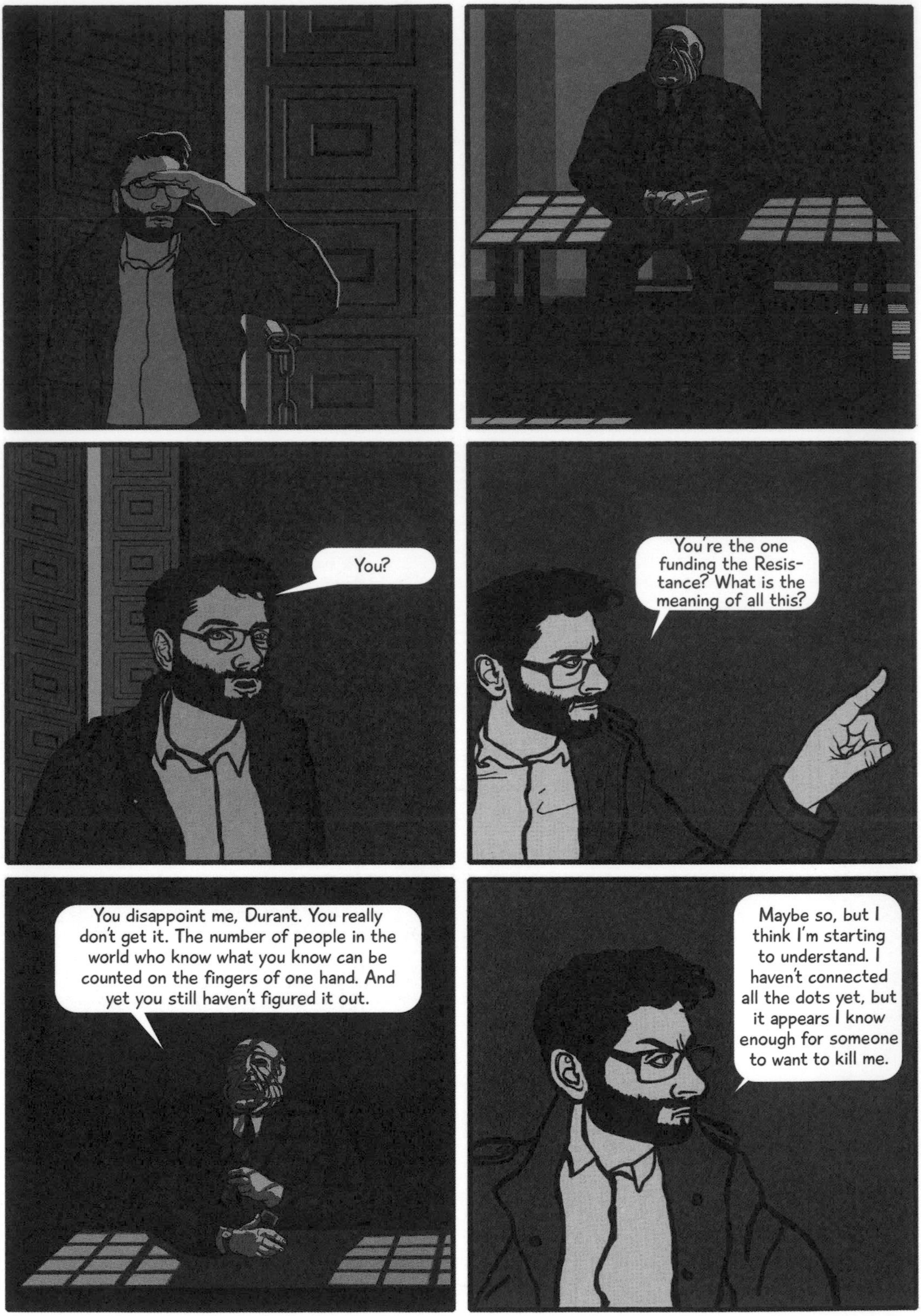

You?
You're the one funding the Resistance? What is the meaning of all this?
You disappoint me, Durant. You really don't get it. The number of people in the world who know what you know can be counted on the fingers of one hand. And yet you still haven't figured it out.
Maybe so, but I think I'm starting to understand. I haven't connected all the dots yet, but it appears I know enough for someone to want to kill me.

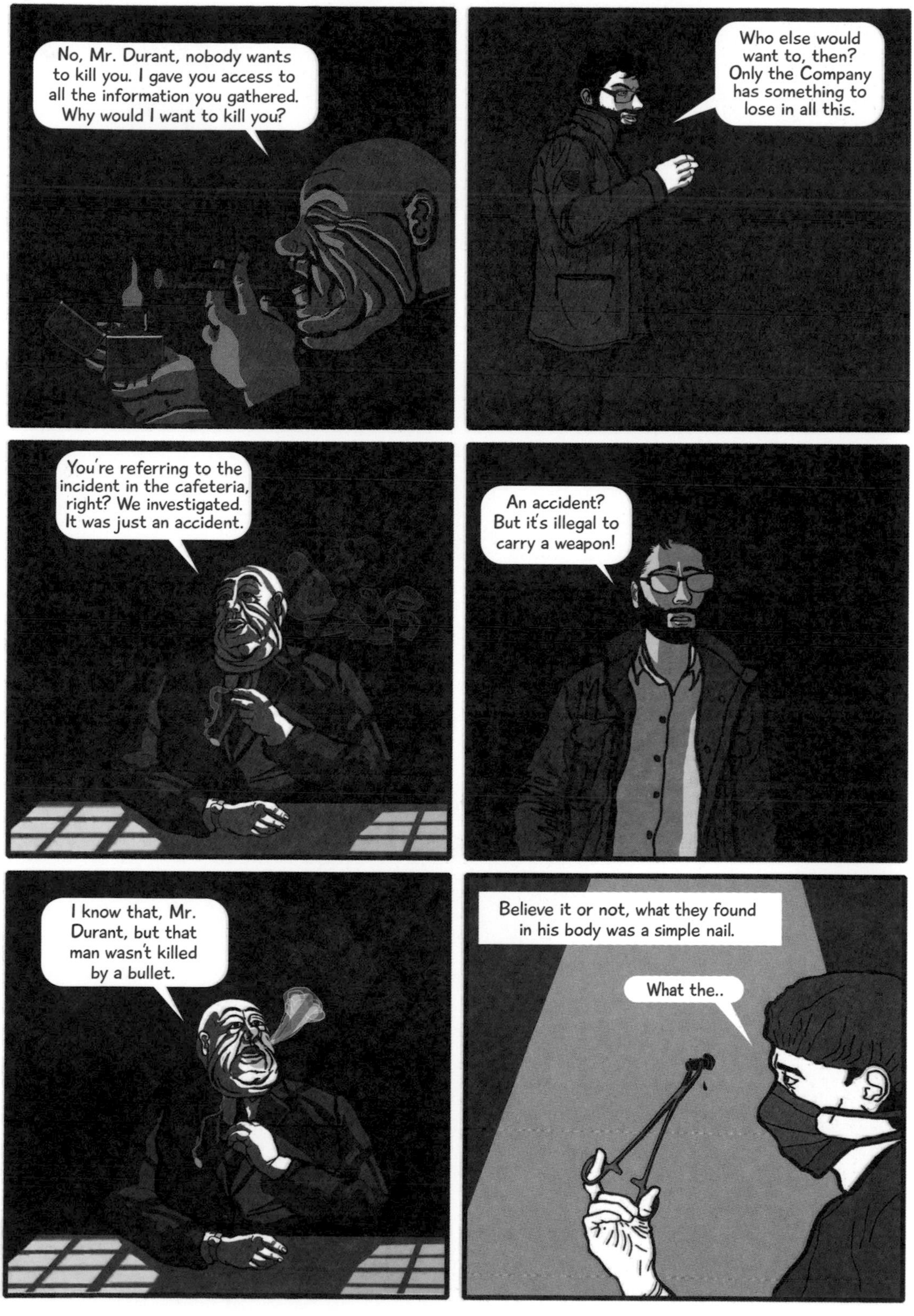
No, Mr. Durant, nobody wants to kill you. I gave you access to all the information you gathered. Why would I want to kill you?
Who else would want to, then? Only the Company has something to lose in all this.
You're referring to the incident in the cafeteria, right? We investigated. It was just an accident.
An accident? But it's illegal to carry a weapon!
I know that, Mr. Durant, but that man wasn't killed by a bullet.
Believe it or not, what they found in his body was a simple nail.
What the..

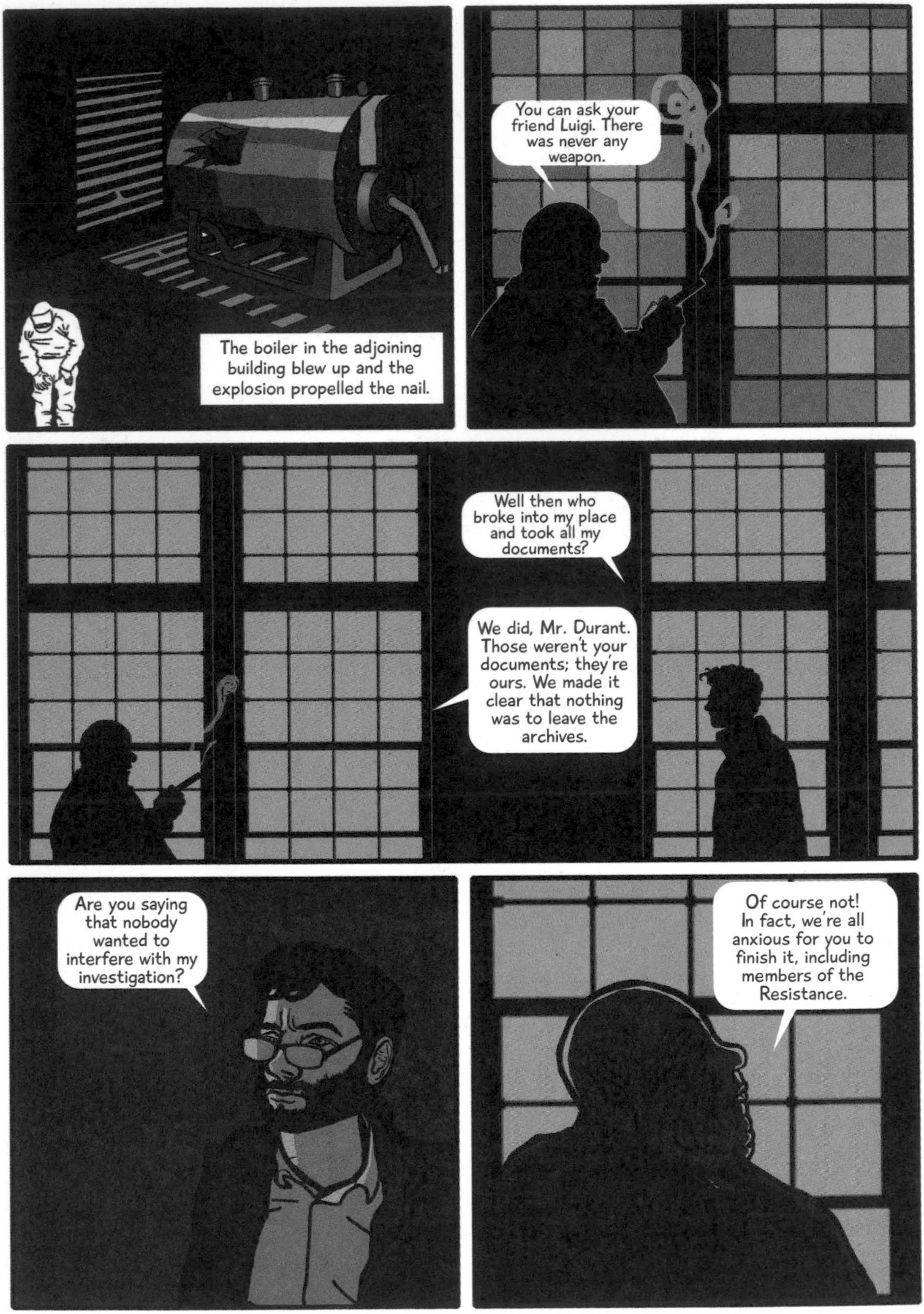
The boiler in the adjoining building blew up and the explosion propelled the nail.
You can ask your friend Luigi. There was never any weapon.
Well then who broke into my place and took all my documents?
We did, Mr. Durant. Those weren't your documents; they're ours. We made it clear that nothing was to leave the archives.
Are you saying that nobody wanted to interfere with my investigation?
Of course not! In fact, we're all anxious for you to finish it, including members of the Resistance.

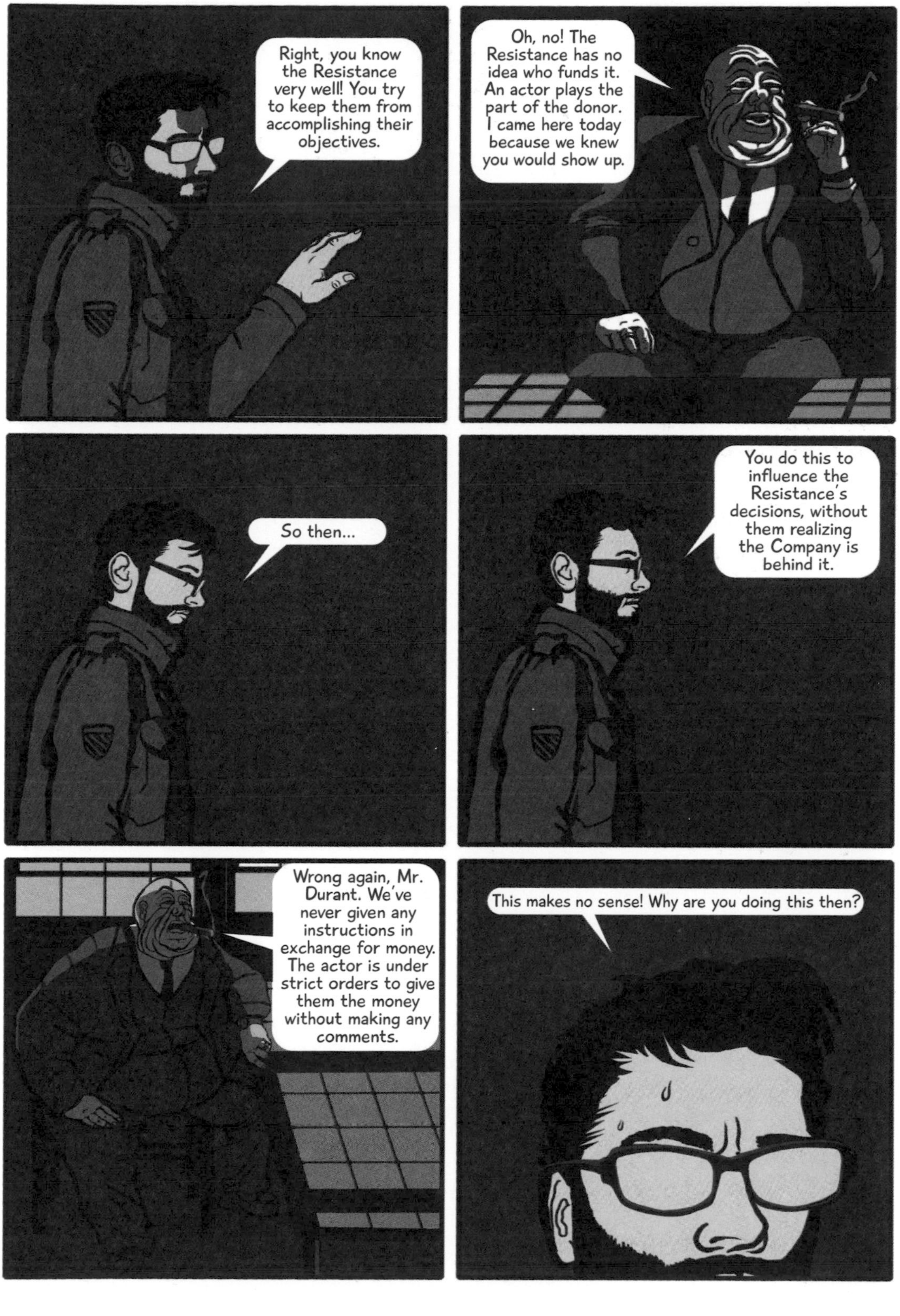
Right, you know the Resistance very well! You try to keep them from accomplishing their objectives.
Oh, no! The Resistance has no idea who funds it. An actor plays the part of the donor. I came here today because we knew you would show up.
So then...
You do this to influence the Resistance's decisions, without them realizing the Company is behind it.
Wrong again, Mr. Durant. We've never given any instructions in exchange for money. The actor is under strict orders to give them the money without making any comments.
This makes no sense! Why are you doing this then?

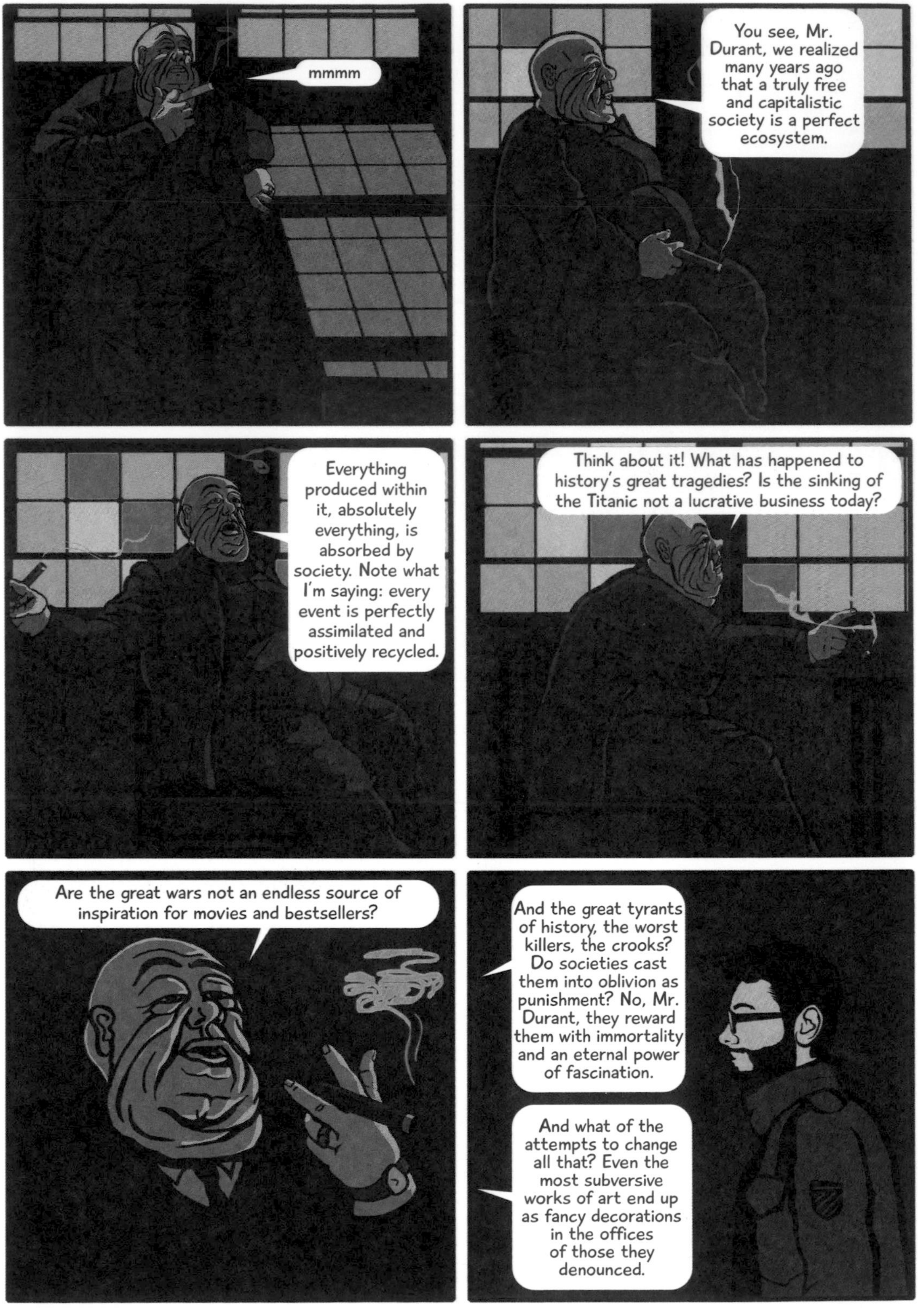
mmmm
You see, Mr. Durant, we realized many years ago that a truly free and capitalistic society is a perfect ecosystem.
Everything produced within it, absolutely everything, is absorbed by society. Note what I'm saying: every event is perfectly assimilated and positively recycled.
Think about it! What has happened to history's great tragedies? Is the sinking of the Titanic not a lucrative business today?
Are the great wars not an endless source of inspiration for movies and bestsellers?
And the great tyrants of history, the worst killers, the crooks? Do societies cast them into oblivion as punishment? No, Mr. Durant, they reward them with immortality and an eternal power of fascination.
And what of the attempts to change all that? Even the most subversive works of art end up as fancy decorations in the offices of those they denounced.

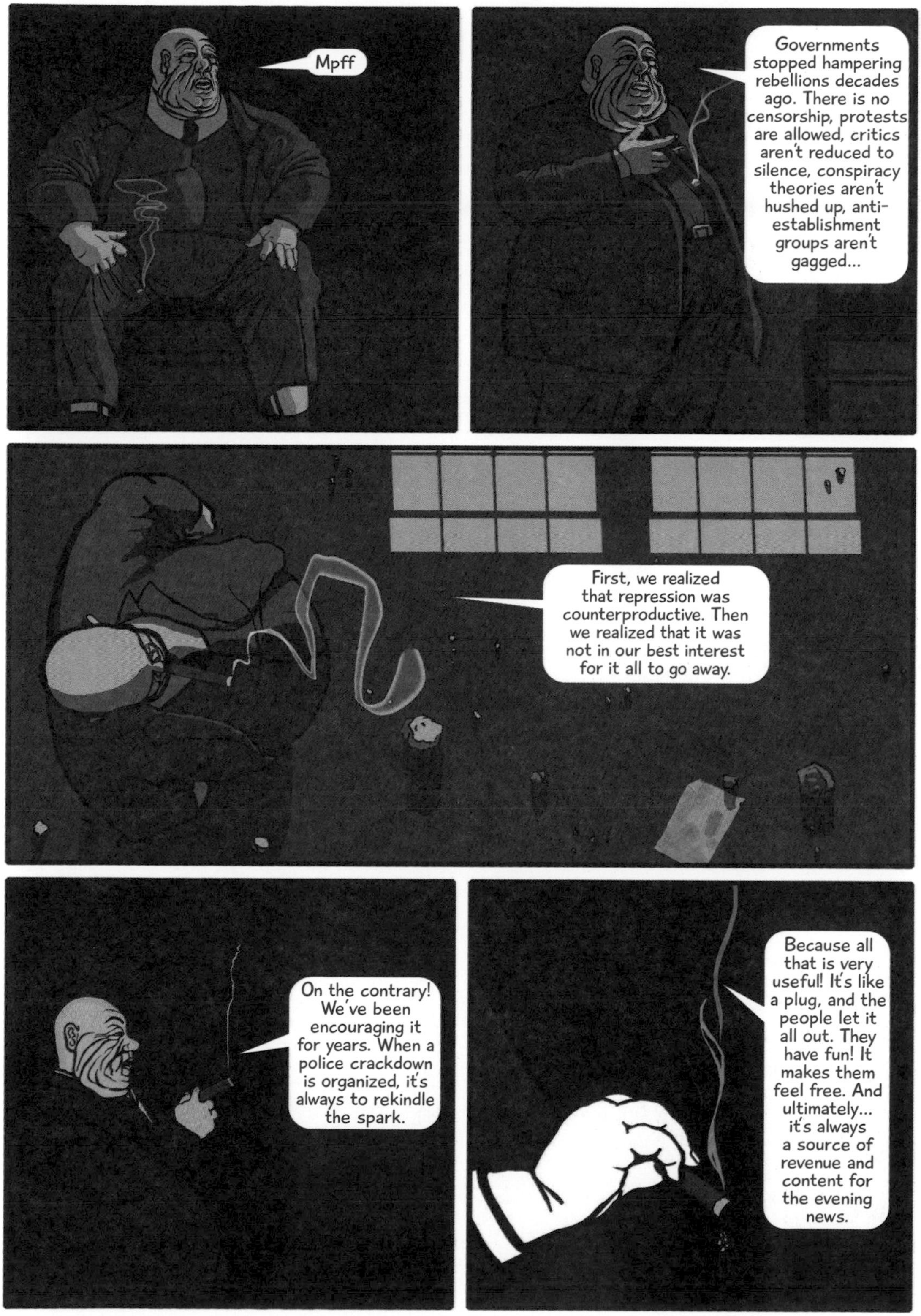
Mpff
Governments stopped hampering rebellions decades ago. There is no censorship, protests are allowed, critics aren't reduced to silence, conspiracy theories aren't hushed up, anti-establishment groups aren't gagged...
First, we realized that repression was counterproductive. Then we realized that it was not in our best interest for it all to go away.
On the contrary! We've been encouraging it for years. When a police crackdown is organized, it's always to rekindle the spark.
Because all that is very useful! It's like a plug, and the people let it all out. They have fun! It makes them feel free. And ultimately... it's always a source of revenue and content for the evening news.

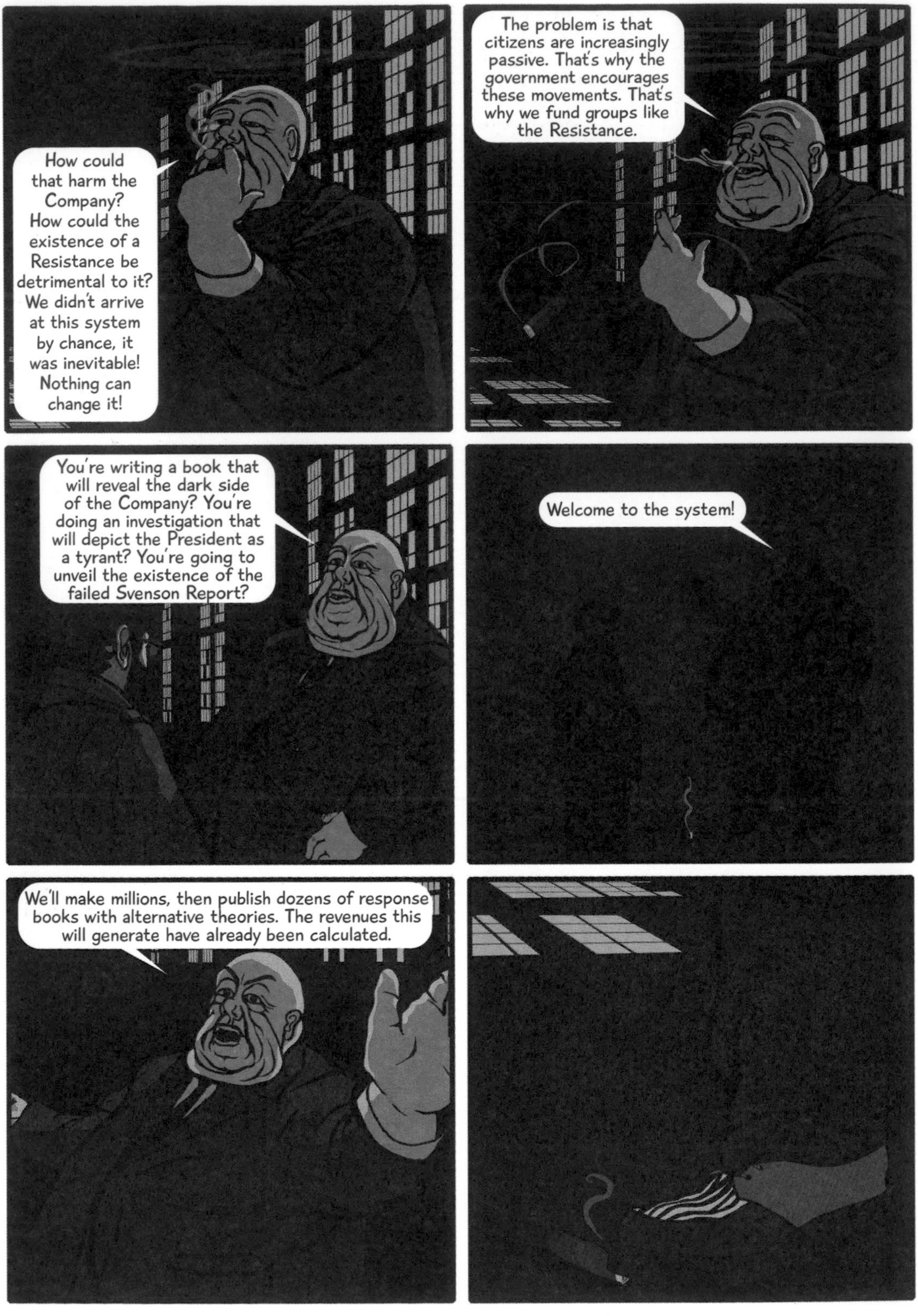
How could that harm the Company? How could the existence of a Resistance be detrimental to it? We didn't arrive at this system by chance, it was inevitable! Nothing can change it!
The problem is that citizens are increasingly passive. That's why the government encourages these movements. That's why we fund groups like the Resistance.
You're writing a book that will reveal the dark side of the Company? You're doing an investigation that will depict the President as a tyrant? You're going to unveil the existence of the failed Svenson Report?
Welcome to the system!
We'll make millions, then publish dozens of response books with alternative theories. The revenues this will generate have already been calculated.

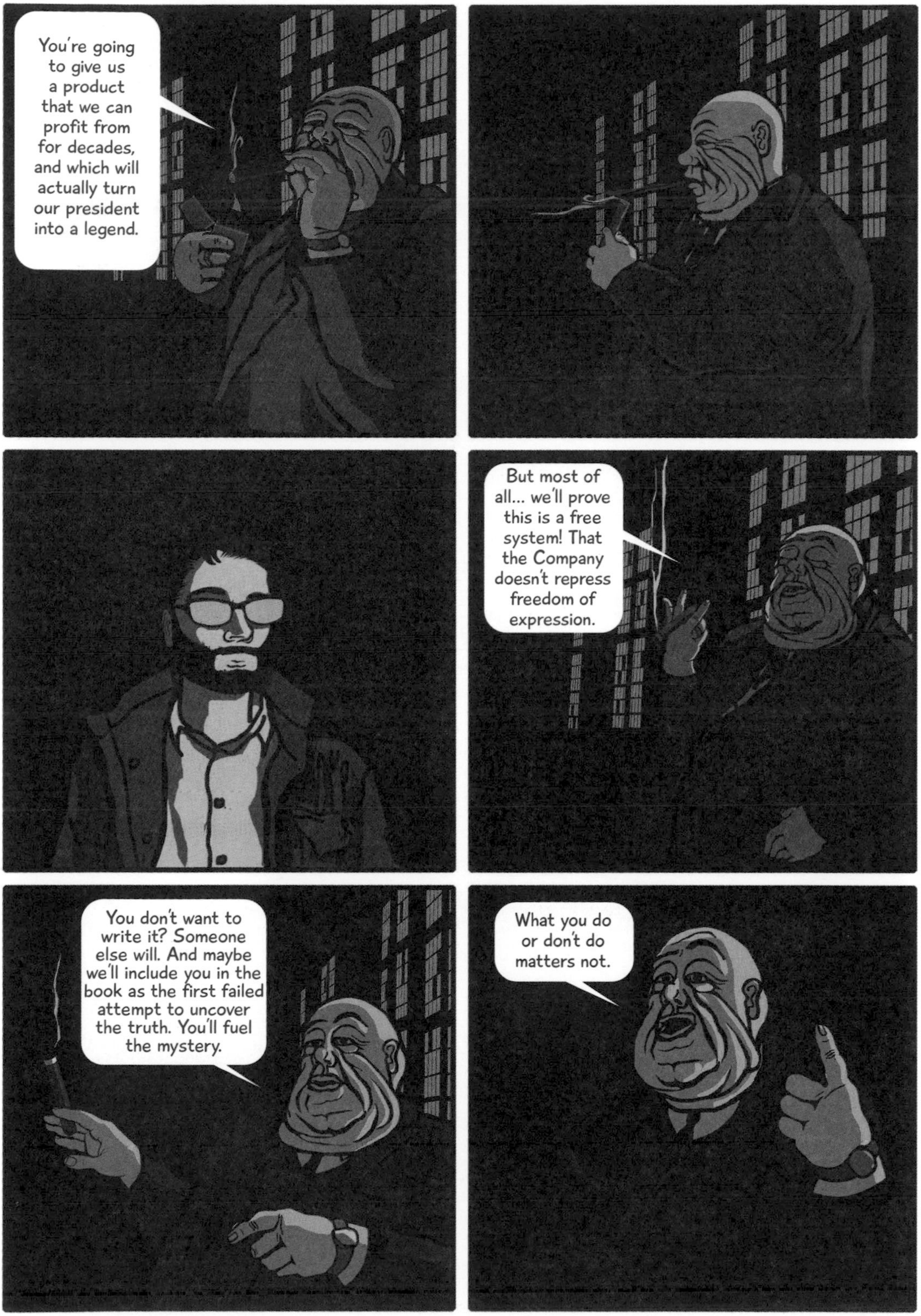
You're going to give us a product that we can profit from for decades, and which will actually turn our president into a legend.
But most of all... we'll prove this is a free system! That the Company doesn't repress freedom of expression.
You don't want to write it? Someone else will. And maybe we'll include you in the book as the first failed attempt to uncover the truth. You'll fuel the mystery.
What you do or don't do matters not.

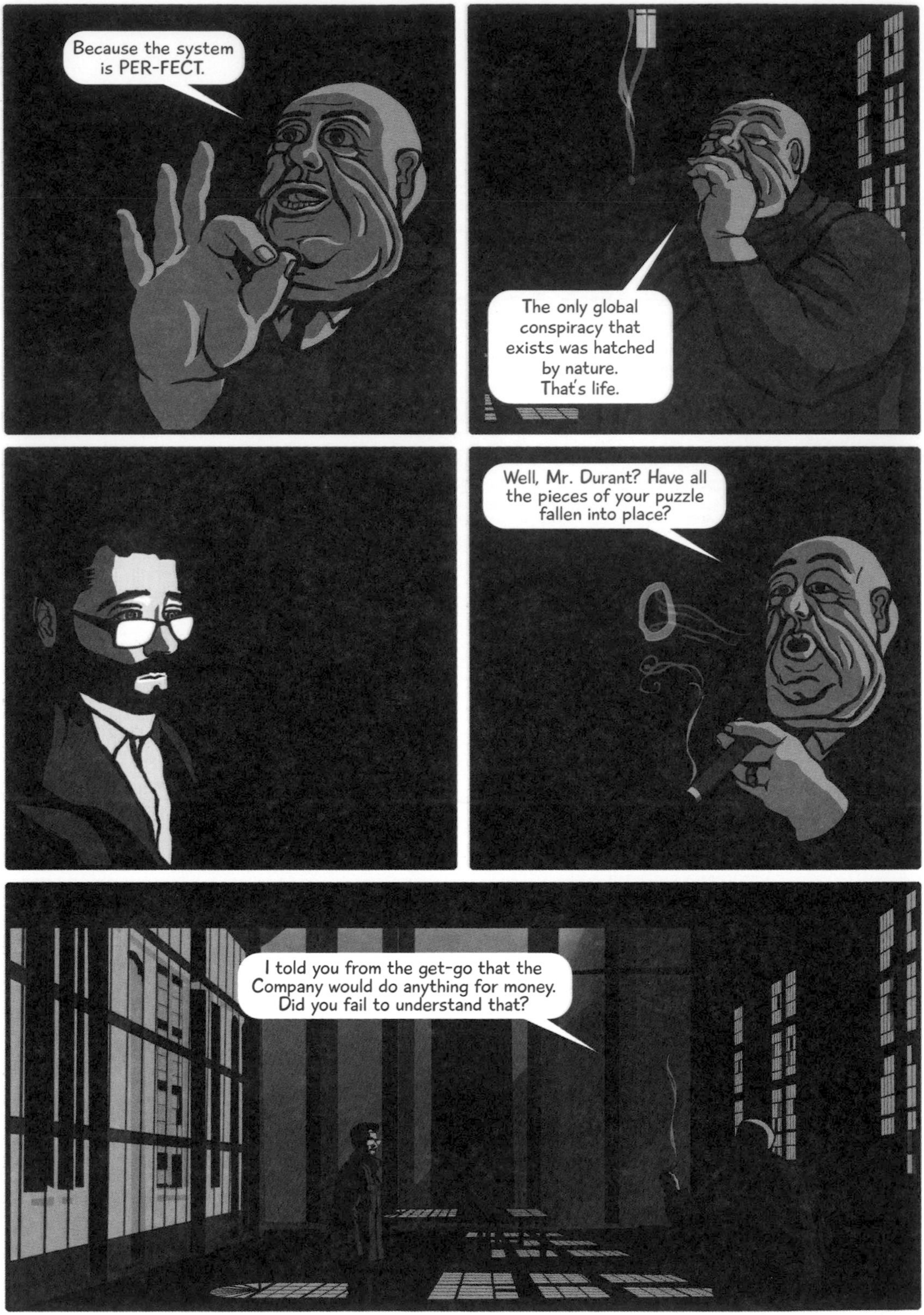
Because the system is PER-FECT.
The only global conspiracy that exists was hatched by nature. That's life.
Well, Mr. Durant? Have all the pieces of your puzzle fallen into place?
I told you from the get-go that the Company would do anything for money. Did you fail to understand that?

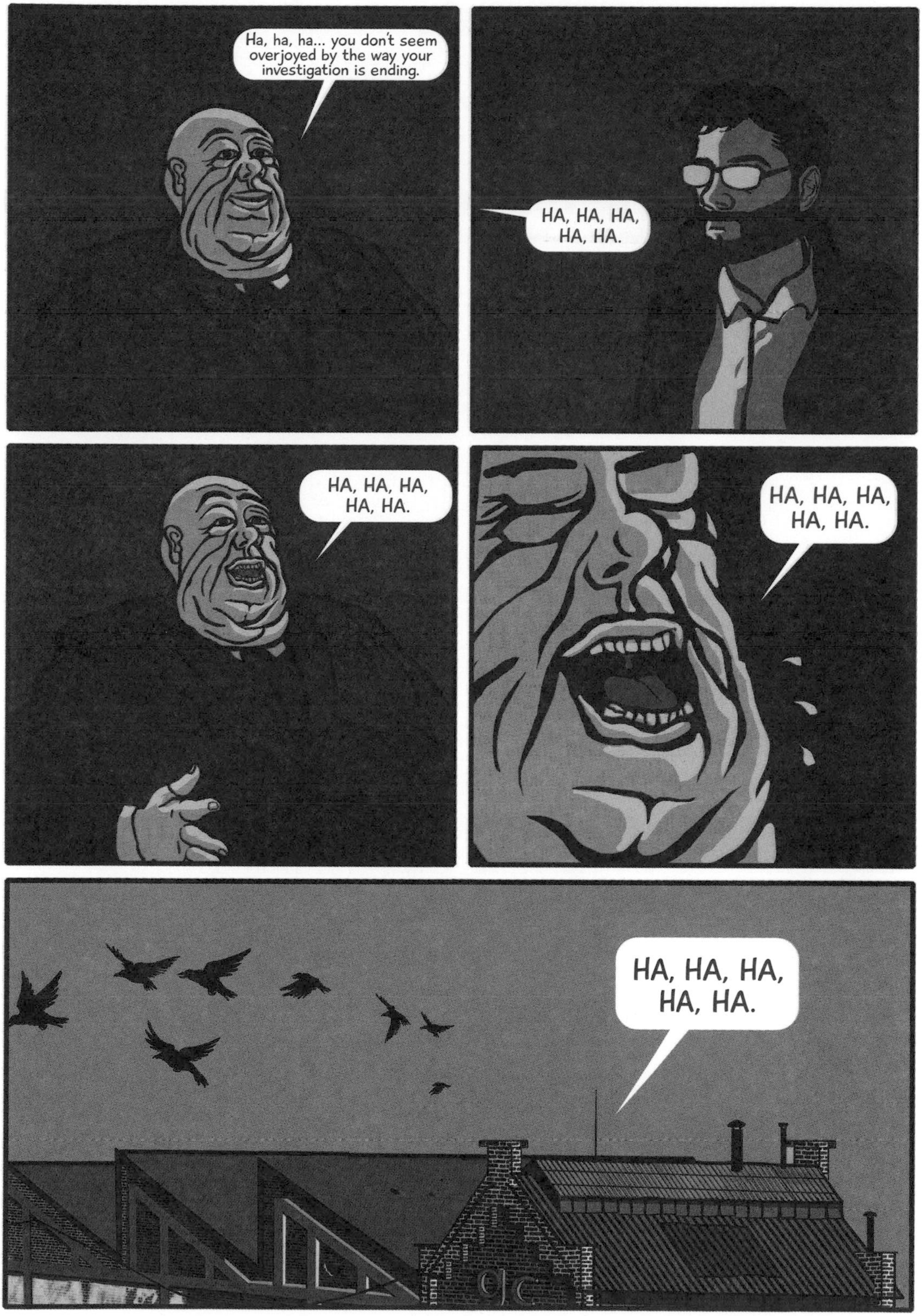
Ha, ha, ha... you don't seem overjoyed by the way your investigation is ending.
HA, HA, HA, HA, HA.
HA, HA, HA, HA, HA.
HA, HA, HA, HA, HA.
HA, HA, HA, HA, HA.

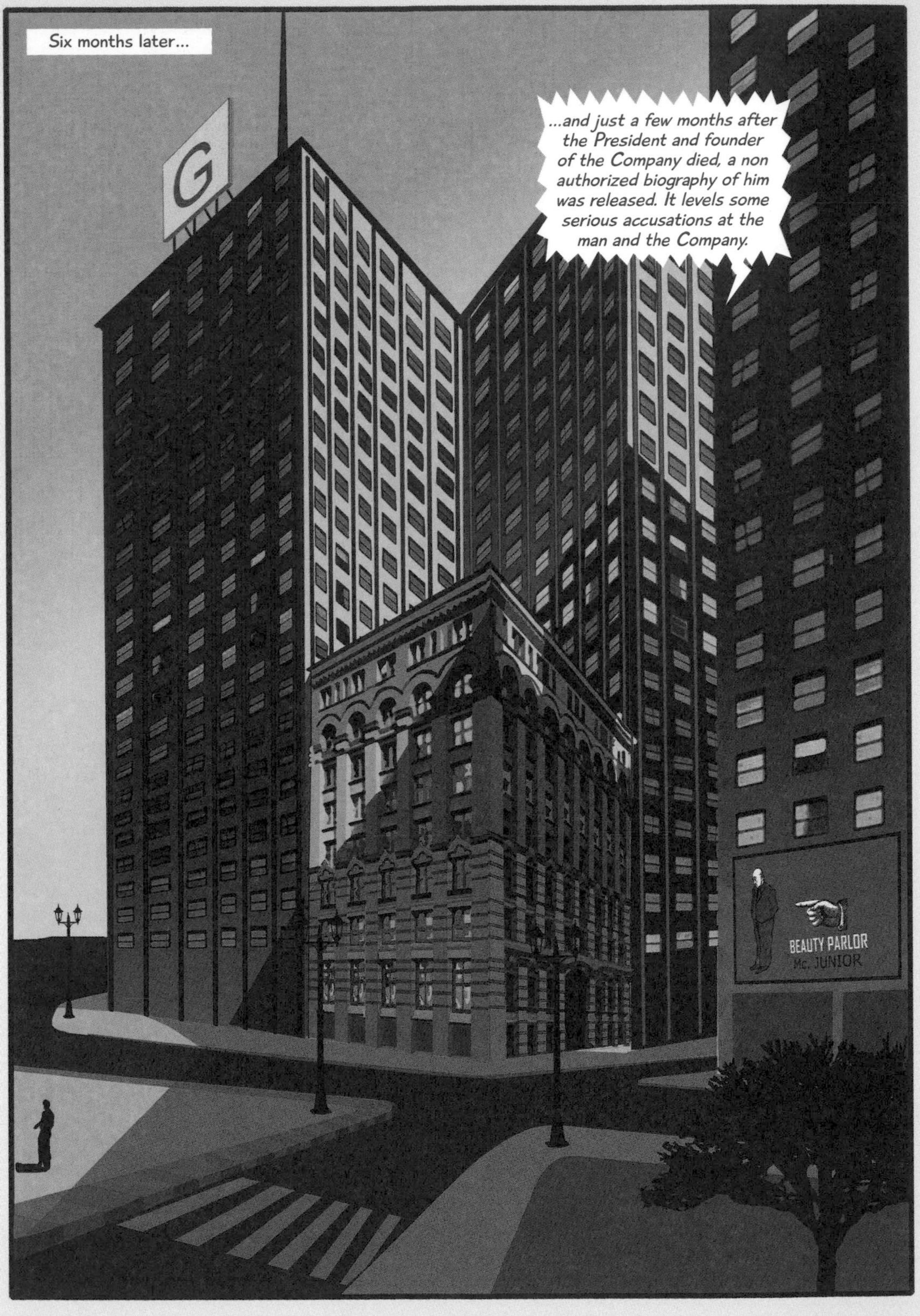
Six months later...
...and just a few months after the President and founder of the Company died, a non authorized biography of him was released. It levels some serious accusations at the man and the Company.
G
BEAUTY PARLOR
Mc. JUNIOR

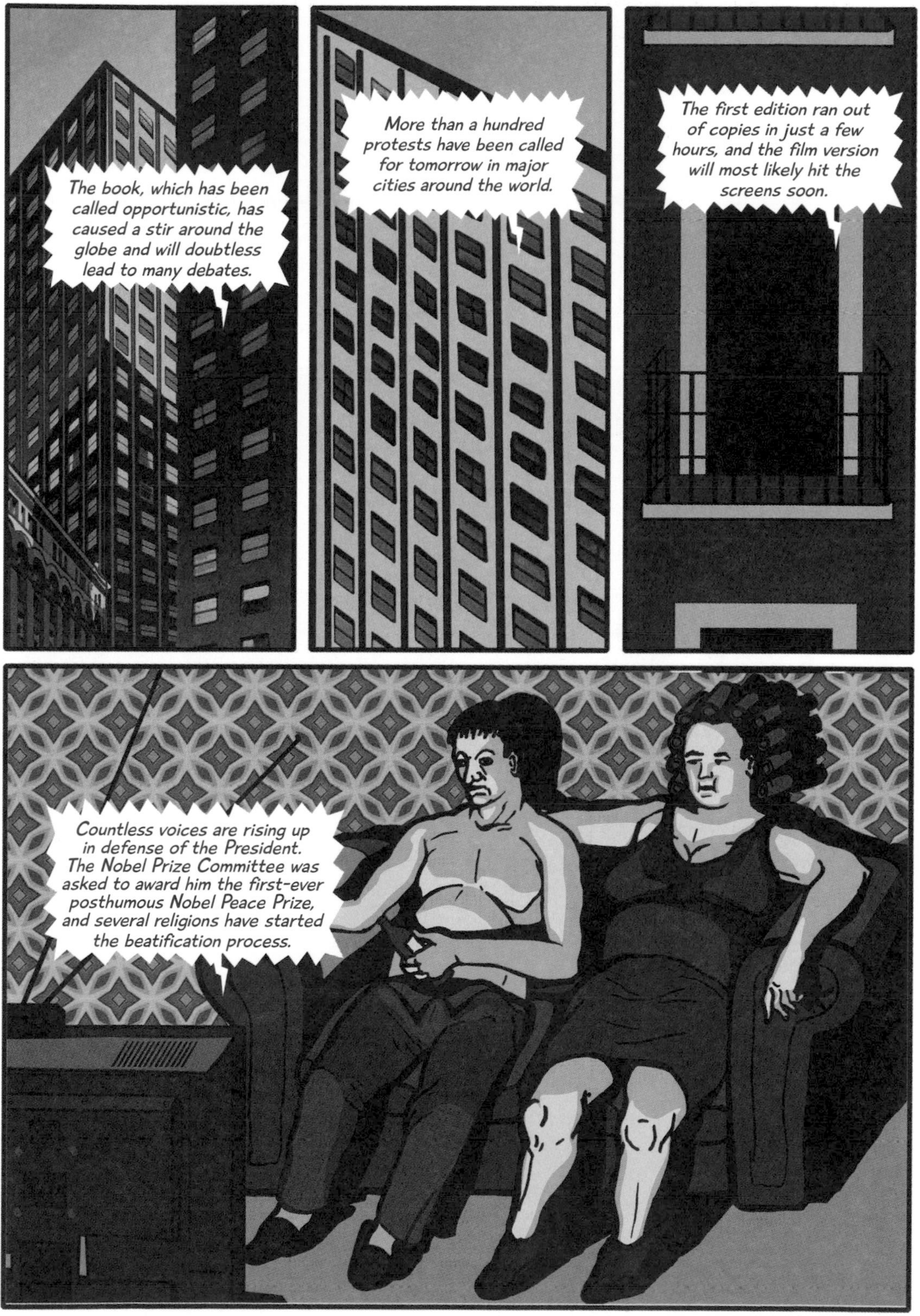
The book, which has been called opportunistic, has caused a stir around the globe and will doubtless lead to many debates.
More than a hundred protests have been called for tomorrow in major cities around the world.
The first edition ran out of copies in just a few hours, and the film version will most likely hit the screens soon.
Countless voices are rising up in defense of the President. The Nobel Prize Committee was asked to award him the first-ever posthumous Nobel Peace Prize, and several religions have started the beatification process.

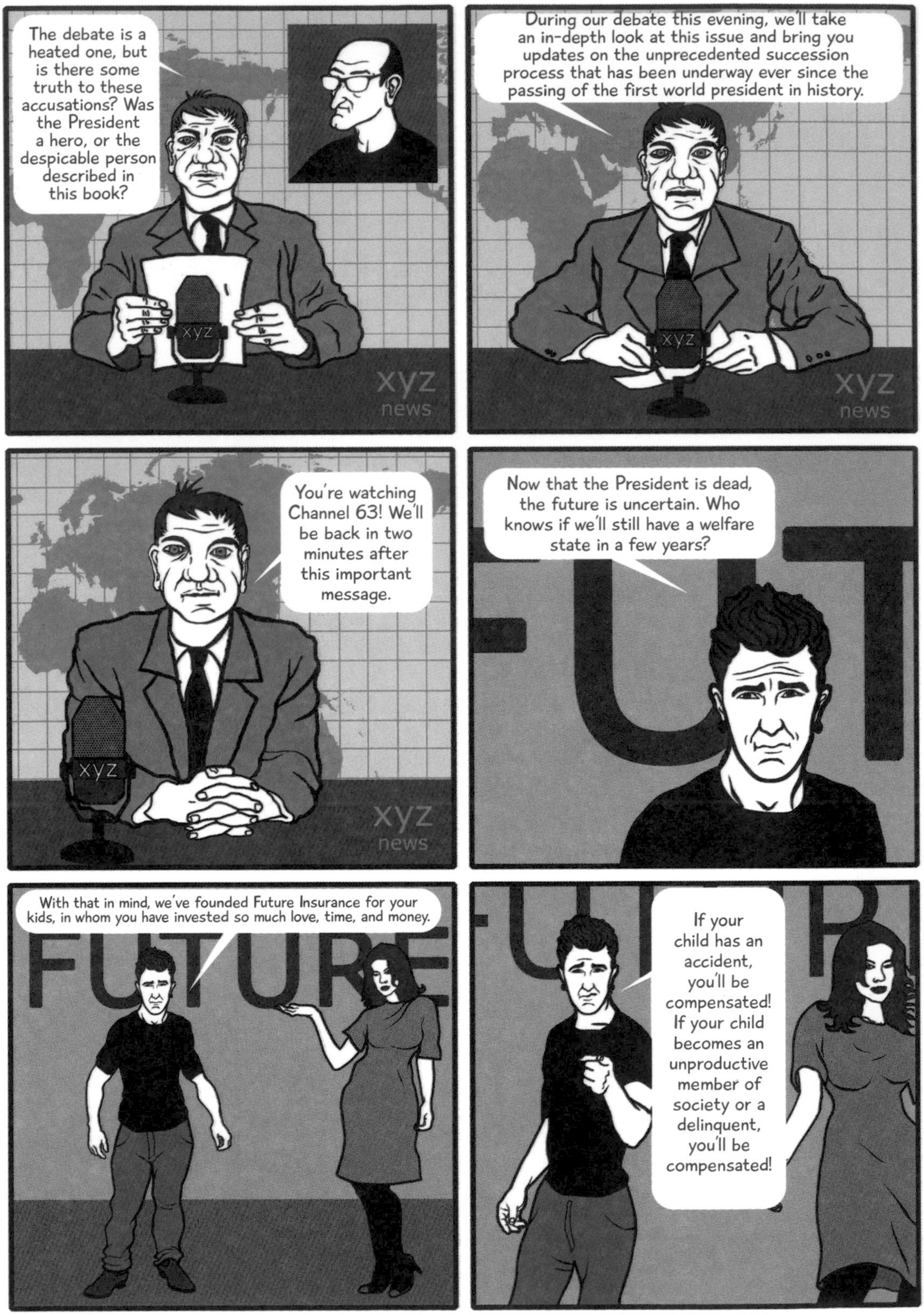

The debate is a heated one, but is there some truth to these accusations? Was the President a hero, or the despicable person described in this book?
xyz
xyz news
During our debate this evening, we'll take an in-depth look at this issue and bring you updates on the unprecedented succession process that has been underway ever since the passing of the first world president in history.
xyz
xyz news
You're watching Channel 63! We'll be back in two minutes after this important message.
xyz
xyz news
Now that the President is dead, the future is uncertain. Who knows if we'll still have a welfare state in a few years?
With that in mind, we've founded Future Insurance for your kids, in whom you have invested so much love, time, and money.
FUTURE
If your child has an accident, you'll be compensated! If your child becomes an unproductive member of society or a delinquent, you'll be compensated!

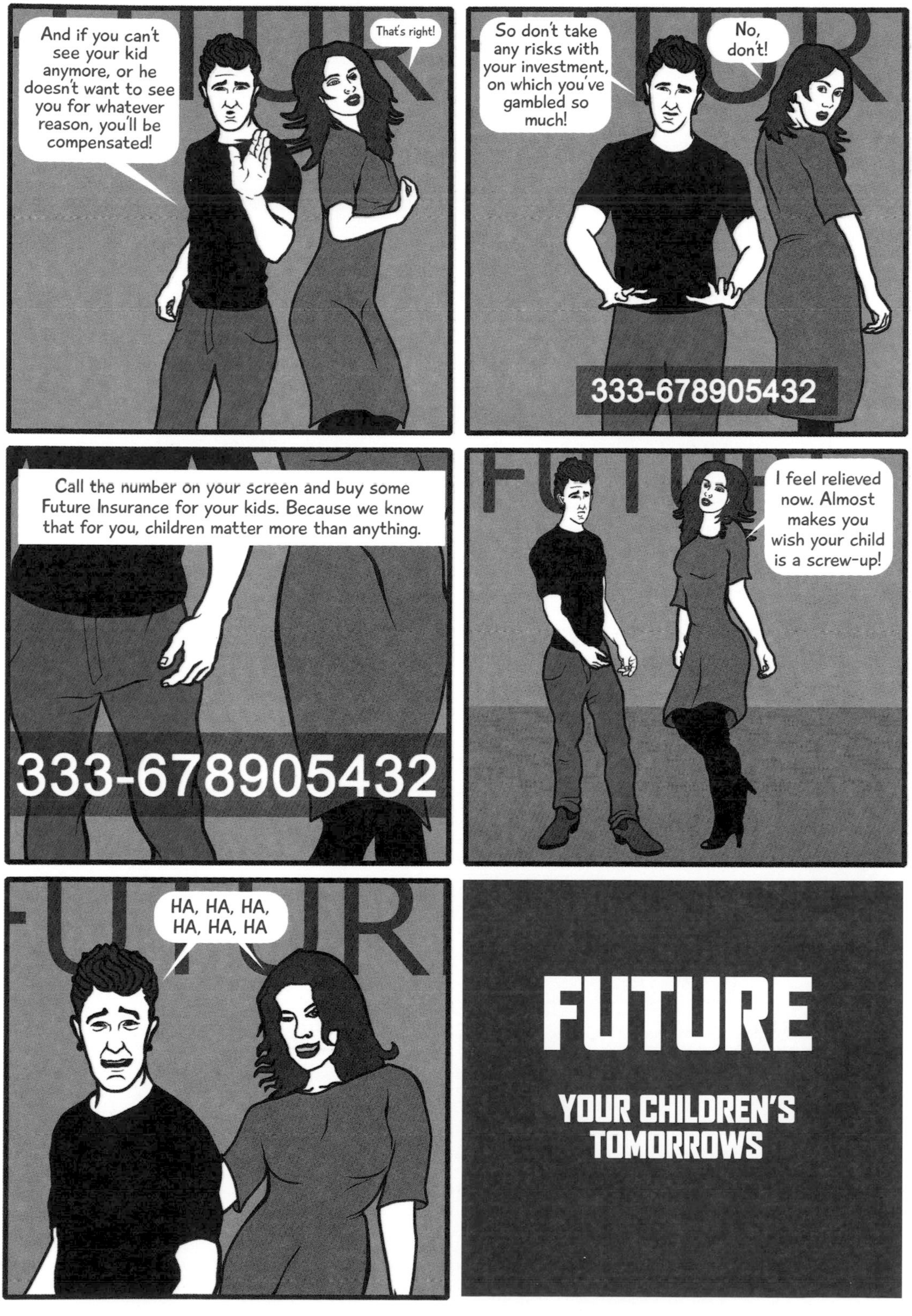
And if you can't see your kid anymore, or he doesn't want to see you for whatever reason, you'll be compensated!
That's right!
So don't take any risks with your investment, on which you've gambled so much!
No, don't!
333-678905432
Call the number on your screen and buy some Future Insurance for your kids. Because we know that for you, children matter more than anything.
333-678905432
I feel relieved now. Almost makes you wish your child is a screw-up!
HA, HA, HA, HA, HA, HA
FUTURE
YOUR CHILDREN'S TOMORROWS

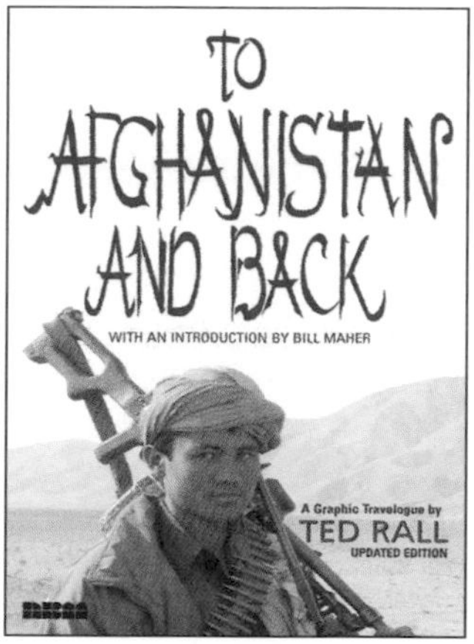
TO
AFGHANISTAN
AND BACK
WITH AN INTRODUCTION BY BILL MAHER
A Graphic Travelogue by
TED RALL
UPDATED EDITION

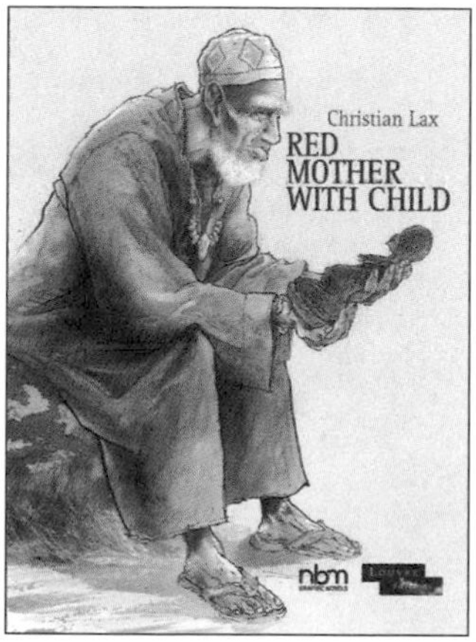
Christian Lax
RED
MOTHER
WITH CHILD
nbm

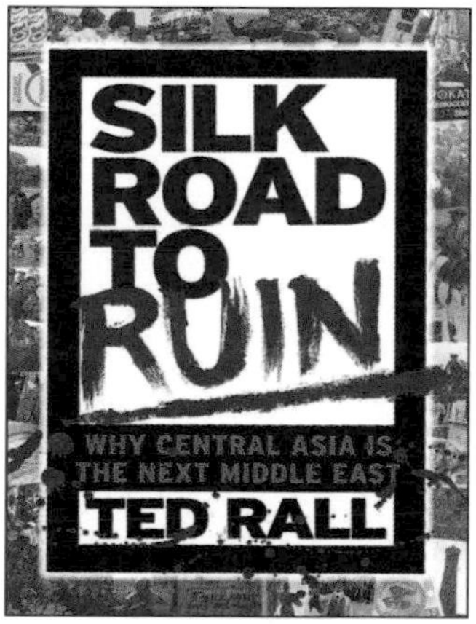
SILK
ROAD
TO
RUIN
WHY CENTRAL ASIA IS
THE NEXT MIDDLE EAST
TED RALL

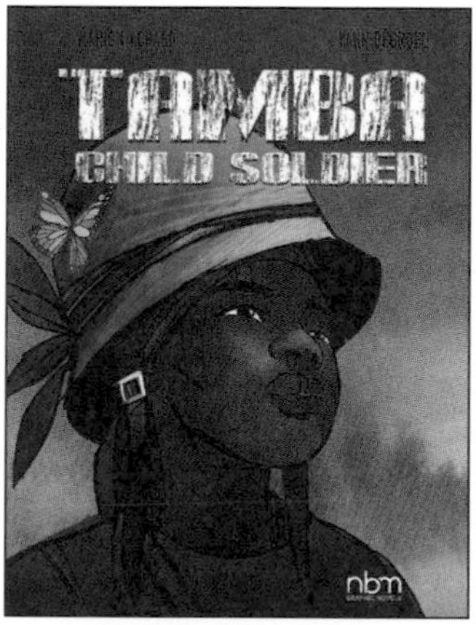
TAMBA
CHILD SOLDIER
nbm

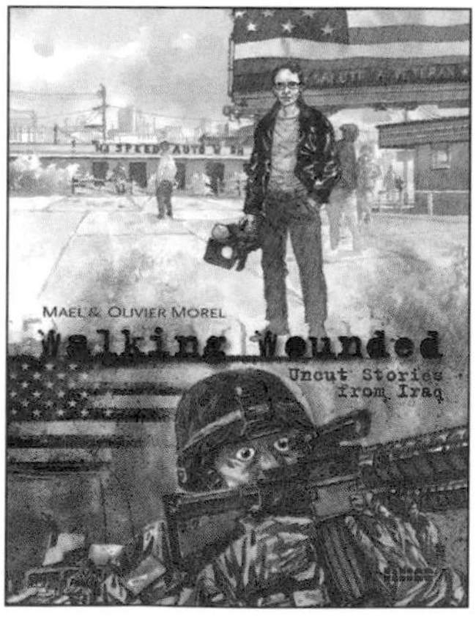
MAEL & OLIVIER MOREL
Walking Wounded
Uncut Stories
From Iraq

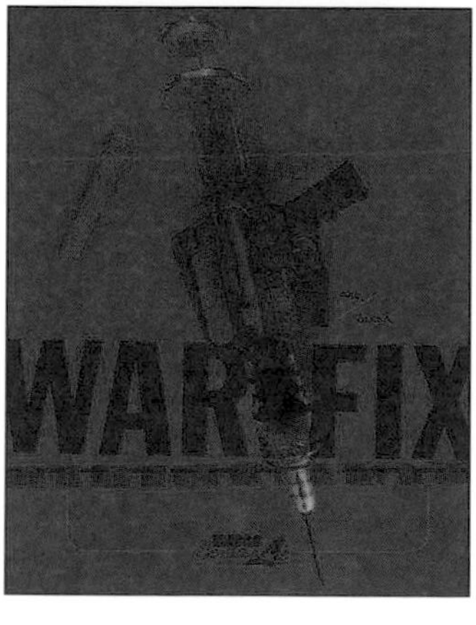
WARFIX

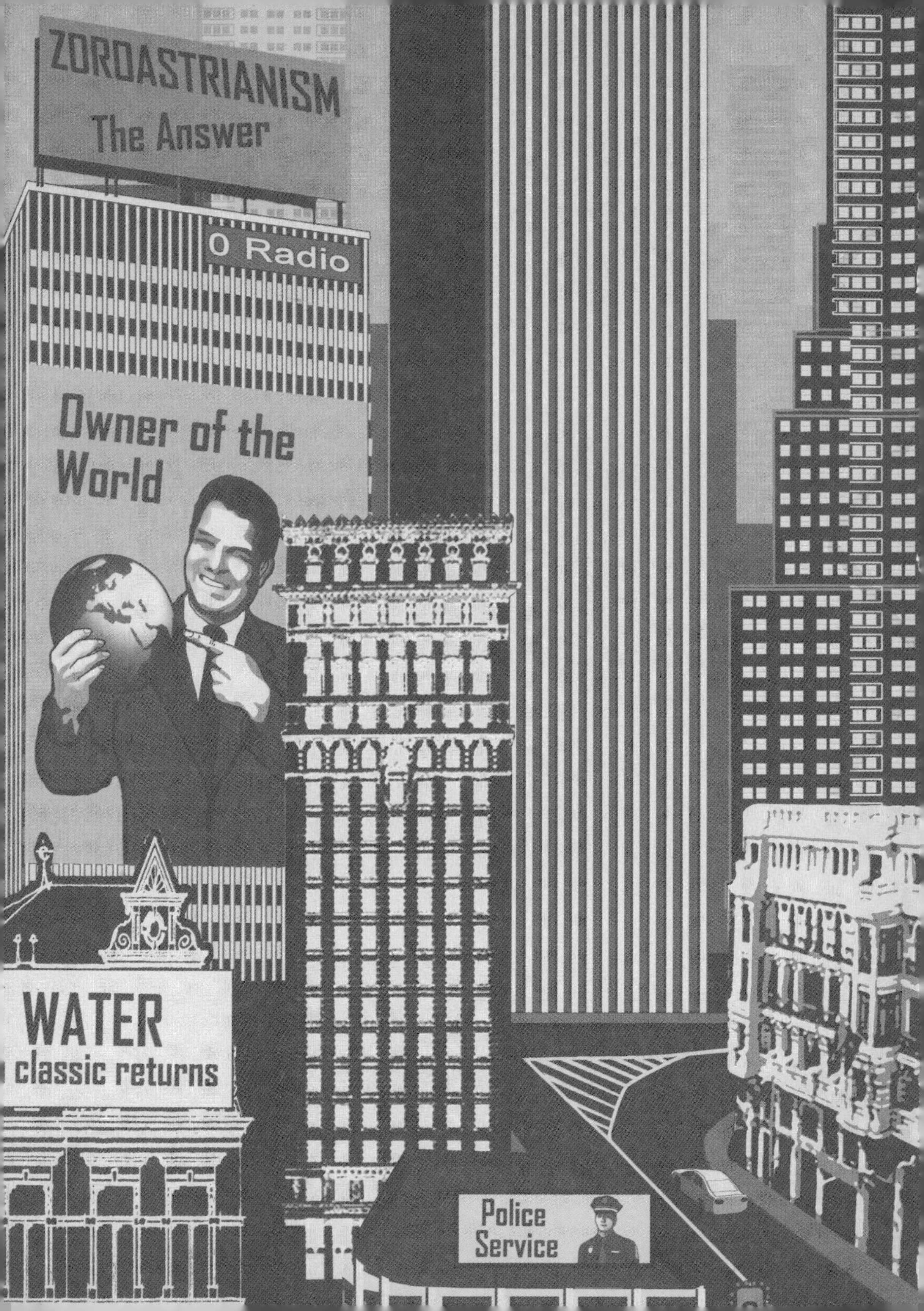
ZOROASTRIANISM
The Answer
0 Radio
Owner of the
World
WATER
classic returns
Police
Service